Communications
in Computer and Information Science   1278

More information about this series at http://www.springer.com/series/7899

Michael Freitag · Aseem Kinra ·
Herbert Kotzab · Hans-Jörg Kreowski ·
Klaus-Dieter Thoben (Eds.)

Subject-Oriented Business Process Management

The Digital Workplace – Nucleus of Transformation

12th International Conference, S-BPM ONE 2020
Bremen, Germany, December 2–3, 2020
Proceedings

 Springer

Editors
Michael Freitag (iD)
University of Bremen and Bremer Institut
für Produktion und Logistik GmbH
Bremen, Germany

Aseem Kinra (iD)
Universität Bremen
Bremen, Germany

Herbert Kotzab (iD)
Universität Bremen
Bremen, Germany

Hans-Jörg Kreowski
Universität Bremen
Bremen, Germany

Klaus-Dieter Thoben
University of Bremen and Bremer Institut
für Produktion und Logistik GmbH
Bremen, Germany

ISSN 1865-0929   ISSN 1865-0937   (electronic)
Communications in Computer and Information Science
ISBN 978-3-030-64350-8   ISBN 978-3-030-64351-5   (eBook)
https://doi.org/10.1007/978-3-030-64351-5

This Springer imprint is published by the registered company Springer Nature Switzerland AG
The registered company address is: Gewerbestrasse 11, 6330 Cham, Switzerland

Preface

The 12th International Conference on Subject-oriented Business Process Management (S-BPM ONE 2020), was originally planned to be held in Bremen, Germany, at the beginning of July 2020. Due to the COVID-19 pandemic, it was first postponed to the end of the year and then decided to run the conference online during December 2–3, 2020. The former S-BPM ONE conferences were held in Lisbon (Portugal) in 2019, Vienna and Linz (Austria) in 2012 and 2018 respectively, and in Karlsruhe, Ingolstadt, Deggendorf, Eichstätt, Kiel, Erlangen, and Darmstadt (all in Germany) starting from 2009.

The motto of the conference is "Digital Workplace – Nucleus of Transformation." In the mission statement of the German Ministry of Economics for 2030 on the topic of Industry 4.0, we find the following target: sovereignty, interoperability, and sustainability. The flexible networking of different players to form agile value-added networks is one of the central core components of digital business processes in Industry 4.0. The interoperability of all players is a key strategic component for the design of such complex, decentralized structures. Only a high degree of interoperability, to which all partners in an ecosystem are committed and contribute equally, guarantees direct operative and process-related networking across company and industry boundaries. According to Katie Costello's contribution at Gardner on March 18, 2019 (https://www.gartner.com/smarterwithgartner/top-10-technologies-driving-the-digital-workplace/) "How artificial intelligence, smart workspaces, and talent markets will boost employee digital dexterity in future digital workplaces," competitive advantage for 30% of organizations will come from the workforce's ability to creatively exploit emerging technologies such as Deep Learning and Internet of Things applications. Hence, the average work day is becoming filled with interactive technologies that are transforming how work gets done. Business processes – including production and logistics processes – are keys as their representation provide the baseline of operating these technologies and thus (implementation-independent) context for exploring and embodying upcoming developments such as Internet of Behavior.

The 12th S-BPM ONE conference focused on how organizations can help their stakeholders become more engaged in driving competitive advantage framed by or based on (subject-oriented) process technology. Topics of interest are:

- Portfolio development through digital processes as services
- Cloud-based decentralization of organizations
- Autonomous digital workplace design
- Self-sovereign identity development
- Patterns of workforce engagement
- Growing of digital dexterous culture
- Business value generation through process digitalization
- Data-driven process transformation
- Process-sensitive data transformation

- Use of mobile technologies and smart products in logistic networks
- Dynamic smart contracting and tokenization
- Explainable process designs
- Sensor-based sense-making
- Contextual integration of things into business processes
- Process-empowered business analytics
- Horizontal and vertical integration of autonomous entities
- Interoperability networks
- Internet of Actors

All submissions underwent a double-blind peer reviewing of three members of the International Program Committee. Finally, 15 submissions with a high score were accepted. The conference program has been structured into a keynote session and five sessions of three presentations each on:

- Subject-oriented business processing – syntax and semantics
- Cyber-physical and assistance systems
- Process mining and the Internet of Actors and Behaviors
- Industry 4.0
- Various views on business process management

The proceedings are organized accordingly.

We are grateful to the members of the Program Committee for their thorough work. Particular thanks go to Aleksandra Himstedt for her very helpful support in the conference organization. We would like to thank Allgeier IT Solutions GmbH for their financial support. Moreover, we would like to acknowledge the smooth cooperation with the publisher Springer and as our direct contacts Alla Serikova and Aliaksandr Birukou.

September 2020

Michael Freitag
Aseem Kinra
Herbert Kotzab
Hans-Jörg Kreowski
Klaus-Dieter Thoben

Organization

Conference and Program Committee Chairs

Michael Freitag	University of Bremen and Bremer Institut für Produktion und Logistik GmbH, Germany
Aseem Kinra	University of Bremen, Germany
Herbert Kotzab	University of Bremen, Germany
Hans-Jörg Kreowski	University of Bremen, Germany
Klaus-Dieter Thoben	University of Bremen and Bremer Institut für Produktion und Logistik GmbH, Germany

Steering Committee

Albert Fleischmann	InterAktiv Unternehmensberatung, Germany
Werner Schmidt	Technische Hochschule Ingolstadt, Germany
Christian Stary	Johannes Kepler University Linz, Austria

Program Committee

Perdro Antunes	Victoria University of Wellington, New Zealand
Stefanie Betz	Furtwangen University, Germany
Anke Dittmar	University of Rostock, Germany
Matthes Elstermann	Karlsruhe Institute of Technology, Germany
Selim Erol	University of Applied Sciences Wiener Neustadt, Austria
Herbert Fischer	Deggendorf Institute of Technology, Germany
Albert Fleischmann	InterAktiv Unternehmungsberatung, Germany
Michael Freitag	University of Bremen, Germany
Andreas Gadatsch	University of Applied Sciences Bonn-Rhein-Sieg, Germany
Stijn Hoppenbrouwers	HAN University of Applied Sciences, The Netherlands
Christian Huemer	Vienna University of Technology, Austria
Udo Kannengiesser	Johannes Kepler University Linz, Austria
Aseem Kinra	University of Bremen, Germany
Stefan Koch	Johannes Kepler University Linz, Austria
Herbert Kotzab	University of Bremen, Germany
Florian Krenn	Compunity GmbH, Austria
Hans-Jörg Kreowski	University of Bremen, Germany
Matthias Kurz	Qualitäts- und UnterstützungsAgentur – Landesinstitut für Schule, Germany
Matthias Lederer	International School of Management, Germany
Francesco Leotta	Sapienza University of Rome, Italy

Contents

Keynote

Business Process Management Based on Subject Orientation from an Economic/Industrial Perspective

How the Coronavirus Highlights the Huge Advantages of Subject Orientation

Herbert Kindermann[✉]

Allgeier IT Solutions GmbH, 28307 Bremen, Germany
herbert.kindermann@allgeier-it.de

Abstract. In the business we are experiencing digital transformation by a higher speed of change and increasing complexity. Especially in the area of BPM this causes more projects which fail. The reasons are manifold but well known and point to the usage of more than 40 years old paradigms of software development. The gap between people formulation new requirements for processes and those creating the software for digitization and automation is getting larger. A solution is to involve business practitioners directly in programming. This disruptive approach is shifting the old software development paradigms and only possible if the basis for programming by businesspeople is based on subject-orientation and on a very simple and easy to use programming environment. Metasonic® Process Suite and Touch provides exactly this environment for coding the business logic of a process by businesspeople. The created process model serves both business and IT. Many examples realized on subject-oriented BPM prove this new concept pays off and is created big success. A comparison of TCO between S-BPM projects and projects using conventional approaches shows the financial advantages in more details. For BPM projects, using the S-BPM methodology and the metasonic® Process Suite & Touch yield significant time and cost savings. The savings are a direct result of the essential capabilities that set the S-BPM methodology and the metasonic® Process Suite & Touch apart from other approaches it focuses on subjects and their communication – the two key elements that are essential to any organization's success.

Keywords: Subject-oriented business process management · Industrial perspective · Digital transformation

1 Introduction

Digital transformation is driving many changes in business and organizations – changes that are very closely related to increase of quantum leaps in complexity and to a dramatical increase in the very rate of change. In business-as-usual scenarios, we sometimes get a vague sense that this is happening, but we do not perceive it as an urgent, real need.

© Springer Nature Switzerland AG 2020
M. Freitag et al. (Eds.): S-BPM ONE 2020, CCIS 1278, pp. 3–20, 2020.
https://doi.org/10.1007/978-3-030-64351-5_1

Enter the coronavirus pandemic, however, and the realization becomes immediate and pressing. It is suddenly an undeniable, present reality.

How should businesses and organizations respond to these challenges?

These days, many companies already operate de facto as "IT companies" even if they run a totally different core business. Accordingly, these challenges are often simply passed on to IT departments, who are expected to come up with a solution!

But what exactly should IT units do?

Program faster? Recruit more programmers? Optimize requirements engineering? Adopt more agile software engineering practices? Should software be written by AI systems?

These are all interesting aspects. Many techniques to optimize software engineering are already in place. Others are still in their early days. Few companies, however, are even considering the possibility of a paradigm change in this area. The basic way in which business areas develop software has not changed materially for decades. The road from time-consuming requirements analysis and engineering via agile or waterfall programming (or the specialized customization of standard software) to the final, complex, monolithic software application is still a very long and arduous one. The consequences are all too familiar: Many software development/customizing projects miss their deadlines and/or devour as much as double the original budget.

2 Reasons Why BPM Software Projects Fail

On the surface, the managers responsible for these software projects point to widely differing reasons for failure. Deeper analysis nevertheless reveals that one core reason is a misunderstanding of both the business and the IT aspects. Subject area specialists and IT experts still routinely struggle to "speak each other's language". Neither side sees the world through the eyes of the other. The result? Misunderstandings and wrong assumptions cause the essence and purpose of countless software projects to be "lost in translation".

Up to now, this issue has been tackled in two basic ways.

The first approach is to conduct a very intensive requirements engineering phase to ensure that exhaustive information is available and double-checked before coding even begins. The problem is that, if this exercise takes too long, new requirements arise in the meantime that have to be slotted into those that have already been described and aligned. This is the stage at which many participants on both the business and IT sides start to lose interest: Essentially, they no longer believe that the ultimate solution will be worth the hassle or fit for purpose. From this moment on, requirements engineering gets stuck in a rut. The feeling spreads that it might be worth looking for a reason to leave the project team… One of two things now happens: Either the requirements engineering phase becomes a never-ending story, or it is stopped abruptly by decree. In the latter case, the software coding/customizing phase begins with a significant risk that the final outcome will be a disaster. A raft of serious change requests is predestined to accompany the solution's launch.

The second approach involves a more agile software project strategy. Coding/customizing starts very early on, but then requires many iterations in the development cycle. At times, this process involves jumping back and forth between different iterations – until the team realizes that, because of what they know, the changes made three iterations back were a waste of time, or even downright wrong...

If this sequence goes on for long enough, developers not infrequently find themselves back at the exact point they had already reached been many iterations ago. They had simply failed to understand that they already had a good solution early on in the process. Further iterations happened because both the business and IT sides did not know the lines along which the other party was thinking, or because the two sides had a different understanding of what was expected from the next steps. The longer such a development cycle progresses, the more complex the solution becomes. Meanwhile, additional requirements consume more time and money than expected – leading to the same kind of disastrous outcomes as with the first approach. Does any of this sound familiar?

If the aim of the software project is to develop a business process application, another point will also be very important: It is vital for all parties to genuinely understand the business process in question. The most fundamental characteristic of a business process has little to do with inputs to and outputs from individual work tasks. It is all about coordination! If we see the behaviors in a process as collections of individual tasks, it is the synchronization and coordination of these behaviors and tasks that make a streamlined business process. The practitioners who actually do the company's business perform tasks that are unstructured, and it is difficult to transform these tasks into code for a computer. Up to now, many business processes have existed neither consciously nor explicitly. Documentation is often sketchy at best. Instead, these processes are more like living entities that have grown within the history of the organization. Where they are documented at all, the "written process" frequently does not reflect the current state of how it is applied. Any such documentation also tends to be maintained independently of the systems that support these processes. One major challenge is therefore how to get the business process described and defined in a way that both the business practitioners and the IT developers are on the same page and share an identical understanding.

3   Involve Business Practitioners in the Programming

We believe the only way to get this done is to enable business practitioners, process owners und process participants to design, code and deploy their own processes. This ensures that the business and IT sides share the same understanding of the process.

This disruptive approach is shifting the following software development paradigms:

– The doctrine that coding/programming must be done by software engineers and coding specialists alone no longer holds true.
– Nor is the concept of control flow for the development of business software applications or workflows necessary anymore.

What does that mean in practice?

Let us dive a little deeper into the development of essential software for businesses: business applications, business processes automation and workflows.

Control flow approaches give the application clearly defined start and end points. Anything that is not described, designed and coded between these points is not in the software, which controls the entire business flow from start to finish. Business Process Modeling Notation (BPMN) is an example of the kind of technologies used for this purpose today. BPMN visualizes the control flow from start to finish using complex swimming lane diagrams with more than 150 different symbols that can be combined in thousands of ways.

But who can actually create these drawings? And who can read them and use them? Who has the capability to change them and add new functionality?

Business practitioners are totally excluded from discussions about the content of these drawings. At best, they need interpreters and guides – which again vastly increases the risk of misinterpretations and misunderstandings.

As long as creating process models requires tools that are almost as complex as a programming language, or as long as someone has to develop software based on process descriptions in Word, Excel or PowerPoint, we will have to rely on specialists: highly experienced process modelers and/or skilled programmers. In other words, there is no way that business practitioners can do this work.

That is why it is time for a little disruption: Let us change the paradigms we use to develop software for business applications.

4 New Paradigms in Software Engineering

Here are the new paradigms that should immediately be applied to software engineering:

– Eliminate the control flow concept and switch to subject orientation.
– Get business practitioners to create much of the software they need themselves.

Does that sound too good to be true? If it really worked, it would obviously be the right answer. Well, the good news is that it *does* work!

Over the past decade, Business Process Management (BPM) has evolved into a comprehensive, integrated approach to managing organizations. It entails understanding, managing and continuously optimizing business processes. Enterprises have invested significantly in both products and services to achieve process improvements that support their strategic and tactical business objectives.

Subject-oriented Business Process Management (S-BPM) is an innovative and unique approach to BPM. It focuses on the actors or practitioners (the "subjects"), driving a process and facilitating communication. This implies a bottom-up approach to process analysis and modeling, rather than the top-down approach used in conventional methods.

In contrast to many existing methodologies, Subject-oriented Business Process Management (S-BPM) uses standard natural language semantics – subject, verb and object – to model business processes.

A subject is the starting point from which to describe a situation or event. Activities are denoted by verbs, and the object is the target of an activity. This approach builds seamlessly on the foundation for existing process modeling efforts: a process description derived from a concept close to natural language in written form. S-BPM also gives an equal weighting to all three elements, thereby avoiding the pitfalls inherent in other methodologies that fail to do so and therefore fail to translate the process description in full.

Modeling with S-BPM begins by identifying the subjects participating in a process. The subjects perform actions and interact with other subjects. This interaction is done in a structured manner via messages. Messages may contain structured or unstructured data that is generated ad hoc or extracted from existing systems or is a combination of both. S-BPM is easy to use as it needs just five symbols to model an entire process. These symbols are:

– Subject
– Message (object)
– Send (verb)
– Receive (verb)
– Internal function (verb)

The natural language approach of S-BPM empowers users to quickly model their processes. Moreover, the models are easy to understand for all participants. There is no need to learn a host of symbols and their semantics, so errors in the model are rare. And if they do occur, they can be detected early and corrected in due course before moving on to process automation.

S-BPM already brings to life one of the Gartner Top Strategic Predictions for **2020** and Beyond – namely, that "workers orchestrate business applications":

> "By 2023, 40% of professional workers will orchestrate their business application experiences and capabilities like they do their music streaming services. Historically, organizations have offered employees a "one-size-fits-all" application solution. Regardless of job description or needs, each employee operated within the same business application. Employees fit their job to the application—sometimes to the detriment of their own job. In the future, business units or central IT will receive capabilities in building block form, enabling them to create individual "playlists" of applications customized to specific employee needs and jobs."

Read more: Gartner Top Technologies and Trends Driving the Digital Workplace https://www.gartner.com/smarterwithgartner/top-10-technologies-driving-the-digital-workplace.

4.1 S-BPM Ensures Unambiguous Semantics

Above all, since S-BPM ensures unambiguous semantics, the process models can be used immediately to experience process behavior and thereby validate the model. In effect, that is like listening to the "playlist" that a process participant has just created and coordinated with other behaviors.

Using S-BPM, the model can be automated without any further design work, ensuring that the automated workflow will ultimately behave exactly as designed in the model. The usual discrepancies between functional design, technical design and final IT implementation are a thing of the past.

The metasonic® Process Suite owned by Allgeier IT Solutions GmbH, Bremen, is based on S-BPM methodology and provides end-to-end capabilities: from process analysis through process design, automation, execution and optimization to process performance monitoring and management. It permits round-trip engineering in real time on a low-code/no-code basis. S-BPM helps process participants to model the process they themselves will work with. Organizational boundaries and behaviors of relevance to a process are addressed early, as are any associated issues. All process-related facts are uncovered during the modeling phase and can be properly considered at the very beginning of the BPM project effort.

The S-BPM method embodies a bottom-up approach, contrasting with the top-down approach used in most other methods. The latter rely heavily on assumptions that are invariably subject to changes in the course of successive interpretations of top-level goals and objectives. Cross-checks against the real situation are possible only to a limited extent. Also, the gradual refinement of processes by a multitude of organizational entities – with each one often acting in isolation – opens the door to inconsistencies and suboptimal results that are very costly to correct in the later stages of a BPM project.

Modeling handled by the process participants themselves is rapid prototyping at its best. Every participant fully understands the rules and results of a process, as well as their individual role in the process. Since they were instrumental in creating the process by modeling it from the bottom up, they also willingly take ownership. That in turn substantially improves the chances of a successful process roll-out. S-BPM constructs are so simple to use that enterprises and their staff can create or modify processes on the fly. Enterprises thus become more agile in responding to the changing demands of their stakeholders and their business environment.

Modeling is done iteratively until all participants agree that the model fully represents reality and/or meets the prescribed process objectives. The model can be validated at each step. Modelers can simply log in and run the model because, in an S-BPM environment, modeling means programming, so there is no need for additional coding. Participants thus experience at first hand the behavior of the process as it will run in future practice. As a result, optimization potential for a process can be identified even during the modeling phase. The model itself thus represents a complete and comprehensive documentation of the process. All updates and changes to the model automatically update the process documentation. Process compliance is therefore designed into the model and carried through without any modification to the resultant workflow.

Once the model has been signed off it will be enhanced by embedding it into the enterprise environment: The organizational structure is mapped into the process organization and the administration of users, roles and groups is defined.

4.2 Orchestration of the S-BPM Process Model

During orchestration, the process model is linked to the existing IT environment. In many cases, business users themselves can link their process model to existing applications and/or cloud services. Additionally, data structures and their layout, as well as forms and display screens, are easy to create and manage by means of "business objects".

Connectors are used to transfer data between the business objects and existing databases and applications. A key element in this phase is the process portal driven by metasonic Flow. Every business user executes their processes exactly as modeled, because the executable application is generated automatically from the business process description.

The workflow in the process portal corresponds exactly to the model. Deviations are not possible, nor is there any room for interpretation. This guarantees that business users will consistently execute processes and services as defined in the model. Each individual knows exactly what their tasks are, what they have to do when and when and with whom they need to communicate.

The status of running processes can be seen at any time with a single click. No more time is wasted searching for information such as: Who has already done what? What is the current process state? What work has already been completed? Everything can be viewed and reviewed at any given time in the process monitor, and the information is always accurate, up to date and complete. Each process step in every executed process instance can be precisely measured and immediately compared with predefined target values in the model. This facilitates timely alerts and delivers real information about throughput times, critical paths or resource bottlenecks on demand.

4.3 Continuous Improvement

Lastly, process participants can utilize the information from the process monitor to implement continuous improvement efforts, as evaluating runtime data can reveal opportunities for optimization.

Subject-oriented BPM (S-BPM) places the focus on process participants and their communication. The simplicity and flexibility of the methodology enables business users to create process models with just five symbols in a language that both business practitioners and IT departments understand.

4.4 A Single Model Serves Both Business and IT

Working with S-BPM yields the following specific benefits:

- Efficient organization gives employee communication a pivotal role.
- Employees can create the applications needed for process execution with only a few steps and in a few hours.
- All process participants understand the importance of their processes and their contributions.
- Acceptance increases, raising the likelihood of successful BPM projects.
- Transparency and simplicity provide process participants with certainty and motivate them to strive for continuous optimization.
- No time or money is lost on endless whiteboard meetings. Process logic is validated immediately, live and interactively. After validation, all process models are based on facts, not assumptions.
- Process models can easily be linked to existing IT applications and integrated seamlessly in the organization. This protects companies' investment in existing IT structures.

– Competencies and responsibilities are very clearly defined. All process steps can be assigned unambiguously, even for highly flexible collaboration between knowledge workers.
– Real-world process = process model = documentation.
– Processes can be adapted very quickly in real time. High-quality processes are guaranteed.
– As a compliance tool, processes guarantee strict adherence to all specifications and rules.
– Employees understand the importance of automatized processes and a new working culture.

To summarize: A Subject-oriented Business Process Management Suite provides the capabilities for an end-to-end round trip. It also shifts the BPM paradigm from a top-down approach that relies heavily on assumptions and consumes a lot of time and resources to an innovative, communication-centric, fact-based bottom-up approach that is both efficient and effective.

5   Does the S-BPM Approach Really Pay off?

After working with the subject-oriented approach for more than a decade, I have personally experienced the following advantages, outcomes and customer testimonies time after time.

A global chemical enterprise was struggling with business process design, changes, alignment, optimization and execution in the form of agile workflows.

Analyzing their workflow history over a twelve-month period, they discovered that digital transformation had yielded very few efficient processes. Workflows to support business practitioners in their daily work were underperforming. These very poor results were found to be due to too many design iterations and alignment workshops undertaken in a vain attempt to get the process model accepted and confirmed by all stakeholders. During these iterations, business users were often asked to confirm the quality and correctness of the business process models created. In response, the business users would repeatedly conduct workshops to supply all relevant information to the BPM/IT experts, explaining the business processes again and again from different angles. After this time-consuming procedure, the business users reasonably expected that the correct process model – and ultimately an initial prototype of the workflow – would bring the BPA/BPE phase of the workflow application project to a successful conclusion. After several iterations failed to progress beyond this point, however, the business users and BPM/IT experts began to argue about the reasons for the poor results. Many of the reasons described at the beginning of this paper came up, triggering endless discussions about mistakes, necessary changes to the model creation phases, the performance of the BPM tools used, the lack of training/education for the business users, and so on.

After being introduced to the subject-oriented approach and briefly analyzing the methodology, the company started to use a S-BPM tool with what they called "the most innovative modeling user interface they had ever seen". The tool was metasonic® Process Touch, an interactive multi-touch display that recognizes tangible modeling building blocks and thus allows employees' behavior patterns to be defined within executable workflow models. Creating applications thus becomes child's play.

metasonic® Process Touch allows those involved to describe the behavior and interactions of one or more participants in the process. A selection tool block permits simple alternation between the different actors. Pushing the modeling building blocks (send, receive, act) together establishes connections between them which are then projected onto the table interface. This is no problem even for teams spread across different locations. Even multiple metasonic® Process Touch tables can communicate with each other. The completed workflow descriptions (including inherent IT support) are seamlessly integrated in the metasonic® Process Suite and can be executed immediately as a web application for the purpose of validation. During validation, data forms, system interfaces and more features can be added to the workflow models to turn them into self-contained applications.

metasonic® Process Touch lowers the inhibition threshold for employees who are often put off by the seemingly complex computer science. In addition, the modeling table promotes communication between IT experts and business users. The workflow models can be changed quickly and infinitely, encouraging everyone to assume greater responsibility and become more involved.

After just two weeks' training, the chemical company's BPM team was able to use this innovative technology to align, design, adjust and validate more the 90 process models in about six months. Working out at an average of 1.5 workdays per process, that adds up to unbelievable success.

A telecom provider in Europe created a proactive incident and problem management system for its small and medium-sized enterprise (SME) customers.

The SME division of a European telecom provider had no real-time view of the state of the telecom infrastructure based on which it delivered relevant products and services to customers. To determine the cause of a fault, customers' only option in most cases was to contact the call center. Repeated inquiries thus became a constant source of irritation on the telecom provider's hotline. Whenever problems occurred, wait times in the hotline queue surged dramatically. Conversely, staff at the customer support center had to seek out and collect information independently from various sources gain a clear overview of each problem. The time delay before this information actually reached the SMEs was inacceptable. Lacking complete and up-to-date information about faults, customers and partners became increasingly dissatisfied – not to mention the high costs incurred by the telecom provider.

To resolve these issues, the telecom provider needed a simple solution that could be implemented and adapted quickly. The aim was to create a mobile app for the most common smartphones that would execute the background processes for proactive incident and problem management. Fault messages therefore had to be processed and localized automatically.

An app was therefore created to give employees, partners and customers a consolidated, up-to-date summary of their service status. The various data sources providing fault information were integrated using metasonic S-BPM Suite and edited as efficiently as possible. Users had the option of sending "push" fault messages in keeping with their app profile. They could also specify which product/service groups, locations, areas and regions they wanted to view and receive push notifications for. Even voice and user data (such as telephone numbers for enquiries) could be stored, which was particularly important as a channel for negative feedback when checking if a fault had been resolved. If the telecom provider reports a fault as "Resolved", the app user had two hours to confirm whether or not this was indeed the case by pressing the appropriate button. If users reported a fault as "Unresolved", it was checked immediately. If necessary, the app user was then contacted and fault processing was reopened.

To optimize the solution, it was necessary to experiment with various combinations of processes and workflows, and also to involve business users in the process of developing this solution. Thanks to the subject-oriented approach, this presented no difficulty. S-BPM's smart complexity management capability always leads to the fast, effective and efficient coordination of business processes.

- Breaking the process down into the encapsulated behaviors of the subjects (i.e. the individuals and systems) involved makes it possible to coordinate the different manageable behaviors in sections.
- Clear interfaces between the subjects are defined by exchanging messages that describe exactly who is sending or receiving what, when and to or from whom.
- In this way, all subjects and their input and output can be modeled systematically in a short time.

The outcome? Thanks to the metasonic® platform's subject-oriented approach, the solution created was already being used by around 1,250 customers, 1,000 partners and 1,500 employees of the telecom provider – around 4,000 users in total – just eight months after its launch. The speed of implementation and adaptation has improved by a factor of four, and the volume of calls linked to disruptions has been reduced by approximately 25%.

This project again demonstrated that Subject-oriented Business Process Management (S-BPM) is a process description method that quickly and easily creates dynamic business applications and rapidly and seamlessly integrates them in existing IT systems. S-BPM helps enterprises maximize their flexibility and delivers effective, efficient and fully compliant business processes.

A subject-oriented approach was used to introduce SAP S/4 HANA at Lufthansa AirPlus International (AirPlus).

Lufthansa AirPlus International is migrating from a legacy, non-SAP-based application landscape assembled over many years to an SAP S/4 HANA environment. Anticipating strong growth in the number of transactions in the future, its aim is to secure real-time transaction speed. SAP has preconfigured, ready-to-use standard processes that are needed to meet the current and future requirements of AirPlus's business areas. To use the business processes provided by SAP productively, several hundred process models had to be analyzed by business specialists and compared with the customer's real business processes. Only then was it possible to decide whether standard SAP processes could be used without modification, whether adaptation was needed or, in exceptional cases, whether a completely new business process had to be defined.

Pilots and airline staff have been using the Universal Air Travel Plan (UATP), the world's first payment system for business trips, since 1936, and AirPlus too has traditionally stood by this system. In 1986, eleven airlines founded the AirPlus Limited Card Services and upheld the venerable brand. AirPlus itself was created three years later, in 1989. Today over 50,000 corporate customers worldwide use the products and solutions of AirPlus to manage their business travel conveniently, effectively and at lower cost. Over the years, this payment solution for airline tickets has evolved into a versatile product range to professionalize corporate travel management.

AirPlus is targeting end-to-end digitalization to automate all its back-office processes with the aim of raising efficiency and cutting costs. Its new, flexible, state-of-the-art IT infrastructure is intended to promote new business models and international growth with improved customer service. As a result, AirPlus is able to design and implement new customer journeys for new potential business models.

The effective and efficient introduction of standard S/4HANA processes plays an important role in this context. Fit-to-standard workshops that are based on complex process model representations take a long time, are expensive and often do not ensure a clear understanding of either the standard SAP processes or the necessary adjustments. Using metasonic® Process Touch technology based on a subject-oriented BPM methodology, it was possible to transform the complex business process diagrams produced by the SAP Solution Manager into a subject-oriented representation. This made business processes more transparent and tangible for the relevant specialist department. Fit-to-standard analysis was thus optimized in terms of time, cost and quality, resulting in processes with a clear and detailed level of alignment.

With metasonic® TIZZARD the Fit-Gap Analysis Accelerator Software Package, AirPlus was able to exchange process models in both directions between the SAP Solution Manager and metasonic® Process Touch. The business users themselves were thus involved in rapidly analyzing and adapting standard SAP processes around an interactive modeling table. This approach both shortened workshop durations and increased the quality of the outcomes.

On the metasonic® Process Touch table, the processes can be physically modeled, analyzed, modified and then validated interactively online. This creates a very high level of transparency and leads to a clear understanding of the process. Process models containing detailed process adjustments are transferred back to the SAP Solution Manager in BPMN (Business Process Modeling Notation) format.

The savings on time and resources are enormous, alongside a massive decrease in change requests when processes go live. The entire procedure is based on a Subject-oriented approach to Business Process Management (S-BPM). Using just a handful of symbols, every business user can describe, analyze and change their behavior in the process on the fly from an individual, first-person perspective. By exchanging messages, they can coordinate their behavior with other process participants, receiving valuable support from the metasonic® Process Touch and its haptic components.

In this case, metasonic's subject-oriented approach considerably reduced the effort involved in hundreds of fit-to-standard/fit-gap workshops in S/4 HANA launch projects, while also improving process quality thanks to the involvement of business users.

6 Comparative TCO for S-BPM Projects

Total cost of ownership (TCO) is a financial estimate that includes all the direct and indirect costs of a given project, product or system. A non-exhaustive list of cost factors associated with a BPM project includes:

- Hardware/software/application infrastructure

  - Initial (one-time) investment
  - Running costs

- Implementation of workflow applications

  - Process analysis
  - Process modeling
  - Process validation
  - Embedding and orchestration
  - Project management
  - Roll-out
  - Training

- Error correction
- Continuous change
- Process execution costs
- Governance costs

  - Process governance setup
  - Process governance operation

The following pages provide a comparative view of the TCO of S-BPM-based projects and BPM projects that use a different methodology (widely referred to today as the standard methodology). Since items such as the infrastructure cost (hardware, software and application costs, both one-time and ongoing) can be assumed to be approximately the same irrespective of the BPM methodology employed, the comparative view provides an in-depth examination only of those cost factors that differ significantly due to the methodology used.

Major cost differences can be identified for process implementation, error correction, continuous change, process execution and process governance.

The discussion below spells out the superior resource utilization and cost/benefit ratios of the S-BPM methodology called BPMN. Furthermore, the metasonic® Process Suite constitutes a highly integrated BPM environment that delivers an unmatched increase in efficiency and effectiveness in the area of dynamic BPM.

For the process design and execution phases, the advantages of using the metasonic Suite as opposed to another BPM tool set can be summarized as follows:

- Vendor lock-in cost reduction

– Process execution cost reduction
– Cost reduction for correcting errors in workflow applications
– Reduction in the cost of changes
– Compliance cost reduction, cost of non-compliance

6.1 Vendor Lock-in Costs

"Vendor lock-in" is defined as the amount of resources that are needed to have a software application customized, modified and deployed so that it can be used as a solution for a specific business purpose. In the context of software such as ERP and workflow systems, a host of different time-consuming activities are indispensable to get the software up and running. It is estimated that for every dollar's worth of system software, approximately an additional ten dollars must be spent to make the software ready to use.

Today, it is standard practice in BPM to start with the discovery phase, gathering process knowledge from different resources and people. Specialists (business analysts) conduct interviews with people from the business departments, and the findings are documented in text form. From these interview reports, a consolidated document is then normally created containing all requirements for the process that is later to be executed and supported by IT. This document serves as input for process model creation. The model should be validated in several meetings with business practitioners and IT people, during which exercise further details should be established to prepare for IT implementation. If all agree that the process model contains every detail necessary for execution, the discovery phase is completed. Statistics indicate that resource expenditure for the discovery phase works out at 40% of the total cost of creating and automating a process (the whole lifecycle representing 100%).

The detailed process model is then transferred to the IT department. Here, it is translated into an IT implementation description that is then coded ready for testing. Necessary changes are implemented after initial tests with the business users. Once this has been done, the software – the business process application – can be commissioned for live production. On completion, the implementation and deployment phase will have consumed another 40% of the overall cost of the BPM lifecycle. Importantly, every change made during process automation project has to follow the same procedure.

The S-BPM based metasonic® Process Suite makes implementation times much shorter. This is because the discovery and implementation phases are merged into a single phase. All unnecessary documentation and meetings are skipped. The process knowledge and the relevant business logic are built into the process model directly by the practitioners who will work with it – the people who know the content of the process exactly. Moreover, the model can already be executed at this stage, allowing for testing and validation during the modeling phase. Once the business objects (i.e. data structures and corresponding forms) have been defined, the business process application is ready to run. Any subsequent changes work in the same way. Changes are implemented in a single workshop and then, after sign-off by the individual responsible for the process, the modified process is ready for use again.

Comparison of the two different approaches (standard and S-BPM) for creating a business process application that is ready to use for business practitioners shows that time savings also depend on existing knowledge and experience with S-BPM and the S-BPM tool used.

Using the metasonic® Process Suite, the cost of creating a business process application can be cut by as much as 50% compared to the expenditure needed using the standard BPM methodology.

6.2 Process Execution Costs

The S-BPM concept strongly supports iterative process improvements based on measurable KPIs and results that are analyzed and executed by process participants. Using an S-BPM tool, the long and time-consuming phases that normally precede process implementation (involving the analysis of process models and their optimization based on assumptions) are eliminated. As described in the section above, creating the executable model is fast and easy. The objective is to start process execution and performance measurement as early as possible. After only a short time, initial performance data can be analyzed so that possible opportunities for improvement can be identified and implemented rapidly. Process measurement can then be resumed and the continuous improvement cycle can begin. Because the analysis of improvement opportunities is based on real measurable results and is conducted by the people who actually work with the process, all recommendations for improvements are precise and based on the best available process knowledge and experience. Necessary changes in the process models are implemented rapidly and, after the execution of the changed models, new performance measurement results can immediately be compared with the previous ones. If further improvements are needed or unexpected changes still make process execution suboptimal, the next iteration in the improvement cycle can be initiated.

Process execution times, related resource consumption and execution costs are reduced iteratively and step-by-step to the predefined minimum targets. Any deviations from target are identified quickly and countermeasures can be implemented without delay. Data supplied by experienced users of S-BPM and the associated BPM tool show that optimization can reduce process execution costs by 50% and more compared to other methodologies and tools. The S-BPM method thus powerfully supports ongoing efforts toward continuous improvement in day-to-day operations.

6.3 Cost of Errors in IT and Process Application Software

Many studies and analyses of software engineering indicate that the cost of error correction is closely related to the point in the development cycle at which errors are detected. Seven major phases are defined for software and application development:

– Rough solution concept creation
– Business requirements definition
– IT implementation specification
– Implementation
– Integration testing
– Installation and ramp-up
– Maintenance

Errors are obviously detected in one or other of these phases. However, the later an error is detected, the more it costs to correct it.

Developing business process applications in a dynamic environment requires methods and tools that support early error and problem detection. If they slip through the net, process errors can result in significant business losses during production, not to mention the high cost of mitigating the business impact of such errors and eventually correcting them.

An S-BPM-based tool makes it possible to execute the process model at any time during the development process. It is therefore much easier to detect errors in the business logic in particular, which tend to be the most expensive errors. And the later business users get to execute and test the process by themselves, the later they will be able to detect these expensive errors. In the metasonic S–BPM environment, business users, process participants and the managers responsible work together to develop and test the process in an integrated environment. Using this unique technology on a large scale, error detection becomes an integral aspect even from the very earliest phase of the application software development lifecycle. This can reduce the total cost of error correction by as much as 60% compared to conventional methodologies and approaches.

6.4 Continuous Process Change Costs

The costs associated with changing a business process can be grouped into two categories:

– Cost of strong resistance to the change: The solution is created by "other specialists" but is not accepted by the people actually affected by the change.
– Cost of a non-sustainable change: After some time, the business process reverts to exactly what it was before the change. Everything invested in the entire process change represents sunk costs, because the intended effect has not been achieved. Any projected business gains from the change are also lost.

The S-BPM approach supports an environment that is conducive to change. It is communication-based, involving the people affected by the intended changes from the very beginning. It also helps them to find the right solutions for changes themselves. Because any changes in the process model are immediately available as changes in the business process application, changes are sustainable and immediately effective.

In a continuously changing BPM environment – which is the standard today – using the S-BPM methodology and an S-BPM-based tool can reduce the costs caused by ineffective changes by up to 50%.

6.5 Compliance and Non-Compliance Costs

Today, the most common approach to compliance management is to first describe policies, rules and regulations that govern process execution and then to check whether process execution fully or partially complies with all these stipulations.

Working with S-BPM and an S-BPM-based tool, all necessary and process-related aspects of existing policies, rules and regulations can be built into the process model in advance. Models can then be tested, executed, validated and signed off by the compliance team before they are approved and released for productive use. This approach provides the guarantee that, once released for live production, processes will be executed with full, no-gaps compliance.

Where audits are required, only the detailed documentation of each executed process needs to be checked.

Methodologies and environments that allow compliance elements to be embedded in the processes themselves naturally reduce the cost of non-compliance, which can be significant and pose serious risks to an organization. Using the S-BPM methodology and a related tool, the cost of compliance management can be reduced by 30% compared to other methodologies and tools.

7 Summary of the Key Advantages of Metasonic® Technology

For BPM projects, using the S-BPM methodology and the metasonic® Process Suite yields significant time and cost savings. These savings are rooted in the end-to-end delivery of business processes (from analysis and modeling through automation, execution and monitoring to continuous optimization) and can amount to up to 60% of the cost of creating comparable fully functional process applications using a different methodology and toolset.

The savings listed above are a direct result of the essential capabilities that set the S-BPM methodology and the metasonic® Process Suite apart from other approaches. Why? Because S-BPM and the metasonic® Process Suite focus on subjects and their communication – the two key elements that are pivotal to any organization's success:

– Optimal, high-quality processes are achieved by mobilizing all modeling workshop participants. Every participant is "switched on" and active.

  • Every one of them stand around the metasonic® Process Touch table.
  • Everyone actively participates in the discussion of the process by interacting with the modeling blocks on the table.
  • The behaviors of each subject or participant in the process are clearly visualized and readily understandable. Thanks to this intuitive first-person perspective, individuals with no prior training can make a valuable contribution to the discussion.

– Smart complexity management leads to the fast, effective and efficient coordination of business processes.

  • Breaking the process down into the encapsulated behaviors of the subjects (i.e. the individuals and systems) involved makes it possible to coordinate the different manageable behaviors in sections.
  • Clear interfaces between the subjects are defined by exchanging messages that describe exactly who is sending or receiving what, when and to or from whom.
  • In this way, all subjects and their input and output can be modeled systematically in a short time.

– With metasonic, business processes are modeled *and* programmed simultaneously, since modeling takes place in a semantic environment.

  • The use of normal human language immensely simplifies the modeling process. Participants work with subjects (who does something?), verbs (what must be done?) and objects (what data is needed or created?).
  • At the same time, IT developers understand subjects, verbs and objects as clearly defined states that thus represent executable code.
  • This approach allows business users and IT people to work together in one language.
  • Business process models can be executed at any time.
  • Thanks to interactive comparison of the process model and business reality, process models can be optimized and completed during development.
  • At metasonic, business processes are not "dead" diagrams or drawings but can be experienced in live interaction.
  • This approach considerably shortens the time it takes to create an automated workflow.

– Simplicity is vital to both high speed and top quality.

  • The business process (notation) is described with only five symbols.
  • metasonic® Process Touch is a simple and highly innovative modeling interface that frees modelers from the "operating complexity" that would otherwise require extensive training. The mice, drop-down menus, pop-up menus etc. that are normally used in laptop modeling software simply do not exist.

– metasonic® Process Touch uses haptic building blocks that deliberately engage a playful "fun factor" – in sharp contrast to boring workshops where participants sit passively watching slides on a projector.

  • Once kindled, the playful instinct motivates participants to want to "win".
  • The team strives to design the optimal process and everyone plays the "game".
  • In the end, everyone wins – and has had a fun and creative experience.

– Thanks to the advantages described above…

  • …the time it takes to align (or change) a business process across all stakeholders is reduced by more than 50% compared to traditional approaches.
  • …the semantic approach (where modeling is the same as programming) considerably shortens the time it takes to code the process logic.
  • …high-quality business processes are created by mobilizing all participants to enjoy working on the process model. This fuels greater commitment and creativity, assisted by the unified modeling language used by both business users and IT people. The result is an optimized, digital, automated workflow.

We asked earlier whether the S–BPM approach really pays off? For all the above reasons: Yes, it certainly does! This approach can help European companies save millions of euros and fast track their activities in business process management, digital process transformation and workflow automation.

References

1. Fleischmann, A., Oppl, S., Schmidt, W., Stary, C.: Ganzheitliche Digitalisierung von Prozessen: Perspektivenwechsel – Design Thinking – wertegeleitete Interaktion. Springer, Wiesbaden (2018). https://doi.org/10.1007/978-3-658-22648-0
2. Fleischmann, A., Schmidt, W., Stary, C., Obermeier, S., Börger, E.: Subject-Oriented Business Process Management. Springer, Berlin (2012). https://doi.org/10.1007/978-3-642-32392-8
3. Neubauer, M., Stary, C.: S-BPM in the Production Industry: A Stakeholder Approach. Springer, Berlin (2017). https://doi.org/10.1007/978-3-319-48466-2
4. Fleischmann, A., Schmidt, W., Stary, C.: S-BPM in the Wild: Practical Value Creation (English Edition). Springer, Berlin (2015). https://doi.org/10.1007/978-3-319-17542-3
5. Fleischmann, A., Raß, S., Singer, R.: S-BPM Illustrated. Springer, Berlin (2013). https://doi.org/10.1007/978-3-642-36904-9

Subject-Oriented Business Processing – Syntax and Semantics

S-BPM Diagrams as Decision Aids in a Decision Based Framework for CPS Development

Josef Frysak[(✉)]

Institute for Information Engineering, Johannes Kepler University (JKU), 4040 Linz, Austria
josef.frysak@jku.at

Abstract. The development of Cyber-Physical Systems (CPS) require the implementation of context-awareness, adaptability, and connectivity to achieve coherently working systems in real environments. To meet these requirements decisions along the development process, need to be taken. In volatile settings decisions might lead to continuously changing functionalities, the requirement of highly modular system structures and interaction mechanisms for decision-dependent adaption of system architectures. Reference architectures are to represent a basic process design to that respect, and the definition of key characteristics for decision-making patterns. Choosing the best architecture for CPS development through informed decision-making is a challenging task, since decision aids are difficult to be selected due to their lack of standardization application schemes. Although in the literature we can find a variety of tools and techniques, coherent alignment schemes on the process level for CPS have not been identified so far. For this purpose, this paper surveys CPS development processes and the available policies and selection for decision-making support, and presents a first approach for a general framework. In this regard the S-BPM approach and its diagrammatic forms of expression are analyzed regarding their fit into the framework. The results reveal the benefits of integration decision-making processes into CPS development ones.

Keywords: Cyber-Physical system · Model-based development · Decision–making · Reference architecture · S-BPM

1 Introduction

Cyber Physical Systems (CPS) are systems of devices (e.g., controller, actuators, sensors), who together fulfill the purpose to exercise control over another, physical system, most commonly in the form of a feedback loop [1]. A physical system can be, for instance, the environment, a human, or a machine. When designing systems that interact with real world environments, designers and developers have to deal with several problems, which usually do not occur when designing traditional information systems [2]. In this paper we investigate three fundamental criteria of CPS, in particular: context awareness, adaptability, and connectivity (see [3]).

To deal with the particular complexity factors of CPS development a reference architecture framework is required. A reference architecture model is a general model that

© Springer Nature Switzerland AG 2020
M. Freitag et al. (Eds.): S-BPM ONE 2020, CCIS 1278, pp. 23–32, 2020.
https://doi.org/10.1007/978-3-030-64351-5_2

provides an orientation schema for structuration, development, integration, and operation of systems [4]. However, there is consent in literature that classical engineering approaches, such as the Waterfall model or the V–Model, alone are not sufficient to deal with the challenges of CPS development [5].

Frysak et al. propose an approach to CPS development [6], which extends view-based engineering by methods of decision-making to support the negotiations between project participants. Based on this idea, this paper presents a first approach on a generic reference framework based on principles of problem solving and decision-making, which allows to identify decision aids for supporting the development of CPS. For making decisions on CPS design alternatives, model- and view-based approaches are required. S-BPM is well known to provide modeling notations able to decompose a process into separate modules of interactive entities, called subjects [7]. This feature is effective to represent Multi-Agent Systems (MAS) [8], a concept closely related to CPS [9]. This paper therefore further aims at investigating the role of S-BPM and how it contributes to the reference-framework based on view-based engineering and decision-making.

The following sections are structured as follows. First, in Sect. 2 an in-depth look at the challenges of CPS development and available frameworks is given. Section 3 then introduces the proposed framework. Section 4 discusses decision aids and the role of S-BPM as a CPS modeling tool in the framework. Section 5 finally contains the conclusions and provides some future research directions.

2   Challenges of CPS Design and Approaches for CPS Development

In this section, the challenges of developing CPS and the research gap in regard to supporting reference frameworks is discussed. The section closes by presenting viable solution for CPS development in form of a view-based approach extended by principles of decision-making and some of its implications.

2.1   Three Challenges of CPS Design

When designing CPS, designers and developers have to deal with several problems arising from the interaction of a CPS with real world environments. Such problems may consist of time constraints, technical constraints (abstract or virtual solutions may not be technically implementable), economic constraints (solutions may be technically possible, but cost-inefficient), ecological constraints (solutions may be technically possible, but ecologically prohibitive), or human health constraints (e.g., the solution may be technically possible, but prohibitive in terms of meaning harm to human beings). It is these constraints, which are subsumed under the systems context awareness.

Although not directly a core feature of CPS, the future vision of CPS also includes a high degree of flexibility and "adaptability" [3, 10]. These features allow the system components to be scaled and adapted to the respective tasks. Most commonly this argument can be found in the context of industrial systems and the construction of smart factories. Industrial CPS should be able to easily adapt to new circumstances such as changing customer requirements and demand.

To fulfil its purpose, a CPS consists of several components (sensors, control units, actuators). Each has different functionalities and fulfils specific tasks. What is considered a component and which subcomponents it is made up of depends primarily on the level of consideration [3]. Regardless of the viewing plane, the systems components and sub-components must be connected, coordinated and orchestrated to form a consistent and appropriate system. The more components a system consists of and the more components interact with each other, the more complex the development of the system becomes. Ensuring interoperability between the system components, such as logical alignment and orchestration or choosing the most appropriate format for message transmission, is another important feature of CPS. These features are summarized under the term "connectivity".

2.2 CPS Design and the Need for Decision-Making Approaches

CPS consist of a large size of heterogeneous components, making the design of such systems a highly complex task. The research community has developed a number of design approaches based on application-specific concepts and requirements [11]. These however, focus on specific areas or concerns. Which of these approaches is most appro-priate depends on the situation and has to be decided on a case-by-case basis. The desire for a general framework to provide orientation and guidance for CPS develop-ment led the US National Institute for Standards and Technology (NIST) to publish a "Framework for Cyber-Physical Systems" [12]. The framework defines basic terms and concepts for a common understanding of CPS and highlights important aspects and facets of CPS development. In terms of CPS development approaches, the frame-work mainly refers to the international standard ISO/IEC/IEEE 15288 on Systems and Software Engineering - System Life Cycle Processes [13]. For developing CPS, well established and documented approaches, such as waterfall, agile, spiral and iterative approaches are proposed. But as stand-alone concepts, these approaches are regarded as insufficient to meet the challenges of CPS development [5]. According to literature, currently model-based engineering (MDE) approaches are widely accepted as viable solution for designing CPS [4]. In model-based engineering models (often graphical models) are used as main artifacts during the entire engineering process of a software or a system. Their ability for abstraction and focus on important aspects allows to make complexity controllable [14–16]. While MDE basically allows creating different kinds of models and enables multi-disciplinary engineering [17], many approaches in liter-ature neglect non-automated procedures for apportion, but also for the alignment and orchestration of different models.

In a previous research [6], a view-based approach extended by decision-making principles was introduced to provide a viable method for conquering these problems. Following the ISO/IEC/IEEE 42010 standard for Systems and Software engineering – Architecture description [18], the approach extends model-based engineering through a view and viewpoint technique. The technique relates models to views representing the concerns of stakeholders. This allows combining the abstraction power of models with the separation of concerns power from classic engineering methods. More impor-tant, to overcome the problem of apportion, alignment and orchestration of models, the approach was extended through principles of decision-making. The activities of the view-based engineering process was organized according to the well-known 4-phases model of Simon [19] (Intelligence, Design, Choice, Implementation and Review). Stakeholder participation is regulated through principles derived from the Vroom-Yetton contingency framework for leadership behavior (levels between autocratic leader decisions to democratic group decisions) [20]. The resulting approach, depicted in Fig. 1, consists of the view-based creation of models (A1–A5), the proposal of alternative model coupling solutions (A6–A8) and the final the choice which one to apply (A9–A11).

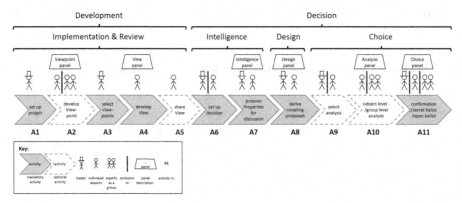

Fig. 1. Visualization of the relevant phases and steps in the decision-making process from [6].

Primarily developed to support negotiations between project participants (domain experts and project leader) when coupling separate models, this idea shows the potential of combining view-based modeling with principles of decision-making to support CPS development.

3   A Decision-Making Based Reference Framework for CPS Development

For supporting decision-making through various forms of decision aids, it is essential to clearly identify the respective decision situation. To identify decision situations during software system design processes, two principles of decision-making are essential [21]: The task (phase) along the decision process and the characteristics of the decision problem. Hence, a reference framework for supporting decision-making in CPS development needs to address these two dimensions to identify the decisions at hand and related potential decision aids. In the following sections, these two dimensions are described in more detail.

3.1   The Decision-Making Processes

In decision-making, especially in management, decisions are understood as a procedure in which an action is selected from a set of at least two alternative actions. The alternatives are mutually exclusive and only one alternative can be selected in a decision.

The decision maker is also forced to make a decision and must select one of the available alternatives. Withdrawing from the decision (not taking action) or postponing the decision can therefore be considered as separate alternative actions. Whether these are viable alternatives strongly depends on the specific decision situation.

A well-known approach for describing decision-making as a process are the four phases proposed by Simon [19]. The four phases consist of:

- **Intelligence.** The Intelligence Phase includes the tasks related to collecting, reviewing and analyzing information from the environment regarding a decision problem. This helps to obtain a clear understanding of the problem characteristics and to define objectives.
- **Design.** In the Design Phase, possible alternative courses of action regarding the problem identified in the previous phase are searched, compiled or even newly designed to solve the decision problem.
- **Choice.** The Choice Phase contains actions related to analyzing and evaluating the set of alternatives previously collected in order to make a choice by selecting a particular alternative.
- **Review.** The fourth phase, sometimes referred to as the Implementation and Review Phase, is concerned with implementing the selected alternative, observing the effects, and comparing the outcomes to the intended objectives.

A criticism of the four-phase approach is its rather simplified and straightforward description of the process with separate phases. Each of these phases represents a much larger and more complex process [19]. In practice, the phases may even overlap (e.g. the ongoing evaluation of individual alternatives during the Design Phase). According to Asemi et al. [22], Simon later extended his model to six phases. A comparison of both models and a figure based on a comparison of decision processes is proposed in Table 1.

Table 1. Comparison of Simon's phase models from [6].

4 phase model	6 phase model
Intelligence	Situational analysis
	Objective setting
Design	Search for alternative
Choice	Evaluation of alternative
	Making the decision
Review	Decision review

Despite the criticism, especially the original four phase approach gained wide recognition in various scientific disciplines and was adopted and extended by other authors (e.g., [22, 23]). Some adaptions even suggest a cyclic approach to problem solving and decision-making (e.g., [24, 25]). That is, after the Implementation and Review Phase, the process enters a new iteration continuing with activities related to the Intelligence

Phase. Approaches using cyclic decision-making processes were already suggested a viable approach for supporting decisions on manufacturing systems (e.g., [26]) and able to consider different stakeholder perspectives (e.g., [25, 27]).

3.2 Dimensions of Decision Problems

In addition to the phase of the decision-making process, information on the characteristics of the decision problem is also an important indicator to identify a suitable decision aid or tool to support a decision. Table 2 presents different dimensions of decision problems and their characteristics from the literature [21]. The first column identifies the dimension of the decision problem, while the second column represents its extremes or characteristics. The dimensions (1-9) were originally adopted from [28]. Dimension (10) originates from [29]. In general, any decision problem can be categorized on the basis of all dimensions given in Table 2. Some characteristics can even be divided into more detailed categories (e.g. the actor-typical dimensions in levels from autocratic to democratic decision problems (see [20])).

Table 2. Dimensions for characterizing decision problems according to [21].

Dimension	Characteristics		
(1) Complexity	Simple	Complex	
(2) Structuredness	Well-structured	Ill-structured	
(3) Solution space	Choice problem	Design problem	
(4) Framing	Threat problem	Opportunity problem	
(5) Interrelatedness	Independent decision problem	Decision problem in a decision sequence	
(6) Problem level	Original decision problem	Meta-problem (Subproblem)	
(7) Actor type	Individual	Collective (Group)	
(8) Goals/Criteria	Single	Multiple	
(9) Certainty levels of alternative outcomes	Decisions under certainty	Decisions under risk	Decisions under uncertainty
(10) Decision scope	Operational	Management	Strategic

4   Decision Aids and the Role of S-BPM as a Decision Aid in the Decision-Making Based Framework

Decision aids are tools, models and techniques that support one, if not many activities of decision-making. There exists a plethora of different tools, depending on the phase and the problem of decision-making. Techniques supporting selections in the Choice Phase are most commonly recognized as decision aids. However, process models, information control and analytics techniques, reasoning methods, representation aids and techniques related to human judgement are also categories of decision aids [30]. Hence, the techniques in S-BPM capable of representing decision relevant information can also be considered as decision aids.

4.1 Benefits of S-BPM as Decision Aid for CPS Development

Subject-oriented business process management (S-BPM) is an approach to describe real-life business processes based on approaches of natural language syntax (subject, predicate and object) and Robin Milner's Calculus of Communicating of System (CCS) [31]. This is achieved through diagrammatic representations of subjects (actors) and their communication interactions (messages) in Subject Interaction Diagrams (SID), and representations of the subject's inherent behavior in Subject Behavior Diagram (SBD). The S-BPM approach and its diagrammatic representations are well suited to represent Service Oriented Architectures (SOA) or Multi-Agent Systems [8]. Latter is a subsection of future systems such as CPS or the Internet of Things (IoT) [9]. S-BPM comes with several capabilities advantageous for CPS modeling:

- **Process representation as mutually interacting subjects:** Allows the representation of CPS components and their communication protocols.
- **The static and architectural way of representing processes in SID's**: Different message sequences in a SID represent adaptable, modular processes.
- **Interpretation of subjects as actors on the execution level:** Allows the identification of stakeholders and domain experts for CPS design. It also allows to represent the Stakeholders involved in the decision, and the information they may contribute.
- **Syntax simplicity (number of symbols) and natural language basis:** Suitable as a means of communication between domain experts.
- **The separation and encapsulation of procedures as subject behavior:** Through encapsulation of procedures in SBDs, S-BPM supports a view-based approach and decentralized data collection.

These capabilities make S-BPM also an excellent candidate for supporting view-based CPS engineering. Nevertheless, the problem of negotiating the connections and messages between subjects remains. Embedding S-BPM techniques as a decision aid in the proposed framework can be a solution. To illustrate the potential of such a solution, two scenarios are provided in Sect. 4.2.

4.2 Two Thinkable Scenarios for S-BPM as Decision Aid in CPS Development

The theoretical scenarios show a company that intends to introduce a CPS to control its production line. After each scenario is described, it is analyzed and linked to the phase and characteristics of the decision based on the framework.

Scenario A) The project is still in its infancy. The manager, responsible for the project needs a team for developing the CPS. He assigns a business analyst the task of recording the process structure that is to be automated by the CPS. The business analyst uses SIDs to represent the business processes. Based on the subjects in the SID, the chief digital officer (CTO) is given the task to identify the relevant team members. The CTO then searches the records for suitable team members. The final choice regarding the team composition is made by the manager. The CTO uses the SID to justify the composition.

Analysis Scenario A) Scenario A shows the use of a SID in the Intelligence Phase. Here it supports the decision by identifying potential team member roles and their qualifications. Due to the vast amount of possibilities, composing a team is an ill-structured design problem. The manager makes an autocratic and single dimensional choice by accepting or denying the proposal. The problem for the CTO, when to stop to search and compose suitable team members can be considered a dynamic meta-decision.

Scenario B) Later in the design process, the CPS team has to define the procedure for exchanging data from the control center to a specific machine. The mechatronics engineer (machine) and the application programmer (control center) each propose an interaction protocol using a SID. The SIDs are then presented to the whole team. Screening the SIDs, the database expert remembers a standard solution for a similar problem and proposes a third procedure. With the three defined alternatives, the CTO starts a vote. The third procedure wins the relative majority and is implemented.

Analysis Scenario B) Scenario B shows the use of a SID in the Design and in the Choice Phase. Here, it is used to carry proposals for the communication structure. Due to the three distinguishable proposals, the decision problem is structured and a choice (vs. design) problem. This time the decision is taken democratically through a team vote. A relative majority voting procedure is used as another decision aid to support the choice.

5   Conclusion

This paper identified three inherent problems of CPS development and the inadequacy of currently known approaches to address them. To this end, a first approach was presented in the form of a general framework that attempts to address these challenges. Combining the strengths of model- and view-based design with principles of decision-making shows great potential in this respect. But only the use of S–BPM as a practical approach for representing design and coupling proposals will allow this potential to be unleashed. Especially the capabilities of the S-BPM method, which supports CPS and Multi-Agent Systems, make the combination of the two approaches a promising one.

However, being a first approach, the proposed framework and its decision aids must be derived further. Additional investigations of the decision process and dimensions of decision problems are required. Probable techniques for decision aids need to be identified, and their basic characteristics, their relationship to the decision process and the dimension of the decision problem investigated. For guiding the selection of viable decision aids, several factors (e.g., cognitive load, effort, task fit) must also be researched. In addition, the role of S-BPM and how it addresses the discussed challenges of CPS design has to be examined in more detail. In this regard, future research should also focus on the potential of S-BPM, especially SBDs, to represent the decision-making processes themselves.

References

1. Lee, E.A.: The past, present and future of cyber-physical systems: a focus on models. Sensors **15**, 4837–4869 (2015)

2. Lee, E.A.: Cyber physical systems: design challenges. In: 2008 11th IEEE International Symposium on Object and Component-Oriented Real-Time Distributed Computing (ISORC). pp. 363–369. IEEE (2008)

3. Broy, M.: Engineering cyber-physical systems: challenges and foundations. In: Aiguier, M., Caseau, Y., Krob, D., Rauzy, A. (eds.) Complex Systems Design & Management, pp. 1–13. Springer, Heidelberg (2013). https://doi.org/10.1007/978-3-642-34404-6_1

4. Harrison, R., Vera, D., Ahmad, B.: Engineering methods and tools for cyber-physical automation systems. Proc. IEEE **104**, 973–985 (2016)

5. Biffl, S., Lüder, A., Gerhard, D. (eds.): Multi-Disciplinary Engineering for Cyber-Physical Production Systems: Data Models and Software Solutions for Handling Complex Engineering Projects. Springer, Cham (2017). https://doi.org/10.1007/978-3-319-56345-9

6. Frysak, J., Krenn, F., Kaar, C., Stary, C.: Decision-making support for view-oriented I4.0 system architecture design. In: Proper, H.A., Strecker, S., Huemer, C. (eds.) 2018 IEEE 20th Conference on Business Informatics (CBI), pp. 186–195. IEEE Computer Society, Vienna (2018)

7. Fleischmann, A., Schmidt, W., Stary, C.: S-BPM in the Wild: Practical Value Creation. Springer, Heidelberg (2015). https://doi.org/10.1007/978-3-319-17542-3

8. Kannengiesser, U., Muller, H.: Towards agent-based smart factories: a subject-oriented modeling approach. In: 2013 IEEE/WIC/ACM International Joint Conferences on Web Intelligence (WI) and Intelligent Agent Technologies (IAT), pp. 83–86. IEEE, Atlanta (2013)

9. calvaresi, d., marinoni, m., sturm, a., schumacher, m., buttazzo, g.: the challenge of real-time multi-agent systems for enabling IoT and CPS. In: Proceedings of the International Conference on Web Intelligence, pp. 356–364. ACM, New York (2017)

10. Hermann, M., Pentek, T., Otto, B.: Design principles for industrie 4.0 scenarios: a literature review (2015)

11. Khaitan, S.K., McCalley, J.D.: Design techniques and applications of cyberphysical systems: a survey. IEEE Syst. J. **9**, 350–365 (2015)

12. Griffor, E.R., Greer, C., Wollman, D.A., Burns, M.J.: Framework for Cyber-Physical Systems: Volume 1, Overview (2017)

13. ISO/IEC/IEEE: ISO/IEC/IEEE International Standard - Systems and software engineering – System life cycle processes. ISO/IEC/IEEE 15288 First edition 2015-05-15, pp. 1–118 (2015)

14. Suri, K., Cadavid, J., Alferez, M., Dhouib, S., Tucci-Piergiovanni, S.: Modeling business motivation and underlying processes for RAMI 4.0-aligned cyber-physical production systems. In: 2017 22nd IEEE International Conference on Emerging Technologies and Factory Automation (ETFA), pp. 1–6. IEEE, Limassol (2017)

15. Berardinelli, L., Mazak, A., Alt, O., Wimmer, M., Kappel, G.: Model-driven systems engineering: principles and application in the CPPS domain. In: Biffl, S., Lüder, A., Gerhard, D. (eds.) Multi-Disciplinary Engineering for Cyber-Physical Production Systems, pp. 261–299. Springer, Cham (2017). https://doi.org/10.1007/978-3-319-56345-9_11

16. Thramboulidis, K., Bochalis, P., Bouloumpasis, J.: A framework for MDE of IoT-based manufacturing cyber-physical systems. In: Proceedings of the Seventh International Conference on the Internet of Things - IoT 2017, pp. 1–8. ACM Press, Linz (2017)

17. Wimmer, M., Mazak, A.: From AutomationML to AutomationQL: a by-example query language for CPPS engineering models. In: 2018 IEEE 14th International Conference on Automation Science and Engineering (CASE). 1394–1399 (2018)

18. ISO/IEC/IEEE: ISO/IEC/IEEE Systems and software engineering – Architecture description. ISO/IEC/IEEE 42010:2011(E) (Revision of ISO/IEC 42010:2007 and IEEE Std 1471–2000), pp. 1–46 (2011)

19. Simon, H.A.: The New Science of Management Decision. Prentice Hall PTR, Englewood Cliffs (1977)

20. Vroom, V.H., Jago, A.G.: On the validity of the Vroom-Yetton model. J. Appl. Psychol. **63**, 151–162 (1978)
21. Haendler, T., Frysak, J.: Deconstructing the refactoring process from a problem-solving and decision-making perspective. In: Maciaszek, L.A., van Sinderen, M. (eds.) Proceedings of the 13th International Conference on Software Technologies, ICSOFT 2018, Porto, Portugal, 26–28 July 2018, pp. 397–406. SciTePress (2018)
22. Asemi, A., Safari, A., Asemi Zavareh, A.: The role of management information system (MIS) and decision support system (DSS) for manager's decision making process. Int. J. Bus. Manag. **6**, 164 (2011)
23. Mora, M., Forgionne, G., Cervantes, F., Garrido, L., Gupta, J.N.D., Gelman, O.: Toward a comprehensive framework for the design and evaluation of intelligent decision-making support systems (i-DMSS). J. Decis. Syst. **14**, 321–344 (2005)
24. Te'eni, D., Ginzberg, M.J.: Human-computer decision systems: the multiple roles of DSS. Eur. J. Oper. Res. **50**, 127–139 (1991)
25. Courtney, J.F.: Decision making and knowledge management in inquiring organizations: toward a new decision-making paradigm for DSS. Decis. Support Syst. **31**, 17–38 (2001)
26. Felsberger, A., Oberegger, B., Reiner, G.: A review of decision support systems for manufacturing systems. In: SAMI@ iKNOW (2016)
27. Shim, J.P., Warkentin, M., Courtney, J.F., Power, D.J., Sharda, R., Carlsson, C.: Past, present, and future of decision support technology. Decis. Support Syst. **33**, 111–126 (2002)
28. Grünig, R., Kühn, R.: Successful Decision-Making. Springer, Heidelberg (2013). https://doi.org/10.1007/978-3-642-32307-2
29. Gorry, G.A., Morton, M.S.: A framework for management information systems. Sloan Manag. Rev. **30**, 49–61 (1989)
30. Zachary, W.: A cognitively based functional taxonomy of decision support techniques. Hum.-Comput. Interact. **2**, 25–63 (1986)
31. Fleischmann, A., Stary, C.: Whom to talk to? a stakeholder perspective on business process development. Univ. Access Inf. Soc. **11**, 125–150 (2012)

Performance Investigation and Proposal for Updates on the Exchange Standard for PASS

Matthes Elstermann[1] and André Wolski[2(✉)]

[1] Karlsruhe Institute of Technology, Karlsruhe, Germany
`matthes.elstermann@kit.edu`
[2] Technische Universität Darmstadt, Darmstadt, Germany
`andre.wolski@stud.tu-darmstadt.de`

Abstract. In this paper we examine the technical performance of the current version of the semantic exchange standard for the subject-oriented process-modeling language PASS (Parallel Activity Specification Schema). Based on our findings we propose changes to the standard that have the potential to significantly increase the reasoning performance.

Keywords: S-BPM · PASS · OWL · Exchange standard

1 Introduction

Currently the Parallel Activity Specification Schema (PASS) as proposed by [9] and [11], is the only explicit subject-oriented (business) process modeling language in existence.

There are currently various modeling tools in existence that allow to create according process models and/or use them [10]. Most have slightly different focus and technical foundations.

Originally proposed in [6] and further explored in [7], an official exchange standard format, founded on semantic-web technology and the Web Ontology Language (OWL) [5] was created in a research community effort, in order to be able to exchange process models in between the various tools.

The official standard has been published and is available at the I2PM community GitHub [4].

While not the most simplistic language in contrast to other possible technical solutions such as XML or JSON, OWL was chosen for various reasons: It comes with existing programming frameworks in various programming languages. It provides a logical provable foundation including tools such as so-called reasoners that provide syntactical and partial semantic checks.

And OWL also is very powerful when it comes to the integration of extensions. The open world assumption behind OWL allows it to store (and exchange) incomplete models, without violating any constraints. Further, OWL documents

© Springer Nature Switzerland AG 2020
M. Freitag et al. (Eds.): S-BPM ONE 2020, CCIS 1278, pp. 33–45, 2020.
https://doi.org/10.1007/978-3-030-64351-5_3

can include or reference additional OWL document specifications, which makes it possible to include tool-specific model aspects and extensions while still being compatible with tools that do not understand the widened scope and then consider only the commonly shared model elements as defined by the standard.

The practicality of this approach has been discussed and agreed on, as can be seen in the current standard document. However, while not necessarily the main focus so far, the technical performance of import, export, and model checking is also an important topic that so far has not been investigated.

Our investigation is motivated by reasoning times of several minutes, which we experienced during the development of an OWL extension and a corresponding OWL process model parser for the process evaluation environment introduced in [12].

2   Application Scenario

As conceptually envisioned [6], loading a process model from an .owl-file requires several steps. The general idea is that in addition to the actual process model, also the information of the standard PASS ontology as well as ontologies, containing the specifications for all aspects an importing tool can handle, need to be loaded to generate the overall relevant knowledge graph.

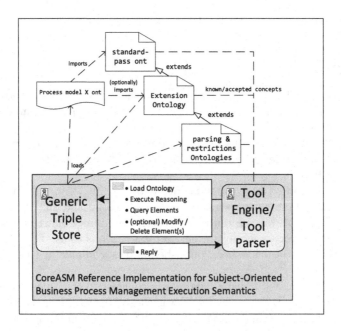

Fig. 1. Setup sketch of loaded ontologies

The Standard PASS Ont contains the specifications for correct PASS model semantics, while other specifications define possible extensions to the standard and how they relate to the standard model. An example of this is shown in Fig. 1, where the Standard PASS Ont is not only imported by the process model, but also extended by tool-specific ontologies.

If all is present, a generic reasoner, a generic logic algorithm or program, can be executed to analyze or reason about the given information in the knowledge graph. The first task here is to validate the syntactical correctness of the given process model and to verify that it is not contradicting the standard definitions. Additionally, based on the given specifications, the reasoner adds all additional links and connections to the knowledge graph. For example, if the model structure only contains the information that a *subject belongsTo* a *subject interaction diagram* (SID), the reasoner will add the information that the SID *contains* the corresponding subject.

This gives parsing tool programmers the great freedom of being able to traverse all elements in a process model in a way they see fit for their purposes without having to worry about the structure of the model that was exported to OWL. As long as a model adheres to the standard and contains sufficient information, a reasoner is able extrapolate and populate a process model with all required information.

Due to its generic approach, reasoning is however a computational complex task that, depending on model size and complexity of the extensions, may take considerable time.

2.1   Concrete Application Setup

In contrast to a modeling tool, the CoreASM execution and evaluation environment requires process models that are not inconsistent and ideally are executable. Here the open world assumption (OWA) is problematic[1].

To avoid the problems, the CoreASM application setup needs to impose further requirements for process models before they can be evaluated. While such requirements can be checked during the parsing (and lead to a RuntimeException), many requirements can be formulated directly in OWL. This way such restrictions can be shared with other tools, which enables any tool, that supports running a reasoner, to check those requirements beforehand.

For example: *"State hasOutgoingTransition max 1 UserCancel Transition"* - this axiom leads to an inconsistent ontology if there is a state with two outgoing user-cancel transitions, which can be checked easily even without an advanced reasoner.

As OWL allows many degrees of freedom in how process models are stored, the parser needs additional help to read OWL process models. This can be expressed in OWL as well, with the help of SWRL rules. For example the

---

[1] The open world assumption used in OWL explicitly allows incomplete descriptions, under the assumption that missing parts are defined somewhere else or at least can be provided later on without causing inconsistencies. For validation purposes the opposite of this assumption is required, to know if the current model is correct or not.

SWRL rule "$SubjectBehavior(?b)$, $EndState(?e)$, $contains(?b, ?e)- > hasEnd$ $State(?b, ?e)$" is used to transfer the knowledge about $EndStates$.

Furthermore, a long-time goal of the evaluation environment is to perform an automatic process model verification, with the focus on interaction soundness that goes beyond the capabilities of e.g. the SiSi approach [8]. The verification of interaction soundness requires further restricted process models, especially no potentially unbounded constructs must be present. For example, a $Macro$ that recursively calls itself can possibly lead to an infinite state space during the verification. The knowledge, which macros are called, can be inferred with a transitive property "$hasCallAbleMacro$" and the SWRL rule "$SubjectBehavior(?m1)$, $MacroState(?s)$, $SubjectBehavior(?m2)$, $contains(?m1, ?s)$, $referencesMacro$ $Behavior(?s, ?m2) - > hasCallAbleMacro(?m1, ?m2)$". Later on, the property "hasCallAbleMacro" can be further investigated before the start of the verification.

2.2 Concrete Ontologies

In the following performance evaluation, **Standard-PASS-Ont** references a slightly modified version of the Standard PASS Ontology, accessed in October 2019. The axiom "$State\ hasOutgoingTransition\ some\ Transition$" has been changed to "$State\ hasOutgoingTransition\ min\ 0\ Transition$" in order to avoid an inconsistency, that results from a currently unresolved conceptional incompatibility of the CoreASM implementation with the Standard PASS definition regarding the restart of subjects, and therefore whether an $EndState$ may have outgoing transitions (explicit restart, as defined in the standard) or must not have any outgoing transitions (implicit restart, as currently implemented in CoreASM).

The **Extensions Ontology** defines additional language elements, that are supported by the CoreASM interpreter but are not (yet) part of the Standard PASS Ont. For example, 18 Functions have a concrete ASM specification, as shown in Fig. 2. Additionally, the CoreASM implementation introduces a scope for DataObjectDefinitions and a concept to copy data objects between Macros via a "DataObjectBinding".

The additional requirements to parse, evaluate, and verify process models are currently stored in three ontologies: the **Parsing Ontology**, the **Callable Ontology** and the **Restrictions Ontology**. The actual definition of the requirements, where they are stored and how they are processed, is currently researched by us.

2.3 Measuring Reasoning Performance

The process models used for the evaluation are a variant of the standard example processes for a travel request and hotel booking often encountered in the literature regarding PS. The process "travelRequest" $contains$ three $FullySpecified$ $Subjects$ "applicant", "supervisor", "administration" and an $InterfaceSubject$

Table 1. Ontology metrics (1)

Metric	Standard	Extensions	Callable	Parsing
Axiom	795	220	9	98
Class count	95	34	0	2
Object property count	46	17	1	0
Data property count	31	2	0	1
Individual count	16	6	0	0
SubClassOf	211	84	1	68
DisjointClasses	24	8	0	0
GCI count	0	0	0	0
Hidden GCI Count	7	0	0	0
ClassAssertion	16	6	0	0
ObjectPropertyAssertion	0	0	0	0
DataPropertyAssertion	0	0	0	0

Table 2. Ontology metrics (2)

Metric	Restrictions	hotelBooking	travelRequest
Axiom	53	105	637
Class count	2	0	0
Object property count	0	0	0
Data property count	0	0	0
Individual count	8	18	113
SubClassOf	15	0	0
DisjointClasses	2	0	0
GCI count	0	0	0
Hidden GCI Count	2	0	0
ClassAssertion	8	33	206
ObjectPropertyAssertion	4	32	207
DataPropertyAssertion	1	14	86

"hotelBookingInterface". The process "hotelBooking" *contains* the FullySpecifiedSubject "hotelBookingDesk" and the InterfaceSubject "hotelBookingClient".

In Table 1 and 2 we list some selected metrics for each ontology, as calculated by Protégé Desktop 5.5.0.

For the performance evaluation we developed a small test bench, that uses OWLAPI 5.1.12 to pre-load the various ontology combinations and then sequentially executes the reasoning for each defined ontology combination. We used a variant of the Openllet reasoner [1], that works around a bug [2] with the small change suggested in the issue description, that should not affect the performance

Fig. 2. TUD PASS extensions

measuring. Then the duration of the call of `reasoner.precomputeInferences`
(`InferenceType.CLASS_HIERARCHY`) was measured between two calls of `System`
`.nanoTime()`.

For comparison, we executed the tests on two different systems:

- A mobile PC with an Intel Core i7-6820HQ CPU, Windows 10 1903, Open-
  JDK 64-Bit Server VM AdoptOpenJDK (build 11.0.5+10, mixed mode)
- A desktop PC with an Intel Core i7-860 CPU, Debian 10.2, Linux 5.4.8-
  1~bpo10+1, OpenJDK 64-Bit Server VM (build 11.0.6+10-post-Debian-
  [4]1deb10u1, mixed mode, sharing)

To take into account, that the Java Virtual Machine uses an optimizing JIT
compiler, we executed the tests in a second run in reverse order.

3   Possible Improvements

In scenarios where reasoning is something that will only be done once with the import of a process model, performance may not be the most crucial criteria. However the referential implementation makes use of the OWL technology far more central for validation and verification purposes, this is a huge issue. Especially if in future iteration constant monitoring and checking during modeling are envisioned. And even if not, still over several minutes for rather small process models and the potential of exponential run-time growth with larger, realistic process models is at the least concerning.

3.1   Existential Explosion and Large Cardinality

Trying to find potential to improve the performance we analyzed the documentation [1] of the Openllet reasoner.

Reasoners are general purpose logical engines that in essence are still deterministic programs that have to cope with the Open World concept of OWL. In consequence and as is described in the documentation, reasoners in general, or at least tableau-based reasoners such as the used Openllet, need to generate a lot of anonymous individuals for various axioms and/or classes in order to be able to actually execute the reasoning.

Especially existential restrictions such as *some*, *min* and *exactly*, *"may generate an intractable number of individuals"* [3] during reasoning *"which grows exponentially when these axioms interact with the others in a recursive [and complex] manner"* [3].

3.2   Measuring Changes

Due to these circumstance it is hard to determine exact causalities and effects or to quantify them. Instead the chosen method for an initial assessment was to apply changes and observe the run-time differences.

As indicated before, the two process model ontologies import the *Extensions Ontology* for additional PASS concepts, which then includes the *Standard PASS Ont*. The OWL process model parser of the run-time environment imports three additional ontologies, to enable the parsing and to determine whether a process model can be executed.

In a first step, we noticed that the OWL class *"PASSProcessModelElement"* is the parent of most of the used OWL classes and is therefore present on almost all individuals. With the background knowledge described in the previous Sect. 3.1 this was obviously the first class to look at, as this central definitions are likely to have a global impact. It contains three subclass definitions: *"hasAdditionalAttribute some AdditionalAttribute"*, *"has ModelComponentID exactly 1 xsd : string"* and *"hasModelComponentLabel min 1 xsd : string"*. All three definitions are *existential restrictions*. Therefore our first step was to change the definitions to avoid the existential restrictions, referenced below as *Standard - minimal changes*: *"hasAdditionalAttribute min*

0 *AdditionalAttribute*", "*hasModelComponentID max* 1 *xsd* : *string*" and "*hasModelComponentLabel min* 0 *xsd* : *string*" (Fig. 3).

Fig. 3. Example for change from *some* to *min 0*

Going further, we were interested in the total impact of existential restrictions. In the second step we replaced most existential restrictions in both the *Standard PASS Ont* and *Extensions Ontology* with either "min 0", "max 1" or "only". While the changes of this second step make semantically not much sense, they should demonstrate the run-time impact of existential restrictions and set a lower threshold of what can be achieved.

Table 3. Change metrics: Standard PASS Ont

Metric	Before	Minimal changes	Maximal changes
minQualifiedCardinality	9	10	26
qualifiedCardinality	37	36	28
maxQualifiedCardinality	25	26	35
someValuesFrom	27	26	7
allValuesFrom	7	7	9

Table 4. Change metrics: Extensions Ont

Metric	Before	Maximal changes
minQualifiedCardinality	0	14
qualifiedCardinality	19	12
maxQualifiedCardinality	0	9
someValuesFrom	16	0
allValuesFrom	1	1

Table 3 lists the changed metrics of the Standard PASS Ont. Table 4 lists the changed metrics of the Extensions ontology.

4   Results of Changes and Combinations

We were also interested in the impact of the additional three ontologies that are used by the parser, which is why we tested some combinations without them being included.

Table 5. Changes of custom extensions.

Extensions	Callable	Parsing	Requirements	Case
UNCHANGED	UNCHANGED	UNCHANGED	UNCHANGED	A1
UNCHANGED	UNCHANGED	UNCHANGED	NONE	A2
UNCHANGED	UNCHANGED	NONE	NONE	A3
UNCHANGED	NONE	UNCHANGED	UNCHANGED	B1
UNCHANGED	NONE	UNCHANGED	NONE	B2
UNCHANGED	NONE	NONE	NONE	B3
MAXIMAL_CHANGES	UNCHANGED	UNCHANGED	UNCHANGED	C1
MAXIMAL_CHANGES	UNCHANGED	UNCHANGED	NONE	C2
MAXIMAL_CHANGES	UNCHANGED	NONE	NONE	C3
MAXIMAL_CHANGES	NONE	UNCHANGED	UNCHANGED	D1
MAXIMAL_CHANGES	NONE	UNCHANGED	NONE	D2
MAXIMAL_CHANGES	NONE	NONE	NONE	D3

Table 5 shows the combinations that were executed for each change of the Standard PASS Ont.

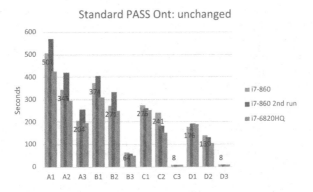

Fig. 4. Performance measuring without changes to Standard Pass Ont

As shown in Fig. 4 the different extensions have a different impact. Although the process models use no macros the removal of the *Callable Ontology* has a noticeable impact, as seen between the cases A and B resp. between C and D. The removal of the *Parsing Ontology* has the biggest impact, as shown between the cases B2/C2/D2 to B3/C3/D3.

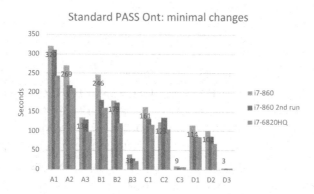

Fig. 5. Performance measuring with minimal changes to Standard PASS Ont

The run-time differences between Fig. 4 and Fig. 5 demonstrate, that even the small change in the Standard PASS Ont for just the *PASSProcess ModelElement* alone already greatly reduces the run-time by a factor of 35% to 45%, across all extensions combinations.

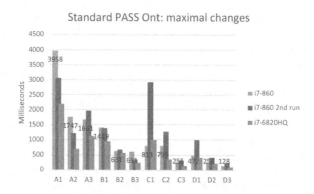

Fig. 6. Performance measuring with maximal changes to Standard PASS Ont

With the relaxation of most existential restrictions in the Standard PASS Ont a performance improvement by the order of two magnitudes can be archived, as demonstrated in Fig. 6 (note the different scale). Note however, that this "blind" approach is semantically questionable and was only chosen to investigate the technical possibilities and limitations.

What can also be seen is the general exponential decrease in run-time in general if the complexity of the knowledge graph is reduced by relaxing.

The improvements of the changes are mainly consistent between the two different machines, with some variations.

The execution order of the first run on both machines was first in the order of the figures and then in the order of the columns. As the Java Virtual Machine uses an optimizing JIT compiler one could expect, that cases that are executed later perform better. The second run on the desktop PC was executed in reverse order, to investigate this factor.

In Fig. 6 we see that the run in reversed order takes 17% longer, which would support this idea. However, the second run is faster in the tests with the minimal changes to the Standard PASS Ont, whereas the first run should benefit from the already executed cases with the unchanged ontology. The second run should benefit most from the JIT optimizations in the cases with the unchanged Standard PASS Ont, but is even 8% slower. We therefore presume that other causes than the JIT optimizations influence the performance measuring variations.

5 Discussion of Proposed Changes and Impact

Based on the findings, it seems obvious to propose the transfer of the made changes into the to the official standard.

The question remains if the according changes are valid on a semantic level and do not negate or change the fundamental concept of the PASS standard.

5.1 *"some"* Vs. *"min 0"*

In OWL, to link to elements via an existential restriction with *"some"* is the most general idea. It means that there can be a link but there must not be, e.g. a *PASSProcessModel contains "some" Subject*[2] [elements].

"Some" was chosen to describe that e.g. *Subjects* are what is supposed to be within a process model. However, **empty or unfinished models**, models that contain only *MessageExchanges* are not wrong. There is no technical reason to state that a model without subjects is invalid or incorrect. The restriction via *"some"* represents that best, especially for human readers who otherwise may think that a model can only be transferred or saved in the exchange format if it fulfills the requirement of containing subjects[3].

Natural language-wise, the quantification of *"some"* is not explicitly defined. Subjectively for the authors at least, it carries however the notion of *"at least 1"* with *"less than one"* as the an exception in rare cases. It better expresses what should be the case without restricting it.

---

[2] Using terms/notation from the standard-PASS-ont directly.

[3] This would be different if the goal was to define constraints and conditions for *"complete"* or *"executable"* process models. Though for the purpose of model exchange such much more strict definitions are not required.

From a logical point of view, *"some"* and *"min 0"* are equal or at least almost equal, as far as can be discerned for our purposes.

So relatively huge, potential performance gains for practical applications indicated by our tests make the transition here more than viable with only potential elegance of expression within the exchange standard being slightly dampened.

5.2   The Case of "min 1"

One of the important aspects of OWL is its open-world-assumption (OWA). This leads to the argument that instead of *"min 0"*, *"min 1"* existential restrictions could be used to quantify relations between elements.

Under an OWA, models not containing elements quantified with *"min 1"* are not wrong per se and a general purpose reasoner would not created error messages, as it assumes that the missing elements may exist but are unknown within the current context.

For some elements or the quantification of their relation this may potentially be true. But here it gets complicated quite quickly.

E.g. Any SBD state will have a function specification and only if it is a default condition and there could be quantification with *min 1* even if it is the default function.

With outgoing and incoming transitions of SBD states it is quite different as there are start and end states in regular PASS diagrams that either have no incoming or outgoing transitions.

To summarize, the usage of *"min 1"* as a general quantifier to replace the *"some"* quantifier is not possible as it does change the semantical description of the standard in contrast to the usage of *"min 0"*.

6   Summary and Outlook

In this work we have examined the possibilities and consequences of improving the runtime performance with reasoning over subject-oriented PASS process models using the PASS owl standard described in the standard-PASS ontology.

We found that certain changes with the quantification of certain attributes in the description may greatly improve the technical performance of the standard in every day application without changing the nature or content of the standard.

Based on our measurement under the stated conditions we therefore propose to discuss the adoption of these changes into the formal exchange standard and greatly encourage this.

Alternatively, we would encourage other researchers to test the proposed changes with other tools that make use of different programming frameworks such as the JAVA based Jena framework in order to verify these result.

References

1. Openllet is an owl 2 reasoner in java, build on top of pellet. https://github.com/Galigator/openllet. Accessed 13 Jan 2020

2. Openllet issue: Nullpointerexception in rete.joincondition.test. https://github.com/Galigator/openllet/issues/39. Accessed 23 Feb 2020
3. Openllet-pellint patterns. https://github.com/Galigator/openllet/blob/integration/tools-pellint/PATTERNS.txt. Accessed 23 Feb 2020
4. A standard for subject-oriented specification of systems. https://github.com/I2PM/Standard-Documents-for-Subject-Orientation. Accessed 13 Jan 2020
5. The web ontology language (2012). https://www.w3.org/TR/owl2-overview. Accessed 14 Jan 2020
6. Elstermann, M.: Proposal for using semantic technologies as a means to store and exchange subject-oriented process models. In: S-BPM ONE 2017 - Darmstadt, Germany, 30–31 March 2017 (2017)
7. Elstermann, M., Krenn, F.: The semantic exchange standard for subject-oriented process models. In: S-BPM ONE 2018 - Linz, Austria, 4–6 April 2018 (2018)
8. Elstermann, M., Ovtcharova, J.: Sisi in the ALPS: a simple simulation and verification approach for pass. In: Proceedings of the 10th International Conference on Subject-Oriented Business Process Management, S-BPM One 2018. Association for Computing Machinery, New York (2018)
9. Fleischmann, A.: Distributed Systems - Software Design and Implementation. Springer, Heidelberg (1994). https://doi.org/10.1007/978-3-642-78612-9
10. Fleischmann, A., Borgert, S., Elstermann, M., Krenn, F., Singer, R.: An overview to S-BPM oriented tool suites. In: Proceedings of the 9th International Conference on Subject-Oriented Business Process Management, S-BPM ONE, ACM (2017)
11. Fleischmann, A., Schmidt, W., Stary, C.: Subjektorientiertes Prozessmanagement. Hanser Verlag, Munich (2011)
12. Wolski, A., Borgert, S., Heuser, L.: A coreASM based reference implementation for subject-oriented business process management execution semantics. In: S-BPM ONE. ACM (2019)

Mapping Execution and Model Semantics for Subject-Oriented Process Models

Matthes Elstermann[1] and André Wolski[2(✉)]

[1] Karlsruhe Institute of Technology, Karlsruhe, Germany
matthes.elstermann@kit.edu
[2] Technische Universität Darmstadt, Darmstadt, Germany
andre.wolski@stud.tu-darmstadt.de

Abstract. For the subject-oriented (business) process modeling language PASS (Parallel Activity Specification Scheme) there are currently two kinds of formal specifications, one for the execution semantics and one for the digital exchange of model descriptions. One uses the Abstract State Machine (ASM) modeling concept, the other is created using the Web Ontology Language (OWL).

An open question is, if and how they fit together, especially given their peculiar different natures.

In this work we analyze how both are related, where there may be confusions or contradictions, and what future work could comprise based on the findings of the analysis. Thereby this work provides an insight to both specifications, fosters understanding, and helps to avoid miss conceptions about both.

Keywords: S-BPM · PASS · OWL · ASM · Formal standards

1 Subject-Oriented Process Models with PASS

This work is concerned with the subject-oriented Process-Modeling language PASS (Parallel Activity Specification Schema) as first defined by Albert Fleischmann in [11] and later in [13].

Subject-Orientation. Subject-Orientation as a paradigm for describing processes is to be understood in the sense of the grammatical concept of subject as active entity in simple natural language sentence. In almost all natural languages/grammars in this world this construct (S - Subject) is the first element to be stated. Only afterwards objects (O) or verbs/predicates (P) follow in the information flow in that order (SOP)[1]. Consequently, in subject-oriented description first the (possibly abstract) active elements in a process must be defined. Or rather, they must not be omitted! Only afterwards the (information) objects

---

[1] SOP is the dominant structure of 50% of the world's natural languages [4] while e.g. the English language's SPO structure is only present in 30% of the languages.

© Springer Nature Switzerland AG 2020
M. Freitag et al. (Eds.): S-BPM ONE 2020, CCIS 1278, pp. 46–59, 2020.
https://doi.org/10.1007/978-3-030-64351-5_4

exchanged between the subjects can be defined, followed by process relevant activities[2].

Being the currently only[3] explicit subject-oriented modeling language in the world, PASS follows this principle.

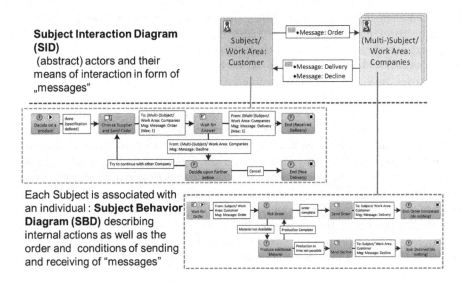

Fig. 1. Main components of PASS

Elements of PASS. The five core elements of PASS are spread across two types of diagrams. A process model first consists of at least one Subject Interaction Diagram (SID, shown in the top part of Fig. 1) that contains information about what active entities are involved in a process - the subjects - and what information they exchange - the objects.

Only after these two elements are described, the activities - predicates/verbs - of each subject are described in individual Subject Behavior Diagrams (SBD, shown in the bottom part of Fig. 1). Here a subject's independent activities are described with so called Function or Do-States, while the acts of sending and receiving messages are stated in according Send- and Receive-States, making it an essential requirement to explicitly model the interaction between subjects.

---

[2] This concept has principle advantages over more classical approaches, as extensively investigated in [6].

[3] It is possible to follow subject-oriented principles by using, e.g. the Business Process Model and Notation (BPMN) [10], however the language itself is not subject-oriented and a possibly subject-oriented workflow can be broken quite easily.

1.1   Execution Semantics

Originally, the execution logic of PASS only existed informally as described by [11] and in the form of the - formerly jCom1 - now Metasonic Workflow Modeling Suit and execution engine.

Over time, more execution engines were developed, extending PASS with their own elements and semantics [12]. In congruence with that there have been attempts to extend and formalize PASS, for example as Borgert did when he proposed an extended Parallel Activity Specification Scheme for the Internet of Services (ePASS-IoS) in [2] formalized with the π-calculus.

However, no single effort has taken hold or was agreed upon in the community or by tool vendors.

This changed to some degree with the release of [13] in 2012 that included the *Börger Interpreter* in its appendix, thereby being somewhat accepted as the de-facto standard. This specification in the notation or formalism of Abstract State Machines (ASM) [3] was devised by Prof. Egon Börger, hence for its name.

Due to the book [13] carrying the label of Subject-Oriented Business Process Management (S-BPM) and S-BPM being a strong term, extensively used as the label of and for the research domain[4], the interpreter model claims to be an S-BPM interpreter model. However, this name is somewhat misleading, as the interpreter is not interpreting the domain and all aspects of Subject-Oriented Business Process Management but rather it is an interpreter specification for a single PASS SBD.

The ASM specification describes an abstract algorithm for the execution of a single Subject in a PASS workflow engine, assuming that other subjects in a PASS process model will be executed equally by other instances of the interpreter.

PERFORM(subj ;COMACT; state) =
 if *NonBlockingTryRound(subj ; state)* **then**
  if *TryRoundFinished(subj ; state)* **then**
   INITIALIZEBLOCKINGTRYROUNDS(*subj ; state*)
  else TryAlternative.____(*subj ; state*)
 if *BlockingTryRound(subj ; state)* **then**
  if *TryRoundFinished(subj ; state)*
   then INITIALIZEROUNDALTERNATIVES(*subj ; state*)
  else
   if *Timeout(subj ; state; timeout(state))* **then**

Fig. 2. Excerpt from the ASM specification of the `PERFORM COMACT` rule

Figure 2 shows an excerpt from the specification. A visual representation of this rule is shown in Fig. 3.

---

[4] E.g. the specialized series of research conferences are called S-BPM ONE.

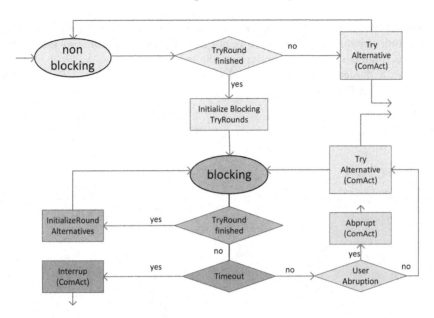

Fig. 3. Graphic showing the principle control flow of the `PERFORM COMACT` rule (from [13])

The Börger execution semantics do not explicitly describe the structure of PASS formally. However, their implicit assumptions define the existence and execution concepts of almost all standard PASS elements at that time.

1.2   Model Description and Exchange

Next to the algorithmic definition of the interpreter, a formal, ontological specification (the Standard Pass Ontology [15]) for the passive model structure of PASS has been created within the Subject-Oriented (S-BPM) Community using the web ontology language (OWL) [16][5].

Initially proposed in 2017 by [5], and further considered 2018 by [7], the origin and main purpose here is the practical need to exchange Process Models between multiple tools on a technical level. Prior to that initiative, there only existed the proprietary format of the Metasonic Workflow Suit as the most extensive PASS model format, as well as the various other [12]. The *Standard Pass Ontology*

---

[5] As argued in [5] and [7], while not the most simplistic technology in contrast to other possible solutions such as XML or JSON, OWL was chosen for various reasons: It comes with existing programming frameworks in various programming languages. It provides a logical provable foundation including tools such as so-called reasoners that provide syntactical and partial semantic checks. And OWL, as non tree-, but rather graph structure, is also very powerful when it comes to the integration of extensions or other tool specific considerations without forcing other tools to be able to handle them.

defines the semantic structures for PASS models and how they should be saved. This includes incomplete and therefore not necessarily executable process models as well as models containing vendor specific extensions.

Figure 4 depicts a small graphical excerpt of the structure defined in the Standard PASS Ontology.

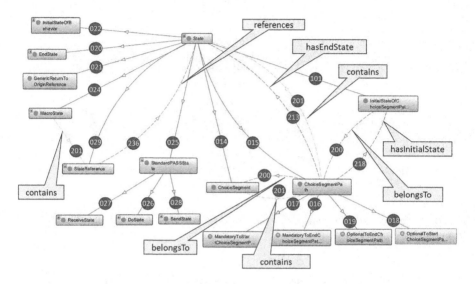

Fig. 4. Graphical excerpt from the Standard PASS Ontology [15]

1.3   Research Motivation

Time, circumstances, method, and goals have been different for both definition approaches. The interpreters are formalized execution logics for algorithmic verification purposes of a workflow engine. In contrast, the by 6 to 8 years younger OWL standard was based on the needs and aspects of process modelers, contains elements not necessary for the execution, and was created with its own vocabulary.

The investigated hypothesis is, that the ASM and OWL specifications fit together. Or if they do not fit, to investigate where differences are or what is not considered by one or the other.

2   Comparison/Mapping

In our analysis we thoroughly investigated both specifications, grouped concepts and tried to map important concepts to one another. Due to the somewhat better comprehensibility of the OWL Specification and their more intuitive denominations, in our matching we decided to start with aspect on the ASM interpreter and describe their purpose with a general natural language *Description* as well as *corresponding OWL model elements.*

Due to the greatly different nature of both, one being an active algorithmic description the other being the specification of a passive data structure, a simple 1:1 match was basically not possible. Rather it is described how the concepts and terms of the OWL standard are supposed to be interpreted.

We have summarized the analysis in matching tables (Figs. 5 to 11). Due to the format of this paper the tables are compactly displayed which may hinder legibility. For better comprehensibility a full accessed copy can be found at [14].

The principle categories are: Basic Model Elements, Main Execution Rules, Functions, and Input Pool Handling Concerns.

As stated, the orientation is done with the ASM spec, therefore the categories where chosen to group certain aspects and formulations in the ASM spec that follow a similar implicit logic. Their meaning is explained at the beginning of each of the following sections.

2.1 Basic Model Elements

Basic Model Elements are terms used in the ASM spec (mostly placeholders) that stand conceptually for passive storage structures[6] and therefore have mostly direct conceptual and terminological equivalents in the OWL standard. See Fig. 5.

2.2 Rules

The interpreter ASM Spec has main-functions or rules that are to be executed. They make up the main interpreter algorithm for PASS SBDs and therefore have no corresponding direct model elements but rather are or contain the instructions of how to interpret a model. See Fig. 6.

2.3 Functions

In ASM Logic, functions return or determine some element (places). Dynamic functions can be considered as "variables" known from programming languages, they can be read and written. Static functions are initialized before the execution, they can only be read. See Fig. 7 and Fig. 8.

2.4 Input Pool Handling Concerns

An implicit assumption of PASS is, that during execution each subject has its own message inbox that receives and stores message instances until taken out by a receive activity specified in the behaviour (see Figs. 9 and 10).

---

[6] The ASM formalism does not have a specific notion or concept of a *"variable"*. Rather, functions and rules have arguments, which use call-by-name semantics and it cannot be statically known whether an argument has an explicit value or is another function.

Interpreter Spec	Description	Corresponding OWL-Model Element
SID_state	Execution concept – no model representation, Not to be confused by a model "state" in an SBD Diagram. State in the SBD diagram define possible SID_States.	X - Execution concept – the state the subject is currently in as defined by a State in the model
D	A Diagram that is a completely connected SBD	SubjectBehavior – under the assumption that it is complete and sound.
node	A specific element of diagram D - Every node 1:1 to state	State
state	The current active state of a diagram determined by the nodes of Diagram D	State
initial state	The interpreter expects and SBD Graph D to contain exactly	InitialStateOfBehavior
end state	one initial (start) state and at least one end state	EndState
edge / outEdge	"Passive Element" of an edge in an SBD-graph	Transition
ExitCondition	Static Concept that represents a Data condition	TransitionCondition
subj	Identifier for a specific Subject Carrier that may be responsible for multiple Subjects	Execution Concept – ID of a Subject Carrier responsible possible multiple Instances of according to specific SubjectBehavior
ExternalSubject	A representation of a service execution entity outside of the boundaries of the interpreter (The PASS-OWL Standardization community decided on the new Term of Interface Subject to replace the often-misleading older term of External Subject)	Represented in the model with InterfaceSubject
subject-SBD / SBD_subject	Names for completely connected graphs / diagrams representing SBDs	SubjectBehavior or rather SubjectBaseBehavior as MacroBehaviors and GuardBehaviors are not covered by Börger
service(state) / service(node)	Rule/Function that reads/returns the service of function of a given state/node:	Object Property: hasFunctionSpecification (linking State, and FunctionSpecification --> (State hasFunctionSpecification FunctionSpecification)
function state	The ASM spec does not itself contain these terms. The	DoState
send state	description text, however, uses them to describe states with	SendState
receive state	an according service	ReceiveState

Fig. 5. Matching Table 1: basic model elements

Interpreter Spec	Description	Corresponding OWL-Model Element
BEHAVIOR(subj;state)	Main interpreter ASM-rule/Method	Execution concept
BEHAVIOR(subj;node)	ASM-Rule to interpret a specific node of Diagram D for a specific subject	Execution concept
Behaviorsubj (D)	Set of all ASM rules to interprete all nodes/states in a SBD(iagram) D for a given subj (set of all BEHAVIOR(subj;node))	Execution concept
PERFORM(subj ; service(state); state)	The main Perform ASM Rule/Method that prompts an PASS interpreter to execute functions defined for states	State hasFunctionSpecification FunctionSpecification Specialized in: DoFunction and. CommunicationActs with ReceiveFunction SendFunction There exist a few default activities: DefaultFunctionDo1_EnvoironmentChoice DefaultFunctionDo2_AutomaticEvaluation
PERFORM(subj ;ComAct; state)	ASM-Rule specifying the execution of a Comunication act in an according state)	CommunicationActs with ReceiveFunction SendFunction DefaultFunctionReceive1_EnvironmentChoice DefaultFunctionReceive2_AutoReceiveEarliest DefaultFunctionSend

Fig. 6. Matching Table 2: rules

Interpreter Spec	Description	Corresponding OWL-Model Element
SID_state(subj)	Dynamic ASM-Function that stores the current *state* of a *subj*	Function that the return state should correspond to/be derived from one of the multiple State in an SBD model
OutEdge(state) / OutEdge(state;i)	Function that returns the set of outgoing edges of a state or a single specific edge i	State hasOutgoingTransition Transition (input / worked on link / output (Set of Transition) (linking State with)
target(edge) / target(outEdge)	Function that returns the follow up state of an outgoing transition (*outEdge* is a special denomination for an *edge* returned by the *OutEdge* -Function)	Object Property: hasTargetState (linking Transition and State--> Transition hasTargetState State
source(edge)	Function that returns the source state of an *edge*	Object Property: hasSourceState (linking Transition and State--> Transition hasSourceState State (input / worked on link / output)
Determine Follow up state Mechanic		
ExitCond(e) ExitCond(outEdge) ExitCond_i(e) ExitCond(e)(subj,state)	Derived Function that evaluates the ExitCondition of a given edge/outgoing edge	Exit conditions in PASS are defined on their corresponding Transitions and therefore are called TransitionCondition. Transitions have(hasTransitionCondition) (State -> hasOutgoingTransition --> Transition --> hasTransitionCondition --> TransitionCondition)
select_Edge	ASM Function that determines an edged (transition) to follow.	Execution Concept
completed(subj ; service(state); state)	Function that returns true if the Service of a certain *state* is complete IF the *subject* is in that *state*	Execution Concept (connected to: State, and FunctionSpecification)
	Rule/Function that gives that returns the service of function of a given state:	Execution Concept

Fig. 7. Matching Table 3: ASM functions

Interpreter Spec	Description	Corresponding OWL-Model Element
NormalExitCond	is used internally to "remember" that neither a timeout nor a user cancel have happened, so that the correct exit transition can be taken.	Exit conditions in PASS are defined on their corresponding Transitions and therefore are called TransitionCondition. Execution Concept: can be set on. Execution Concept: used to determine the correct exit
Timer/Timeout Mechanic: The evaluation and handling of timeouts is defined (and refined) with several rules and functions. *timeout(state)*, *Timeout(subj , state, timeout(state))*, *SetTimeoutClock(subj ; state)* are used to evaluate the timeout condition, *Interrupt_service(state)(subj , state)* is used to define how the corresponding service should be canceled. *TimeoutExitCond* is used internally to "remember" that a timeout happened, so that the correct exit transition can be taken.		In the model to be interpreted the according aspects are captured by TimerTransitions that have (hasTransitionCondition) a TimerTransitionCondition containing the date. The *timeout(state)* function should read the information.
User Cancel/Abrupt Mechanic: The evaluation and handling of user cancels is defined (and refined) with several rules and functions. *UserAbruption(subj, state)* is used to evaluate the user decision, *Abrupt_service(state)(subj , state)* is used to define how the corresponding service should be abrupted. *AbruptionExitCond* is used internally to "remember" that a user cancel happened, so that the correct exit transition can be taken.		In PASS models the possibility to arbitrarily cancel the execution of a (receive) function and the possible course of action afterwards may be discerned via a UserCancelTransitions
MultiRound / mult(alt) / InitializeMultiRoun / ContinueMultiRoundSuccess (among others)	Definition of Functions and ASM rules for interaction between multiple Subjects at once	With the definition of the data properties hasMaximumSubjectInstanceRestriction The MultiSubject are actually the standard and SingleSubject the special case
AltAction / altEntry(D) / altExit(D) AltBehDgm(altSplit) altJoin(altSplit)	Rules for the semantics/handling of ChoiceSegements	Handling of ChoiceSegment & ChoiceSegmentPath
Compulsory(altEntry(D)) and Compulsory(altExit(D))		Combination of isOptionalToStartChoiceSegmentPath and isOptionalToEndChoiceSegmentPath data properties

Fig. 8. Matching Table 4: further ASM functions

Interpreter Spec	Description	Corresponding OWL-Model Element
P /InputPool	The input pool of a subject instance	Execution concept – the model consists of Subject that hasInputPoolConstraints InputPoolConstraints wich are applied to Pool
MsgToBeHandled(subj ; state)	Place where temporarily messages are stored that will be send or received.	Execution concept

Fig. 9. Matching Table 5: places for input pool handling

Börger Interpreter Function	Description	Corresponding OWL-Model Element
constraintTable(inputPool)	Function that Returns the set of all input Pool constrains	Refers to a set of InputPoolConstraints of Subject that has hasInputPoolConstraints – for its Input Pool
sender/receiver	Identifiers for possible subject instances trying to access an input pool	Execution Concept with evalution relevance for: MessageSenderTypeConstraint and SenderTypeConstraint
msgType	(Data) Type of an Instance of a Message	MessageSpecification Can be used to formulate: MessageTypeConstraint
select_{MsgKind};subj;state;alt;()	ASM Function that determines the message kind ("message type") to be received in a given receive state.	Execution Concept
{Blocking; DropYoungest; DropOldest; DropIncoming}	Default Input Pool handling strategies for	InputPoolContstraintHandlingStrategy And their individual defaultinstances: InputPoolConstraintStrategy-Blocking InputPoolConstraintStrategy-DeleteLatest InputPoolConstraintStrategy-DeleteOldest InputPoolConstraintStrategy-Drop
P / inputPool	The actual Input Pool	Execution Concept – can be restricted by InputPoolConstraint
synchronous communication	Definition for an input pool constraint set to 0 requiring sender and receiver interpreter to be in the corresponding send and receive states at the same time in order to actually communicate (as messages cannot be passed to an input pool)	

Fig. 10. Matching Table 6: functions for input pool handling

3 Summary and Findings

Our analysis shows that the execution semantics of Börger and the model definition in OWL match very well. To be more precise, we did not find any contradictions between two aspects.

However, the nomenclature between the two differ quite profoundly and may not give the impression that both fit well together though.

3.1 Vocabulary

The ASM specification follows its own naming scheme used there, and is also much older and therefore uses older variants of terms and naming.

This can already be seen by the indiscriminate and somewhat erroneous usage of the term *S-BPM* throughout the whole specification without any explicit mentioning of the actual term *PASS*.

Other examples for older terms in contrast to newer variants are *Function-State* (now *Do-State*) or *External Subject* (now *Interface Subject*).

Finally there is one larger potential for misunderstanding: the term *Action*. It appears in both standards and means different things, but not in a contradicting way. The ASM specification refers to *Actions* simply as activities the abstract interpreter engine may take. An *Action* in the OWL standard is an aggregation of model elements, that groups a single modeled state with all its outgoing transitions together.

3.2 Unmatched

The other important finding of our analysis is, that at this point there are certain aspects in the OWL Model that are not covered in the Börger ASM interpreter (see Fig. 11).

PASS OWL Model Element	
InteractionDescribingComponents / Subject / FullySpecifiedSubject/ MultiSubject	With the exception of InputPool related concepts that belong to the SID of PASS process model, the Börger interpreter is for most parts concerned with the execution of a singular SBD. The specifying and coordinating nature of the SID of a PASS model should have had an influence on the creation of the individual SBDs but therefore is also irrelevant for the ASM interpreter.
FullySpecifiedSubject containsBehavior min 1 SubjectBehavior	The OWL-Model standard envisions a subject to contain possibly multiple behaviors that possess a priority order. This includes GuardBehaviors, MacroBehaviors and ExtensionBehaviors/ExtensionLayer as well as elements to navigate between the different behavior layers such as the GenericReturnToOriginReference.
GuardBehavior MacroBehavior ExtensionLayer GenericReturnToOriginReference	The Börger interpreter cannot execute these Multi-Behavior models. There is however an ASM Spec extending the Börger Spec that envisions the according execution . [7] Interpreter ASM Rules/Mechanisms for the Execution of Guards and Macros assumes these specialized model constructs to be part of the singular SBD. That original concept has evolved and been changed in the new PASS-OWL model standard
ReminderTransition / ReminderEventTransitionCondition	This type time-logic-based transitions did not exist when the original ASM interpreter was conceived. They were added to PASS for the OWL Standard. They can be handled by assuming the existence of an implicit calendar subject that sends an interrupt message (reminder) upon a time condition (e.g. reaching of a calendarial date) has been achieved. (includes the specialized (CalendarBasedReminderTransition, TimeBasedReminderTransition
DataDescribingComponent / DataMappingFunction	The PASS OWL standard envisions the integration and usage of classic data element (Data Objects) as part of a process model. The Börger Interpreter does not assume the existence of such data elements as part of the model. However, the refinement concept of ASMs could easily been used to integrate according interpretation aspects. (Includes Elements such as PayloadDescription for Messages or DataMappingFunction

Fig. 11. Unmatched elements

Most of these non-considerations are due to the evolution of PASS, especially from the community process of the derivation of the OWL standard. The main missing aspects are the following:

Iterative Time Transitions. This type time-logic-based transitions did not exist when the original ASM interpreter was conceived. They were added to PASS for the OWL Standard. They can be handled by assuming the existence of an implicit calendar subject that sends an interruption message (reminder) upon a time condition (e.g. reaching of a calendarial date) has been achieved. (includes the specialized *CalendarBasedReminderTransition* and *TimeBasedReminderTransition*.

Data Mapping. The PASS OWL standard envisions the integration and usage of classic data elements (Data Objects) as part of a process model. The Börger Interpreter does not assume the existence of such data elements as part of the model. However, the refinement concept of ASMs can easily be used to integrate according interpretation aspects.

Multi-behaviour Models. The OWL-Model standard envisions a subject to contain possibly multiple behaviors that possess a priority order. This includes *GuardBehaviors*, *MacroBehaviors* and *ExtensionBehaviors/ExtensionLayer* as well as elements to navigate between the different behavior layers such as the *GenericReturnToOriginReference* as *StateReference*.

This is different from the original concepts that were just in their early conceptual development stages when the Börger Interpreter was devised. At the point in time there was neither a modeling tool/mechanism for these considerations nor any kind of workflow engine able to handle them.

The underlying ideas of the Guards, Macros, and Extensions as such can be matched, however the ASM specification itself does not directly support them and expects these elements to be (implicitly) transformed beforehand; which lacks important features like the Return To Origin.

Especially with the Macro-mechanism there are discrepancies.

What original had been envisioned as a *Macro Table*-Model (compare [13]) element, is now (in the OWL-model standard) considered a normal *Do-State* that, depending on the envisioned mechanism either is calling or is being referred to by the initial state in a *Macro-behavior* which otherwise works as a normal behavior. If subject-internal data should change the behavioral flow of the macro it is not necessary to be defined explicitly since a macro-behavior should have implicit access to all relevant data of the subject. Therefore conceptually, a *MacroBehavior* is similar to the originally envisioned *MacroBehaviorClass*.

However, the OWL standard itself does not envision neither stand alone abstract subjects nor behaviors without corresponding SID specifications that define interaction possibilities for that macro behavior. Rather in the OWL standard Macro behaviors must belong to a subject and therefore are not transferable. For most parts, and especially due to the otherwise undefined interactions, that is the only logical choice from a modeling perspective. The exception would be macros with only Do-States (without interaction) that could be called by any subject without the need to adhere to that subjects defined communication.

All of this boils essentially down to a modeling problem rooted in the somewhat incomplete description concepts for the original Macro-definitions.

One possible solution to this is the Abstract Layered PASS (ALPS) conceptual extension [8] that expects an arbitrating wrapper to Börger interpreter [9]. The concept would allow to specify incomplete (abstract) behaviors such a macros in independent models, that in-turn could be used or referred to in other behaviors.

3.3   Recent ASM Interpreter Development

As analyzed in the previous section, since the original concepts have evolved slightly changed in the new PASS-OWL model standard, the Börger Interpreter cannot execute these Multi-Behavior models.

However, there have been several works that have build upon the Börger Interpreter that can enable the handling of identified discrepancies without contradicting both specifications.

One is the aforementioned Arbitrator-Pattern specification of [9]. That however is only a conceptual idea, yet to be tested.

A more recent ASM interpreter for PASS models is the CoreASM-based interpreter by André Wolski [17,18]. Instead of being simply a formal specification, it is an ASM definition that is also executable in the CoreASM environment and supports such concept as MultiSubjects or External Processes. However due to a different send and receive concept inherited from the work of Bandmann [1] it supports only the InputPoolConstraintStrategy-blocking and does not support synchronous communication.

It supports Data Objects and thereby provides implementations for the Data Mapping Functions and also for various Data Modification Functions. Furthermore, functions are offered for the InputPool handling and to control the subject-internal behavior. These functions map very well to the FunctionSpecification and DataMappingFunction elements of the OWL standards and refine those with tool-specific definitions.

Novel to Bandmann and Börger the interpreter introduces native support for MacroBehaviors, which is the first step to support multiple behaviors in general. The specification of Macros also introduces a scope for Data Objects, so that they can be modified locally in a MacroBehavior.

The GuardBehavior, Extension Layers and return to origin concepts are not supported by the CoreASM reference implementation.

4   Summary and Conclusion

In this work we presented the in-depth comparative analysis of the two specifications that claim to be formal definitions for the subject-oriented modeling language PASS.

We have shown, that the existing ASM interpreter of Börger can be matched with the OWL specification. To be more precise, we did not find any contradictions between them, our initial hypothesis holds for now, which of course can be proven wrong in the future.

Nevertheless, in the detailed comparison between the Börger interpreter and the Standard PASS OWL Ontology we discovered elements that are covered by the more recent OWL standard, but are missing in the older interpreter specification.

These, however, are also not contradictions as the more recent ASM specifications like [18] or [9] that extend, but do not contradict Börger are able to handle almost all of those, with the *IterativeTimeTransitions* the only model elements not covered at all.

In the recent ASM specifications we found concrete implementations for functions, that are (explicitly) not present in the OWL standard, for example Data Modification Functions. These elements underline the goal of the OWL standard to be an extensible framework that is able to cope with vendor-specific extensions.

However, we also discovered that the vocabulary differences between the OWL and ASM descriptions are a major pain point when working with both specifications at the same time. This work therefore also contributes in the way that it is a guide to the different standards and clarifies possible misunderstandings. Nevertheless, based on this finding, we propose to change the ASM specification of the referential implementation to align its vocabulary with the OWL standard.

Another open aspect that needs refinement, is the missing formal agreement on correct modeling of macros, guards, and extensions. In principle the mechanisms are defined and exist in both. Although description and execution concept exist with [8] and [9] to solve the matter the community did not agree on yet. Furthermore, [9] is more an idea than a studied execution concept in the PASS/S-BPM context/domain. A referential implementation of the according concept is therefore another proposed future research goal.

References

1. Bandmann, M.: Spezifikation einer Ausführungs-und Verifikationseinheit mit Abstract State Machines für die Subject-Oriented Business Process Management Modellierungsnotation. Diplomarbeit, TU Darmstadt, July 2014
2. Borgert, S., Steinmetz, J., Mühlhäuser, M.: ePASS-IoS 1.1: enabling inter-enterprise business process modeling by S-BPM and the internet of services concept. In: Schmidt, W. (ed.) S-BPM ONE 2011. CCIS, vol. 213, pp. 190–211. Springer, Heidelberg (2011). https://doi.org/10.1007/978-3-642-23471-2_14
3. Börger, E., Stärk, R.F.: Abstract State Machines: A Method for High-Level System Design and Analysis. Springer, Heidelberg (2003). https://doi.org/10.1007/978-3-642-18216-7
4. Dryer, M.: Chapter order of subject, object and verb. the world atlas of language structures (2017). http://wals.info/chapter/81. Accessed 06 Feb 2017
5. Elstermann, M.: Proposal for using semantic technologies as a means to store and exchange subject-oriented process models. In: S-BPM ONE 2017, Darmstadt, Germany, 30–31 March 2017 (2017)
6. Elstermann, M.: Executing Strategic Product Planning - A Subject-Oriented Analysis and New Referential Process Model for IT-Tool Support and Agile Execution of Strategic Product Planning. KIT Scientific Publishing, Karlsruhe (2019)
7. Elstermann, M., Krenn, F.: The semantic exchange standard for subject-oriented process models. In: S-BPM ONE 2018, Linz, Austria, 4–6 April 2018 (2018)
8. Elstermann, M., Ovtcharova, J.: Abstract layers in PASS – a concept draft. In: Zehbold, C. (ed.) S-BPM ONE 2014. CCIS, vol. 422, pp. 125–136. Springer, Cham (2014). https://doi.org/10.1007/978-3-319-06191-7_8
9. Elstermann, M., Seese, D., Fleischmann, A.: Using the arbitrator pattern for dynamic process-instance extension in a work-flow management system. In: Derrick, J., et al. (eds.) ABZ 2012. LNCS, vol. 7316, pp. 323–326. Springer, Heidelberg (2012). https://doi.org/10.1007/978-3-642-30885-7_23
10. Fichtenbauer, C., Fleischmann, A.: Three dimensions of process models regarding their execution. In: S-BPM ONE 2016 (2016)
11. Fleischmann, A.: Distributed Systems: Software Design and Implementation. Springer, Heidelberg (1994). https://doi.org/10.1007/978-3-642-78612-9
12. Fleischmann, A., Borgert, S., Elstermann, M., Krenn, F., Singer, R.: An overview to S-BPM oriented tool suites. In: Proceedings of the 9th International Conference on Subject-Oriented Business Process Management, S-BPM ONE. ACM (2017)
13. Fleischmann, A., Schmidt, W., Stary, C., Obermeier, S., Börger, E.: Subject-Oriented Business Process Management. Springer, Heidelberg (2012). https://doi.org/10.1007/978-3-642-32392-8
14. I2PM: Standard document for pass (2019). https://github.com/I2PM/Standard-Documents-for-Subject-Orientation. Accessed 22 Jan 2020
15. I2PM: Standard pass ont (2019). https://github.com/I2PM/Standard-Documents-for-Subject-Orientation/blob/master/PASS-OWL/standard_PASS_ont_v_1.0.0.owl. Accessed 22 Jan 2020

16. Org, W.: The web ontology language (2012). https://www.w3.org/TR/owl2-overview. Accessed 14 Jan 2020
17. Wolski, A., Borgert, S., Heuser, L.: A CoreASM based reference implementation for subject-oriented business process management execution semantics. In: S-BPM ONE. ACM (2019)
18. Wolski, A., Borgert, S., Heuser, L.: An extended subject-oriented business process management execution semantics. In: Betz, S., Elstermann, M., Lederer, M. (eds.) Proceedings of the 11th International Conference on Subject-oriented Business Process Management, S-BPM ONE. ACM (2019)

Cyber-Physical and Assistance Systems

Task-Based Design of Cyber-Physical Systems – Meeting Representational Requirements with S-BPM

Georg Weichhart[1,2(✉)], Maximilian Reiser[2], and Christian Stary[2]

[1] PROFACTOR GmbH, Steyr-Gleink, Austria
georg.weichhart@profactor.at
[2] Business Informatics – Communications Engineering,
Johannes Kepler University, Linz, Austria
{georg.weichhart,maximilian.reiser,christian.stary}@jku.at

Abstract. This paper explores representational capabilities of S-BPM for task-based CPS design, in order to meet Cyber-Physical System particularities throughout development and operation. Essential functional properties of CPS are derived from conceptual and empirical studies. As tasks are the foundation for functional design of operational support systems, they need to be captured when developing CPS. In this contribution, we focus on representing tasks that form the basis of stakeholder communication. The analysis of notational S-BPM capabilities reveals the need for contextual introduction and application of interaction and behavior diagrams, when S-BPM models should add value to CPS development activities.

Keywords: Cyber-Physical Systems (CPS) · Task-based design · Design representations · Diagrammatic capabilities · Subject orientation

1 Introduction

The Industry 4.0 (I4.0) initiative and related developments target smart manufacturing in production industry, focusing on more effective and individualized interaction between suppliers, producers, and customers. Production processes should be adaptable and reconfigurable based on the interaction of distributed and autonomous components. These components consist of machines, sensors and actuators and thus, form cyber-physical systems (CPS) [1]. Modern production systems are a network of autonomous (software and physical) components that interact with each other and with humans to achieve business goals through their intelligence [2]. Physical components of a CPS are linked with digital CPS representations, for planning and executing actions [3]. This digital representation is a model termed "digital twin" and enables the simulation of processes in the physical world [4]. As such, executable process models can serves as valid baseline for design, engineering, and development based on CPS.

However, the digitalization of processes must include the possibility of human intervention. Humans are components of a Cyber-Physical System. Therefore interactive

© Springer Nature Switzerland AG 2020
M. Freitag et al. (Eds.): S-BPM ONE 2020, CCIS 1278, pp. 63–73, 2020.
https://doi.org/10.1007/978-3-030-64351-5_5

control panels or user interfaces need to be provided. They are based on the tasks a CPS is designed for, implementing some strategic objectives of organizations [5].

Recognizing the essential role of people as context provider and user, and component of a CPS, the socio-technical nature of CPS, technical aspects of the production industry need to be enriched with human skills in I4.0. Meeting the objective of "creative people and powerful IT" [6] requires skills of people to be combined with physical technology in complex production processes [6, 7]. The challenge hereby is to solve problems on a behavior (i.e. process) level, including socio-technological process planning, and ensure interpretation the same way by humans and machines [7].

Given the nature and diversity of representational needs, CPS development increases the number of requirements on process models. They are headed by continuous integration and combination of embedded systems and distributed manufacturing and aim for accurate modeling at design and runtime [3].

In the following section, we look at the existing gap in process modeling at two levels - physical and the logical (or cyber) level, before detailing resulting research goals and questions. Then, we summarize the CPS-specific modeling requirements, before discussing S-BPM modeling capabilities and their contribution to meet representational requirements for CPS development.

2   The Gap to Be Researched

Stressing the socio-technical aspects of CPS, requires addressing the behavior of human and artificial agents involved. An essential requirement for modeling of CPS stems from the required shift, involving the business and operation level – see Fig. 1. Today different processes are planned on the business and the production level, on both levels design phases need to be run. There is a communication gap between the levels because of the business level notations are not designed for information transfer to production level [8], as confirmed by Seiger et al.: "[…] In the field of and manufacturing, modeling and execution languages for business processes, e.g., BPMN and BPEL, have proven to be well suited […]. However, the on-going integration and combination of embedded systems and distributed cloud-based services into cyber-physical systems (CPS) and smart environments, lead to a number of new requirements for process modeling and execution." [3]

In the context of Industry 4.0, it is becoming increasingly important that manufacturing companies improve their processes in order to achieve better quality at lower costs and at less production time. The increasing demand for individualized products requires additional decrease of the time for setup and modifications of processes [9]. By aligning the business with the production level, as shown in Fig. 1, this time can be reduced [8].

CPSs are socio-technical systems by nature. The second context, where graphical and executable models of CPS are relevant, are processes where human are closely interacting with artificial agents or robots (e.g. in Operator 4.0 scenarios) [25, 27, 28]. In this context, process models need to address details that can be executed by artificial agents (robots) and at the same time must be understood by humans (i.e. require a higher level of abstraction). In these scenarios, similar as above, the integrated view reduces the (re-)planning of processes that span multiple CPS of different kind. We will use the human-robot collaboration scenario as running example in the following.

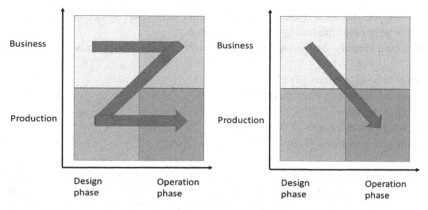

Fig. 1. The suggested shift in [8]

Graphical or visual process representations allow a wide group of stakeholders to understand the behavior of systems (and systems-of-systems). At the same time, such representations can be transferred into executable specifications. The different notational capabilities either stemming from system or software engineering, industrial production, or Business Process Management (BPM) needs to be challenged for suitability of supporting the socio-technical aspects of CPS in an integrated fashion. The features of diagrammatic process modeling languages need to be analyzed with respect to the needs of CPS development support; discussed in the next section.

3 Representational Requirements for CPS Modeling

Two independent research questions have been of interest: Which process notations exist for representing behaviour of systems in a structured way? Which aspects are specific for CPS modelling? Literature from SpringerLink, ScienceDirect, IEEE, ACM, ResearchGate has been found to tackle these questions. To identify modelling approaches we have used the terms: process modeling notation OR language; System modeling notation OR language; Cyber physical systems modeling notation; Business process modeling; Business process notation.

Several graphical notations for modelling processes could be identified in the context of business and technical (production) system development:

- Business Process Modelling Notation (BPMN) [5, 10, 11, 20];
- Subject-oriented Business Process Management (S-BPM) [13, 14];
- Integrated Enterprise Modelling (IEM) [18];
- Unified Modelling Language (UML) [5, 10, 11];
- Systems Modelling Language (SysML) [5];
- Integrated DEFinition Methods (IDEF) [17, 18, 23, 24].

For the second question, we have been using the terms: process principles, modeling, notation, language, process fundamentals, process features. These have been combined with CPS, Cyber-Physical System, Cyber-physical Production System, Industry 4.0. The keywords were combined using Boolean operators.

We could identify the following aspects which CPS modeling needs to capture:

- Aspect of heterogeneity [3, 12]
- Aspects of complexity and abstraction [3, 12]
- Dynamic aspects [3, 15]
- Decentralization aspects [3, 16]
- Detailed data modeling [26]

Aspect of Heterogeneity: Since a CPS consists of a multitude of services and machines. Physical and logical components need to be modelled in an interconnected way, according the provided services. "CPSs are heterogeneous, in the sense that they combine various aspects relying on both physical and cyber world [...] Owing to the increasing integration of cyber capabilities in the physical world, there is a need to develop new design methodologies [...] (i.e. different types of cyber and physical activities) and enable seamless models of integrated activities (i.e. the integration between cyber and physical behaviours)" [12]. Interconnections may also lead to federated system or hierarchies of components: "In a CPS there are usually numerous heterogeneous services and devices integrated into a so-called system of systems. However, when modelling workflows, a unified view on these components would be helpful." [3]. In case of human-robot collaboration, this heterogeneity is to some extent extreme. Both are physical systems but need activity descriptions in a very different level of granularity. A unified view allows modifications of workflows while keeping the worldviews of both consistent.

Aspects of Complexity and Abstraction: From the point of view of complexity, models should be capable to abstract and thus, to display different levels of detail, and to capture multiple perspectives on a CPS: "Processes within CPS can be very complex and contain a large number of process steps, both, composite and atomic, as well as further process elements. This makes means for hierarchical structuring and aggregating process components necessary in order to master high levels of complexity." [3] Thereby, usability matters: a "Future CPS modelling work needs suitable abstractions for intuitive modelling of the CPS behaviour (e.g. processes) and their real-world aspects (i.e. the devices and the physical entities affected by the execution of physical actions). These models need to be intuitive to read and easy to understand. They also should present a detailed view of the CPS behaviour and represent concurrent behaviour while being intelligible to technical and nontechnical stakeholders. The main challenge is to enable designers to specify the CPS processes using a multi-domain modelling approach." [12]. Human-robot collaboration, again demonstrates the need to address this aspect. Human operators working with robots in production systems have (typically) no detailed understanding of the machine. However, this issue needs to be addressed for both agents interacting seamlessly. An intelligible description of the robot's next task as well as the human's next task is required for the design of (socio-technical) workflows.

Dynamic Aspect of the CPS: This requirement indicates that the exact time of service provision and use of components is a modeling topic: "[...] modelling service invocations within processes on the instance level, i.e. the invocation of a concrete service, may not be suitable due to its possible unavailability [...] This way, we do not necessarily need to know at modelling time, which concrete service or device will be executing the process step." [12] The digital twin needs to capture both, happy (i.e. standard), and non-happy paths: "In the context of CPS modelling, there is a need to support both physical and cyber parts. To ensure the communication [...], the control part allows the reception of the monitored data, makes control decisions to find the needed services and sends the instructions to the physical devices." [3]. Humans in human-robot collaborations will not always act precisely according to predefined process models. Mistakes will happen. Re-planning processes and workflows requires the digital representation of collaboration.

Decentralization Aspects: The decentralization in a CPS also affects underlying process models. If smart products know their requirements, production can be self-organizing. Hence, for modeling, the possibility of alternative process paths needs to be provided: "Decentralization refers to the control of the scheduling in how work pieces find their operations and process sequences themselves [...] autonomous and cooperative work pieces determine their way of production, i.e. operations and machines, themselves and negotiate with the machines for the capacity for their operations. [...] The determination of the manufacturing process by negotiation can also mean that every work piece takes an individual route through the production system using different machines or even different production technologies as long as the requirements for product can be fulfilled" [16]. Here again, human-robot collaboration reveals this need in an excellent manner. The human and the artificial agent will act concurrently. There are different degrees of coupling collaborative aspects. The most tightly coupling assumes that both actors work on the same work piece at the same time.

Detailed Object and Data Modeling: Due to the nature of IoT systems, a CPS operates as system of many different physical and logical devices. Their objects of manipulation or data need to be represented as logical units and detailed in models: "Data elements must be described in detail [...]. The domain class model can consider Industry 4.0 aspects like IoT device data sets. The process models use these data objects." [19]. In socio-technical designs, the robot (program) needs to be linked to a camera system responsible for identifying the human and the tasks executed by the human operator. Models need to be detailed to represent the relevant elements in detail to allow the robot to act on the observed situation.

4 Representational S-BPM Capabilities

Although in the literature we could find various notations (see previous section), we will focus on S-BPM and its capabilities in the context of CPS in this paper.

S-BPM provides modeling construct from a decentralized system perspective. S-BPM focuses on the acting process elements termed subjects. Their activities are synchronized by means of message exchange. Semantic information is modeled following fundamental sentence structures "subject - predicate - object". According to the meta-model shown in Fig. 2, each subject encapsulates its activities. Collective behavior is modeled through their interaction, namely by exchanging messages with other subjects. These messages include content of varying complexity, from simple notifications to complex ones (i.e. data structures). The exchange of messages between two subjects either occurs synchronously or asynchronously [14, 21].

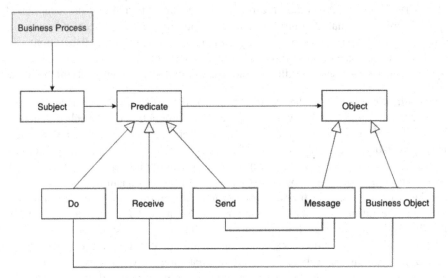

Fig. 2. S-BPM meta model based on [21]

Subject-oriented process models contain two different diagrams: Subject Interaction Diagrams (SIDs) providing the subjects and the messages they exchange, and Subject Behavior Diagrams (SBDs) specifying the exact behavior for each subject of an SID. The behavior is determined through various states that a subject can be assigned to: receive - a subject receives a message, send - a subject sends a message, and function - a subject performs an action on a business object. The latter can check or change business objects through executing actions. Business objects are the content of the messages. Their name is intended to shed light on the purpose of the given message and their content contains information for the recipient.

The following model constructs allow representing complex processes (cf. [15, 21, 22]:

- Connected Processes - If a large amount of subjects communicate with each other, a S-BPM model may become confusing. Therefore, subjects can be outsourced to external processes.
- Service Processes - Service processes are similar to connected processes: they include a so-called interface subject that is visible to all other subjects, however, cannot recognize non-interface subjects. When they receive a message, they pass the name of the sender so that the interface subject can respond.
- Multi-processes - Multi-processes are an extension of connected processes. Each time a message is sent to a multi-process, a copy of this process is generated.

- Hierarchical Process Network – Since more than two processes can be linked together, a hierarchy or a network of processes can be generated.
- Message Observer and Message Guard - The standard scenario of a message transmission is called happy path, but it must also be possible to model deviations from this path. For example, if a message after being sent changes its state, this deviation from the happy path is treated separately - the Message Observer or Message Guard accomplishes this task.
- Choice and Multipath - It is not imperative that actions are executed in a particular sequence, using the choice operator to specify that. Actions can also be marked to make sure they are executed in any case.
- Macros - In some cases behavior specifications of subjects are used on several occasions. Macros allow reusing specifications this way.

5   Representational S-BPM Capacities for CPS Development

In this section, the CPS modeling requirements are discussed in the context of S-BPM modeling capabilities, starting with basic process element and proceeding with more sophisticated concepts capturing complex system behavior. We use basic modeling categories to structure the representational analysis.

Basic Process Elements. S-BPM considers a *task* to be modeled as part of business processes or technical processes, as subjects represent behavior encapsulations of any kind. A subject can be also used as a *resource* and as an *actor*, *role* or *organizational unit* that performs a task. *Information* is handled in S-BPM through messages that are exchanged between subjects. *Entities* and information overlap in their properties, in S-BPM, entities can be determined by subjects. *Events* in a process in S-BPM are considered through the actor itself, as each actor is a kind of event, due to the start and end when executing behavior.

Perspectives and Views. S-BPM focuses on the communication of actors, implemented by modeling the sending and receiving of messages. The *functional* perspective is completed by modeling the execution of business objects. The *information* perspective is captured by describing the generated messages in the unstructured messages process information, while the *organizational* perspective is specified through structuring the interaction between subjects, i.e. through their communication patterns.

The *behavioral* perspective describing the coordination between the process participants and the order in which process steps are carried out. It also shows whether processes can react to internal or external influences to process behavior. S-BPM maps the coordination and tasks to subjects, structuring their behavior in dedicated diagrams. Subject interaction constitutes the *logical* perspective. Since validated SBDs capture the flow of control for executing models, S-BPM models also represent the *dynamic* perspective on CPS.

So far, S-BPM does not explicitly capture the *physical* perspective on CPS beyond behavior encapsulation through subjects. This perspective is taken when S-BPM model are implemented, in the course of assigning technical systems to subjects as subject carriers. From a design view, the *scenario* perspective would also require additional modeling constructs. Currently, S-BPM specifications capture entire process settings. From a coarse grain view, an entire scenario could be represented as single scenario. From a fine grain view, particular threads of message exchanges could establish a specific scenario. Since each subject encapsulates its entire set of functions, it could be part of several scenarios, in case the SID addresses more than a single scenario.

S-BPM representations are embedded into the open S-BPM life cycle. They do not capture the *development* perspective per se. In the course of implementing models, each subject is instantiated from an organizational and technical perspective, thus allowing to proceed with development. In case of assigning information from other parts of the life cycle to the implementation of S-BPM models, additional constructs need to be introduced.

Flows. S-BPM models enable the representation of *control* and *information* flows. The flow of physical objects can only be abstracted in terms of data representations encoded in messages that are exchanged between subjects. The interaction between subjects direct the flow of control, and, at the same time, acts as carrier of information through the adhered content to messages.

Representing CPS Particularities. S-BPM modeling tackles

- **Aspect of heterogeneity**: In S-BPM modeling subjects can be used to represent the provision of services and machines, with subjects representing a single service and the behavior of machines.
- **Aspect of complexity and abstraction**: S-BPM enables this modeling concept in the form of a complex or hierarchical process network, a concept similar to unfolding sub processes.
- **Aspect of dynamics**: The dynamic requirement for CPS process modeling allows to leave open at modeling time the exact service or physical component actually used to operate the CPS. S-BPM modeling meets that requirements in principle due to the abstraction of the nature of actors, but does not provide indicators or a generic placeholder to indicate uncertainties in services or devices provision.
- **Aspect of decentralization**: S-BPM models allow decentralized operation due to parallel subject instantiations.
- **Aspects of detailed data modeling**: Structured data can be modeled using message descriptions, as they can contain attributes.

The decoupling of detailed subject-specific processes allows to represent human and robotic behavior. The message-based synchronization of tasks supports collaboration while maintaining the independence of each subject's behavior. There are currently some shortcomings with respect to the physical perspective. However, the communication-based nature of S-BPM provides a good starting point for an integrated modelling of socio-technical behaviors in CPSs.

6 Conclusion

CPS development requires modeling capabilities that (i) capture their structure and behavior, and (ii) enable recognizing the vertical and horizontal processes due to its tight coupling of business and production operation. Functional tasks build the core of process designs, and need to be embedded in CPS design representation while covering the volatility of CPS operation. In the work partially presented here, we were looking to answer the two questions: Which process notations exist for structured behavior specification? Which aspects are specific for CPS modelling?

While focusing in this work on S-BPM capabilities, our original study has involved six different modelling languages with 28 different diagrams. It enabled thorough understanding on how behavior can be diagrammatically represented.

The second question resulted in an understanding of the particularities of a CPS that need to be modelled. We could identify five aspects that should be captured: heterogeneity, complexity and abstraction, dynamics, decentralization, detailed data models.

The results we have derived so far, help developing the requirements on an integrated process modelling approach, which is required for complex system development, such as for CPS. For CPS development, the behavior of collaborating humans and artificial agents (e.g., robots) needs to be represented in models [25, 26]. The explored representational capabilities of S-BPM enable task-based CPS design, as the elaborated CPS particularities can become part of intelligible and accurate representations for development and operation.

Analyzing S-BPM's modeling capabilities revealed the need for contextual application of modeling elements and the utilization of both types of diagrams. For accurate application both, fundamental modeling elements, and abstract system modeling constructs, such as views and flows, need to be used. It also turns out that CPS development could be fully supported by enriching S-BPM models with CPS-relevant runtime environment information during design time.

Acknowledgements. This work has been supported by Pro2Future (FFG under contract No. 854184). Pro2Future is funded within the Austrian COMET Program - Competence Centers for Excellent Technologies - under the auspices of the Federal Ministry for Climate Action, Environment, Energy, Mobility, Innovation and Technology (BMK) and the Federal Ministry for Digital and Economic Affairs (BMDW) and of the Provinces of Upper Austria and Styria. COMET is managed by the Austrian Research Promotion Agency FFG. It has also received support by the European Union and the State of Upper Austria within the strategic program Innovative Upper Austria 2020, project: Smart Factory Lab.

References

1. Kannengiesser, U., Müller, H.: Towards agent-based smart factories: a subject-oriented modeling approach. In: Proceedings - 2013 IEEE/WIC/ACM International Joint Conferences on Web Intelligence and Intelligent Agent Technologies – Workshop, WI-IATW 2013, vol. 3(S), pp. 83–86 (2013)

2. Roth, A.: Einführung und Umsetzung von Industry 4.0. Springer, Heidelberg (2016). https://doi.org/10.1007/978-3-662-48505-7
3. Seiger, R., Keller, C., Niebling, F., Schlegel, T.: Modelling complex and flexible processes for smart cyber-physical environments. J. Comput. Sci. **10**, 137–148 (2015)
4. Wagner, C., et al.: The role of the Industry 4.0 asset administration shell and the digital twin during the life cycle of a plant. In: IEEE International Conference on Emerging Technologies and Factory Automation ETFA, pp. 1–8 (2018)
5. Petrasch, R., Hentschke, R.: Process modeling for industry 4.0 applications: towards an industry 4.0 process modeling language and method. In: 2016 13th International Joint Conference on Computer Science and Software Engineering JCSSE 2016, vol. Cc (2016)
6. Bauernhansl, T., ten Hompel, M., Vogel-Heuser, B. (eds.): Industrie 4.0 in Produktion, Automatisierung und Logistik. Springer, Wiesbaden (2014). https://doi.org/10.1007/978-3-658-04682-8
7. Wantia, N., et al.: Task planning for human robot interactive processes. In: 2016 IEEE 21st International Conference on Emerging Technologies and Factory Automation (ETFA), pp. 1–8 (2016)
8. Gerber, T., Theorin, A., Johnsson, C.: Towards a seamless integration between process modeling descriptions at business and production levels: work in progress. J. Intell. Manuf. **25**(5), 1089–1099 (2014). https://doi.org/10.1007/s10845-013-0754-x
9. Trstenjak, M., Cosic, P.: Process planning in Industry 4.0 environment. Procedia Manuf. **11**, 1744–1750 (2017)
10. Kluza, K., Wiśniewski, P., Jobczyk, K., Ligęza, A., (Mroczek), A.S.: Comparison of selected modeling notations for process, decision and system modeling, vol. 11, pp. 1095–1098 (2017)
11. Suchenia, A., Kluza, K., Wiśniewski, P., Jobczyk, K., Ligęza, A.: Towards knowledge interoperability between the UML, DMN, BPMN and CMMN models. MATEC Web Conf. **252**, 02011 (2019)
12. Graja, I., Kallel, S., Guermouche, N., Cheikhrouhou, S., Kacem, A.H.: Modelling and verifying time-aware processes for cyber-physical environments. IET Softw. **13**(1), 36–48 (2019)
13. Weichhart, G.: Representing processes of human robot collaboration. In: CEUR Workshop Proceedings, vol. 2074 (2018)
14. Kannengiesser, U., Neubauer, M., Heininger, R.: Integrating business processes and manufacturing operations based on S-BPM and B2MML. In: Proceedings of the 8th International Conference on Subject-Oriented Business Process Management - S-BPM 2016, pp. 1–10 (2016)
15. Jin, G., Jäkel, F.W.: Execution and evaluation of enterprise models in IEM/MO 2 GO based on Petri net. Int. J. Adv. Manuf. Technol. **96**(9–12), 4517–4537 (2018)
16. Meissner, H., Aurich, J.C.: Implications of cyber-physical production systems on integrated process planning and scheduling. Procedia Manuf. **28**, 167–173 (2019)
17. Lin, F., Yang, M., Pai, Y.: A generic structure for business process modeling. Bus. Process Manag. J. **8**(1), 19–41 (2002)
18. García-Domínguez, A., Marcos, M., Medina, I.: A comparison of BPMN 2.0 with other notations for manufacturing processes. AIP Conf. Proc. **1431**, 593–600 (2012)
19. Petrasch, R., Hentschke, R.: Process modeling for industry 4.0 applications: towards an industry 4.0 process modeling language and method. In: 2016 13th International Joint Conference on Computer Science and Software Engineering (JCSSE), pp. 1–5 (2016)
20. Allweyer, T.: BPMN 2.0: Introduction to the Standard for Business Process Modeling. Books on Demand GmbH, Deutschland (2015)

21. Fleischmann, A., Kannengiesser, U., Schmidt, W., Stary, C.: Subject-oriented modeling and execution of multi-agent business processes. In: Proceedings - 2013 IEEE/WIC/ACM International Conference on Intelligent Agent Technologies IAT 2013, vol. 2, pp. 138–145 (2013)

22. Buchwald, H., Fleischmann, A., Seese, D., Stary, C. (eds.): S-BPM ONE 2009. CCIS, vol. 85. Springer, Heidelberg (2010). https://doi.org/10.1007/978-3-642-15915-2

23. Mayer, R.J.: IDEF1 Information Modeling. Knowledge Based Systems, Inc., College Station (1992)

24. Noran, O.: UML vs. IDEF: an ontology-oriented comparative study in view of business modelling. In: ICEIS 2004 – Proceedings of the Sixth International Conference on Enterprise Information Systems, pp. 674–682 (2004)

25. Weichhart, G., Fast-Berglund, Å., Romero, D., Pichler, A.: An agent- and role-based planning approach for flexible automation of advanced production systems. In: IEEE International Conference on Intelligent Systems (IS), pp. 391–399 (2018)

26. Weichhart, G., Stary, C.: Interoperable process design in production systems. In: Debruyne, C., et al. (eds.) OTM 2017. LNCS, vol. 10697, pp. 26–35. Springer, Cham (2018). https://doi.org/10.1007/978-3-319-73805-5_3

27. Weichhart, G., Åkerman, M., Akkaladevi, S.C., Plasch, M., Fast-Berglund, Å., Pichler, A.: Models for interoperable human robot collaboration. IFAC-PapersOnLine 51, 36–41 (2018)

28. Romero, D., Bernus, P., Noran, O., Stahre, J., Fast-Berglund, Å.: The Operator 4.0: human cyber-physical systems & adaptive automation towards human-automation symbiosis work systems. In: Nääs, I., et al. (eds.) APMS 2016. IAICT, vol. 488, pp. 677–686. Springer, Cham (2016). https://doi.org/10.1007/978-3-319-51133-7_80

Mobile AR-Based Assistance Systems for Order Picking – Methodical Decision Support in the Early Phases of the Product Life Cycle

Lukas Egbert[1]([✉]), Moritz Quandt[1], Klaus-Dieter Thoben[1,2], and Michael Freitag[1,2]

[1] BIBA - Bremer Institut für Produktion und Logistik
at the University of Bremen, Bremen, Germany
egb@biba.uni-bremen.de

[2] Faculty of Production Engineering, University of Bremen, Bremen, Germany

Abstract. To support order picking assistance systems are in use, as employees depend on a constant supply of information to guide them through the work process. In addition to conventional assistance systems such as picking lists or handhelds, the first Augmented Reality-based systems are already used, which allow virtual insertions into the field of vision. Since these systems enable new forms of interaction and the choice of the forms of interaction has a significant influence on the choice of hardware, the process-based design of the optimal interaction between humans and the system must be made early in the development process.

Based on sequence analyses and process models of current picking processes, we have methodologically investigated different forms of interaction between human and assistance systems, depending on the work process. For this purpose, we simulated the use of an AR-based assistance system using the Wizard of Oz method based on a representative example process of order picking and derived suitable interaction concepts from this. Furthermore, we identified the requirements of the system users by creating personas.

In this way, we were able to make a process step-dependent selection of suitable forms of interaction, which is the basis for a requirement-based AR hardware decision. The general procedure derived from this allows a transfer to other use cases to methodically support the hardware selection for an AR-based assistance system depending on the selected interaction concept. In this way, well-founded decisions for the design of such an industrial assistance system can already be made in an early phase of the product development process without high development effort.

Keywords: Augmented reality · Order picking · Decision support

1 Introduction

The increasing trend to insert computer-aided networking of products and processes in manufacturing processes characterizes the fourth industrial revolution (Industry 4.0). A

© Springer Nature Switzerland AG 2020
M. Freitag et al. (Eds.): S-BPM ONE 2020, CCIS 1278, pp. 74–87, 2020.
https://doi.org/10.1007/978-3-030-64351-5_6

comparable development can be observed in logistics. The use of modern information and communication technology enables an increasing demand for highly individualized products and flexible services. In the area of warehousing, the focus is mainly on mobile support for order picking, as employees are dependent on a constant supply of information regarding the work process, e.g. the number of the aisle, the shelf and the article where the next item has to be picked by the employee [1].

In practice, various assistance systems are used in order picking. The most common systems include pick-by light, which guides the picker through the process in a light-controlled manner, pick-by-paper, which provides the information on a paper list carried along with the order, or pick-by-display, which displays the information on a mobile data terminal [2]. Another promising technology for the mobile support of industrial processes by providing context-sensitive information is Augmented Reality (AR) [3], which is referred to as pick-by-vision in the context of order picking. Azuma [4] defines AR as the combination of virtual content with the real environment with partial overlay, real-time interaction between user and virtual content, and a three-dimensional relationship between real and virtual objects. By using AR technology, in addition to the insertion of information directly into the user's field of vision, new forms of information input are possible, such as gesture control or the manipulation of virtual objects,. The use of sensor technology enables technical assistance systems to independently record information from the environment and transmit it to the user [5]. In pick-by-vision systems, AR is used, as head-mounted displays (HMDs) and smart glasses offer the possibility of working hands-free. However, the large number of prototypes and concept studies is in contrast to a much smaller number of systems used in practice. This is due to the barriers to the introduction, such as hardware restrictions, the AR-related challenges of software programming, the acceptance of the systems by the users and the costs compared to established systems [6]. The high general potential of AR technology for use in order picking accompanies numerous possibilities of using the technology, such as the possible forms of interaction, the numerous possible hardware configurations, and the possibilities for addressing different senses. Therefore, these factors have a decisive influence on the design of the assistance system [7, 8]. The need for a mobile assistance system is derived from the work process of order picking. With regard to AR technology, this means that the solution is implemented on mobile devices such as smartphones, tablets or data glasses. Compared to stationary AR solutions, e.g. information terminals in museums or AR-based support of operations in medicine, there are different requirements for the tracking procedures and operating concepts used such as possible distractions of the user in motion.

The interaction between humans and systems is a decisive criterion for the acceptance of the systems. The interaction design has a direct influence on the efficiency of the process in which the assistance system is used [9]. For the evaluation of AR-based assistance systems, there is no consistent methodological basis for evaluating them over the development process [5]. Mostly missing guidelines for the development and evaluation of the system and interaction design, especially for mobile AR solutions, have so far led to the predominant use of user-based evaluation methods [8, 10]. In order to ensure a continuous evaluation throughout the entire product development process, and involving the system users in the development, we have integrated the human-centered design process from ISO 9241-210 [11] into the product life cycle (see Fig. 1).

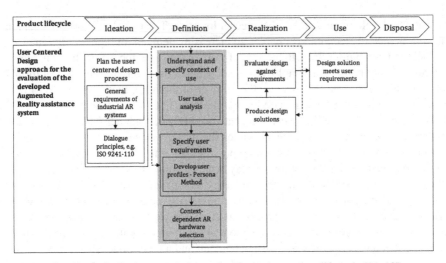

Fig. 1. Methodical approach for evaluation in the product lifecycle [11, 12]

Context-related hardware selection plays a decisive role in the early phase of the development of an AR-based assistance system since the choice of hardware determines the possible forms of interaction between humans and the system as well as the possibilities of process support in the work process. In the planning of the human-centered design process in the first phase of the PLC, we considered the general requirements for the development of industrial AR systems, as examined e.g., in Quandt et al. [13]. In the following phase, "Definition," which is the focus of this paper, we first performed a user task analysis to gain detailed knowledge about the work process and working environment of the order pickers. Besides, we examined the requirements of the order pickers for interaction with assistance systems in the order picking process, employing the persona method. Based on this analysis, we determined the ideal process-dependent forms of interaction for the use of an AR-based assistance system.

In the following, we present an approach to support decision makers in selecting AR hardware for assistance systems in order picking. For this purpose, we compared the identified individual interaction and representation forms of AR systems on the process level with exemplary hardware properties. The subsequent phases of product development are shown in Fig. 1 for the purpose of completeness, but are not discussed in detail in this article, as the hardware selection has a decisive influence on the further phases.

2   Background

Already in 2012, Baumann [14] performed a study on the use of data glasses with a static display in order picking. With the further development of HMDs, AR-based assistance systems for order picking were introduced in practice. These systems base on different AR hardware and software solutions. The focus is on fast, error-free, and user-friendly order processing. However, these solutions do not yet include the integration of virtual elements into the real environment. So far, current systems display picklists statically at the edge of the user's field of vision. The connection between reality and virtuality by superimposing virtual elements on natural perception has not yet been realized [6, 15]. So far, various interaction concepts play a subordinate role in these solutions, since the static information displayed does not allow interaction between user and system. Schwerdtfeger et al. [16] have investigated the use of AR systems in order picking concerning the visualization of coarse and fine navigation of the picker. In user studies, they tested virtual insertions to support the search processes, e.g., highlighting of picking containers and insertion of direction arrows. The insertion of squares that formed a tunnel to guide the view of the required container proved to be the most advantageous way of highlighting relevant objects in the field of view. Besides, the display of a meta navigation arrow supports the search for current displays outside the field of view [16]. The work of Reif and Günthner [17] presents similar results; they also successfully tested the insertion of directional arrows for the guidance within a warehouse to the correct extraction location.

Kim et al. [18] conducted a user study to investigate how different HMDs and UI designs affect the work of the order picker. The user study confirms the potential for the use of HMDs in order picking, but it depends strongly on the selected hardware and the design of the HCI [18]. A recent review paper by Wang et al. [19] examined the current status of the use of AR solutions in intralogistics. The use of AR in order picking is associated with high potentials. However, there is a lack of tools and methods to support decision-makers in logistics when it comes to the broad introduction of AR technologies in practice [19].

From the research work carried out to date on the use of AR in order-picking, the enormous potential of the technology for this application is evident. However, AR technology has not yet become established in practice, even though there is a vast number of the implemented concept studies and proof of concepts. One reason for this is the lack of acceptance by system users of this new technology [20]. On the other hand, the numerous possibilities of hardware and software design give rise to many approaches for designing interaction and visualization of the systems. No standards have yet emerged in this area. The hardware selection determines the further system design since the properties of the hardware determine interaction and visualization possibilities and must be done early in the development process. To incorporate the requirements of the application scenario, decision makers need to consider work processes and working environments, as well as the employees' requirements for this decision. Decision-makers must consider that improved usability and user experience of future AR solutions increase user acceptance [8]. Therefore, we have to answer the following research questions to develop decision support for AR hardware selection to prepare an informed decision about the AR hardware used early in the development process:

- How can we support the introduction of AR-based assistance systems based on the work processes in order picking from the perspective of interaction between employee and assistance system?
- How can we support the hardware selection based on the selection of interaction forms most favorable for the picking process?

3   Methodological Procedure

Based on the proposed approach in Fig. 1, we first analyzed current picking processes at three different warehouses of a logistics service provider. The following processes were analyzed: picking with labeled picking containers, picking with a MDT and picking with a picking list. We carried out the process analyses using the method of workflow analysis, which involves a systematic analysis of the people and equipment involved in the process and their activities. Besides, we created process models according to the BPMN 2.0 standard, which allows the process steps to be divided into different roles, in this case, into the activities of the picker and those of the assistance system. The recorded processes largely correspond to the reference process for order picking depicted by Günthner et al. [21], even if it originates from the year 2009. Therefore, we refer to the reference process for the analyses conducted in this work. From the workflow analyses, the authors determined the process-related requirements for the interaction with assistance systems. In Fig. 2 a reference picking process is depicted in form of a BPMN-model, in which the order picker uses a MDT as an assistance system. The recurring improvement potentials in the use of conventional assistance systems (paper lists, MDTs) that could be identified are colored and explained in Table 1.

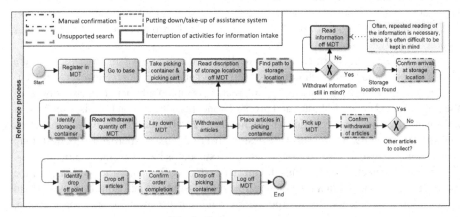

Fig. 2. Reference process

Table 1. Identified potential for improvement in the picking process

Activity	Current problem of the activity
Information intake	To intake information the order picker interrupts further activities
Route search	Route search without support by the assistance system
Identify extraction point	Searching for the extraction point without the support of the assistance system
Article extraction	Handheld assistance system must be put down for article extraction
Confirmation	Manual confirmation by the order picker

For the conception of the process step dependent interaction with an AR-based assistance system in order picking, we used the reference process of Fig. 2. For this purpose, the authors divided the process into the following five sub-tasks: Basic process steps for process preparation, process steps for coarse navigation (route search), process steps for fine navigation (identification of storage container), process steps for material handling and confirmation (e.g. for confirming the withdrawal of articles). The sub-tasks were then run through in test scenarios in which we tested different forms of interaction. We tested both the information transfer to the picker and the information input by the picker to the assistance system.

To methodically support the test runs of the individual scenarios, we used the Wizard of Oz method (WOz). In WOz, (partial) functions of a system are performed by a person (the "Wizard"), in order to simulate the features of the system to a test person, e.g. by registering a voice input of a test person in a test run and triggering the corresponding reaction of the system by the wizard [9]. This method has already been used in other works in the field of AR [22, 23]. In the context of this work, we applied WOz to be able to test different forms of interaction in an early phase of the product design without having to test different hardware and without extensive development work. In the repeatedly performed test scenarios, we simulated the features of an AR-based HMD to test a broad spectrum of interaction forms. The selection of the tested interaction forms were based on literature research on the characteristics of conventional and AR-based assistance systems. Examples of interactions tested for information input to the system are voice and gesture control. For information input, we tested acoustic outputs and virtual insertions into the field of vision, such as directional arrows when searching for a path according to Reif and Günthner 2009 [17] or tunnels for visual guidance according to Schwerdtfeger et al. [16].

To conduct the test scenarios, we set up a test stand, consisting of a base and two shelves, which we equipped with storage containers. Figure 3 depicts a schematic illustration of that test stand.

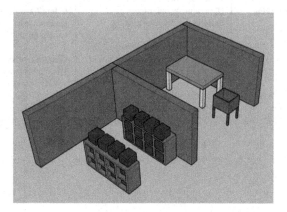

Fig. 3. The test stand

The test person embodied the picker and started from the base to search for the items listed in a picking order. In order to simulate the presentation of information by the HMD, the wizard for instance loudly read the shelf and container numbers while the test person searched for the container. For visual highlighting of containers in AR, the respective containers were marked with colored markers. We evaluated the forms of interaction qualitatively concerning their suitability in the context of the process steps and determined the most advantageous form for the respective process step. That way, we could deliver qualified statements regarding the best possible interaction concept without the use of hardware. This was possible by a process-step-dependent assignment of the best possible way of transmitting information to the picker in the process, respectively the way the picker should enter required information into the assistance system. As an example, the test runs for the subtask "coarse navigation" are described in the Appendix.

In addition to the process requirements, the authors also investigated the user requirements. A survey of warehouse employees resulted as difficult, because there were no AR hardware or operational interaction concepts that could have been demonstrated or discussed at this early stage of development. Without previous experience of AR technology, the order pickers could not define their ideas and requirements towards the use of an AR-based system. Therefore the Persona Method was applied, which enables the creation of fictional user personas, whose characteristics and requirements were used in this work to create a user friendly process. Three user personas were created, which represent the requirements of typical groups of picking employees (see Fig. 4).

Persona 1: Order Picker Trainee	Persona 2: Temporary Worker	Persona 3: Experienced Order Picker
- Starts working in new warehouse - Familiarization phase	- Has picking experience in other companies - Starts working in new warehouse	- Longtime order picker - Familiar with working environment and processes
Age: 20 **IT familiarity:** High **Experience in order picking:** Low **Language skills:** Native speaker	**Age:** 43 **Training:** Outside the industry **IT familiarity:** average **Experience in order picking:** average **Language skills:** German as a foreign language, uncertainties in reading and technical terms	**Age:** 59 **Training:** order picker **IT familiarity:** Low **Experience in order picking:** High **Language skills:** Native speakers
Characteristics: - Increased need for information due to training - Works in new job and unfamiliar surroundings	**Characteristics:** - Language barrier - Works in unfamiliar surroundings	**Characteristics:** - not familiar with IT equipment - Feels unsettled by new technology - Perceives IT-devices to be disturbing at work

Fig. 4. Created personas

The creation of the personas was based on experiences acquired during the process mapping in the warehouses and further researches of statistics and literature on the composition of the workforce in order picking. Persona 1 is a trainee with an increased need for information in the order picking process, persona 2 a temporary worker with a high language barrier and persona 3 an older order picker, who is critical towards the use of new technology. We rerun the test scenarios of the five sub-processes of the reference process, using WOz. This time the individual requirements of the personas were taken into account by the test person and appropriate adjustments regarding the interaction were made for each persona. For the temporary worker, for example, we suggested changing the interaction from voice to gesture control due to his language barrier. For the experienced order picker, we suggested reducing the number of virtual insertions into the field of vision. These user-specific modifications should also be taken into account in the hardware selection. Furthermore, the AR system should feature a settings menu so the interaction forms can be individualized by the employee according to his preferences before starting the picking process.

4   Results and Discussion

As a result of the analyses described above, Table 2 provides a decision support that enables a selection of suitable AR hardware based on process and user requirements. For each of the five sub-processes, it describes the respective information flows, which include the information input and recording by the picker. In the middle column, it displays the most advantageous form of interaction identified in our tests; the two right columns contain possible alternative forms of interaction for this process step. These recommendations regarding the interaction generate a basis for the selection of AR hardware for the process, whereby the selection is based on the forms of interaction made possible by the AR systems.

In our use case, we examined three different hardware configurations. Due to the availability of hardware and the state of the art in order picking we decided to compare a Microsoft HoloLens as a binocular data glasses with the possibility to insert holographic virtual information in the three dimensional space with a Google glass, which is currently used for commercial applications in order picking. A Google glass in combination with an RFID wristband is evaluated as a variant. These hardware characteristics are examples that show the functionality of the process-based evaluation table. In practice, decision-makers can evaluate numerous hardware variants that correspond to the current state of the art.

Based on our exemplary assessment, a binocular HMD best represents the recommended forms of interaction and display since this hardware offers gesture control as well as a three-dimensional presentation of information. This is advantageous, for example, for displaying the tunnel for gaze guidance or the meta-navigation arrows. A monocular HMD cannot fulfill all recommended points due to the limited interaction possibilities and the lack of flexibility in the display of virtual information. However, if this is extended by an RFID wristband, the tracking of the user in the context of coarse navigation, as well as hand tracking for fine navigation, it is possible. In this way, even with a monocular HMD, many of the recommended interaction patterns, as well as the optimal display formats, can be achieved.

For employees whose individual user requirements, e.g., language barriers, high process experience, differ from the forms of interaction identified as ideal, the alternative forms of interaction listed in the two right columns of Table 2 can be selected. This allows for more efficient process design in individual cases.

In summary, the approach developed in this paper can provide a basis for the selection of assistance systems already in an early phase of product design, which can significantly reduce the financial and technical effort for testing different hardware. The proposed decision basis should not replace the execution of tests with real hardware and under real conditions. Due to the numerous implementation possibilities, however, the decision space can be limited in this way.

The evaluation table we have set up is limited in that, due to the priority given to work processes in this approach, appropriate expertise is still required to evaluate the AR hardware. We therefore propose to use the evaluation table as a structured decision support for logistics service providers interested in an AR solution for order picking. For example, in the context of a workshop, they can be supported by an AR expert in the collection and analysis of hardware characteristics. The joint evaluation of the hardware for all main process steps of order picking enables an assessment of whether the selected hardware fulfils all process-related requirements or what compromises can be expected in the implementation due to user requirements. No costs are considered in this early phase. The decision makers can consider possible cost limits for individual devices during the initial selection of the hardware for the evaluation. The high subjectivity of individual evaluations can be mitigated by the discussion of experts from various disciplines in the decision-making process, a survey and analysis of hardware characteristics that is as comprehensive as possible, and a detailed knowledge of the requirements of the own work processes.

Table 2. Decision basis for the AR hardware selection for order picking

Input by order picker   Output from assistance system

Subtask	Information design	Visual/interaction design		
		Recommended implementation	Alternative implementation 1	Alternative implementation 2
Registration of the user in the assistance system, reception of the picking container at the base station, starting the order	Entries for registration, confirmation of the order	Voice input	Gesture input	Touch Input
	Visual guidance through virtual contents	Metanavigation at chest height	Metanavigation on the ground	No metanavigation, due to missing three-dimensional display option
Provision of information to the point of picking, route to the point of picking, repeated provision of information	Provision of picking information (aisle, shelf number), tested with 2 digits	Display at the edge of the field of view	Voice based information provision	-
	Support of the route search (rough navigation)	Visual guidance via navigation arrows	Voice based guidance	-
Confirm arrival at the point of picking, identify point of picking	Confirmation of arrival in the correct aisle row	Automatic position detection via user tracking	Scanning of a reference marker by the user	manual confirmation by the user
	Provision of picking information (shelf no. 2 digits, article no. 6 digits)	Display at the edge of the field of view	Voice based information provision	-
	Support of the identification of the point of picking (detailed navigation)	Virtual tunnel to the point of picking	Virtual frame around the point of picking	-
Determine picking quantity, pick up article(s), place article(s), confirm position	Control and confirmation of the picking quantity	Automatic recognition via hand tracking	Automatic recognition via additional sensors on the user's hand	Manual entry of the removed quantity
	Control and confirmation of the picking quantity	Display at the edge of the field of view	Voice based information provision	-
Identify delivery point, deliver article(s), confirm order, deliver picking container, log off from system	Support of the route search (rough navigation)	Visual guidance via navigation arrows	Voice based guidance	-
	Confirmation of the picking order	Confirmation of the order by scanning a reference point	Confirmation of the order by position tracking	Manual confirmation of the order

Microsoft HoloLens   Google glass   Google glass with RFID wristband

5   Conclusion and Outlook

In the context of this contribution, we present a decision support for the selection of AR hardware in order picking. For this purpose, we investigated the process-related requirements for interaction by analyzing picking processes at different logistics locations in comparison with a reference process. According to the process requirements, we tested different forms of interaction for this reference process for sub-process steps by simulating the interaction using WOz. Furthermore, we examined the user requirements for the interaction based on three personas, which represent the characteristics and needs of particular groups of employees. Based on these requirements, we identified possibilities for individual adaptations to the previously created interaction concepts.

As a result, we have created a basis for decision-making that specifies the best possible form of interaction for each step of the picking process, and suitable alternatives. Based on this, the AR hardware to be tested under real conditions can be selected. The approach developed in this paper reduces the effort and costs for the procurement and testing of the AR assistant system hardware to be used in a picking process.

In our future work, we plan to evaluate the forms of interaction with a larger user group in order to obtain more significant results. Since the concepts developed in this work have not yet been tested under real conditions, we plan to validate them by conducting user tests with the future system users and under as real as possible process conditions. This guarantees a demand-oriented assistance system development. By using the persona method, we could identify the potential individual needs of order pickers regarding interaction adjustments. The resulting influences on the choice of assistance system hardware should be evaluated with system users to evaluate their validity. Based on the results of this work, further criteria for interaction in the process, such as ergonomics or process conditions, e.g., light, noise, or dust, hardware cost, labor law guidelines should also be investigated.

Appendix

Subtask 2 – Coarse Navigation: Information intake of storage location, route to storage location, repeated information intake.

These process steps are passed through by the picker to move to the correct picking location of the next position, e.g. a rack with picking containers. For this, the identification number of the location (e.g. aisle and shelf number) must be taken and the route to this location must be covered. Since the order picker has to remember many numbers during his shift, it becomes hard to keep those numbers in mind. Often he needs to read the same number several times while he is comparing them to the labels of shelves and boxes surrounding him.

Test Setting: The process steps of subtask 2 take place on the way from the base to the aisle row. The test person walks this path and holds the collection container in both hands, simulating the pushing of the picking cart. The change made to the test stand for each form of interaction is described in Table 3.

Potential for Improvement Identified in the Process

I.   Omission of unnecessary processes

   – Eliminate repeated pauses for information intake

II. Reduction of route search time

   – Support route search

III. Reduction of search times and parallel activities

   – Enable information intake parallel to walking to the storage location

Information Design
1. Picking information (aisle and shelf number [tested with 2 digits each])
2. Support for route search (coarse navigation)

Table 3. Test runs of subtask 2

Tested interaction form	Description of the test runs	Results
Acoustic information intake (1.)	Aisle and shelf numbers are spoken aloud by the wizard, the test person tries to find the storage location	Basically suitable, but with an increasing number of processed positions difficulties in memorizing the numbers. When the test person enters the number, a new announcement must be made
Visual information intake (1.)	Aisle and shelf numbers are virtually displayed at the edge of the field of vision [simulated]	Very well suited. Direct comparison of the displayed numbers with inscriptions in the vicinity is possible. Repeated readout always possible
Acustic route search support (2.)	The surround headphones of the HMD emit a repeated sound coming from the direction of the removal container. [A smartphone that emits a repeated tone is placed in the pickup tray you are looking for]	Direction from which the sound is coming is not clearly visible, therefore prone to errors. The sound is perceived as stressful, even for other people in the vicinity
Visual route search support (2.)	Display of virtual direction arrows that lead to the extraction point	Matching the numbers for route finding is no longer necessary. Pathfinding is simplified and accelerated

Recommended Presentation Design of the Required Information

- Text insertion in the edge of the field of view
- Direction arrows displayed

Explanation

The acoustic transmission of the numbers creates the problem that it can only be listened to selectively and just be re-recorded by an input from the picker, which makes it more difficult to memorize. In comparison, the visual display of the identification numbers is always visible and can be directly compared in the field of vision with labels in the surroundings. The information is still taken up repeatedly, but the picker does not have to interrupt his work for this. In the case of acoustic information provision, this must be actively requested by the user at the right time.

Although the routing with direction arrows means that it is no longer necessary for the order picker to match the aisle and shelf numbers, the identification numbers should still be displayed to enable continuous checks and verification of the routing support.

References

1. Barreto, L., Amaral, A., Pereira, T.: Industry 4.0 implications in logistics: an overview. Procedia Manuf. **13**, 1245–1252 (2017)
2. Baechler, A., et al.: A comparative study of an assistance system for manual order picking - called pick-by-projection - with the guiding systems pick-by-paper, pick-by-light and pick-by-display. In: 49th Hawaii International Conference on System Sciences, pp. 523–531. IEEE (2016)
3. Kipper, G., Rampolla, J.: Augmented Reality. An Emerging Technologies Guide to AR, 1st edn. Syngress, Waltham (2013)
4. Azuma, R.T.: A Survey of Augmented Reality. Presence Teleoperators Virtual Environ. **6**(4), 355–385 (1997)
5. Billinghurst, M., Clark, A., Lee, G.: A survey of augmented reality. Found. Trends® Hum. Comput. Interact. **8**(2–3), 73–272 (2014)
6. Stoltz, M.-H., Giannikas, V., McFarlane, D., Strachan, J., Um, J., Srinivasan, R.: Augmented reality in warehouse operations: opportunities and barriers. IFAC-PapersOnLine **50**(1), 12979–12984 (2017)
7. Dünser, A., Billinghurst, M.: Evaluating augmented reality systems. In: Furht, B. (ed.) Handbook of Augmented Reality, pp. 289–307. Springer, New York (2011). https://doi.org/10.1007/978-1-4614-0064-6_13
8. Dey, A., Billinghurst, M., Lindeman, R.W., Swan, J.E.: A systematic review of 10 years of augmented reality usability studies. 2005 to 2014. Front. Robot. **AI5**, 1–28 (2018)
9. Preim, B., Dachselt, R.: Interaktive Systeme. Band 2: User Interface Engineering, 3D-Interaktion, Natural User Interfaces. 2nd edn. Springer, Heidelberg (2015). https://doi.org/10.1007/978-3-642-45247-5
10. Kourouthanassis, P.E., Boletsis, C., Lekakos, G.: Demystifying the design of mobile augmented reality applications. Multimedia Tools Appl. **74**(3), 1045–1066 (2013). https://doi.org/10.1007/s11042-013-1710-7

11. ISO 9241-210:2019: Ergonomics of human system interaction – Part 210: Human-centred design for interactive systems. Geneva (2019)
12. Stark, J.: Product Lifecycle Management. Springer, Heidelberg (2015)
13. Quandt, M., Knoke, B., Gorldt, C., Freitag, M., Thoben, K.-D.: General requirements for industrial augmented reality applications. Procedia CIRP, 1130–1135 (2018)
14. Baumann, H.: Order Picking Supported by Mobile Computing. Dissertation. Universität Bremen (2012)
15. Marks, A.: Wirtschaftliche Mitarbeiterqualifizierung durch lernorientierte Montagesystemgestaltung. Apprimus Wissenschaftsverlag, Aachen (2019)
16. Schwerdtfeger, B., Reif, R., Günthner, W.A., Klinker, G.: Pick-by-vision: there is something to pick at the end of the augmented tunnel. Virtual Reality **15**(2–3), 213–223 (2011)
17. Reif, R., Günthner, W.A.: Pick-by-vision: augmented reality supported order picking. Vis. Comput. **25**(5–7), 461–467 (2009)
18. Kim, S., Nussbaum, M.A., Gabbard, J.L.: Influences of augmented reality head-worn display type and user interface design on performance and usability in simulated warehouse order picking. Appl. Ergon. **74**, 186–193 (2019)
19. Wang, W., Wang, F., Song, W., Su, S.: Application of augmented reality (AR) technologies in inhouse logistics. E3S Web Conf. **145**(1) (2020)
20. Haase, J., Beimborn, D.: Acceptance of warehouse picking systems. In: Bandi, R.K., Kishore, R., Beimborn, D., Sharma, R., Srivastava, S.C. (eds.) Proceedings of the 2017 ACM SIGMIS Conference on Computers and People, pp. 53–60, ACM Press, New York (2017)
21. Günthner, W.A., Blomeyer, N., Reif, R., Schedlbauer, M.: Pick-by-Vision: Augmented Reality unterstützte Kommissionierung. Lehrstuhl für Fördertechnik Materialfluß Logistik, München, München (2009)
22. Lee, M., Billinghurst, M.: A wizard of Oz study for an AR multimodal interface. In: Digalakis, V., Potamianos, A., Turk, M., Pieraccini, R., Ivanov, Y. (ed.) ICMI 2008, Proceedings of the Tenth International Conference on Multimodal Interfaces: Chania, Crete, Greece, Association for Computing Machinery, New York, pp. 249–256 (2008)
23. Alce, G., Wallergård, M., Hermodsson, K.: WozARd: a wizard of Oz method for wearable augmented reality interaction—a pilot study. Adv. Hum. Comput. Interact. **2015**(4), 1–10 (2015)

Functionalities and Implementation of Future Informational Assistance Systems for Manual Assembly

Towards Individualized, Incentive-Based Assistance and Support of Ergonomics

Christoph Petzoldt[1]([⊠]) [iD], Dennis Keiser[1], Thies Beinke[1], and Michael Freitag[1,2]

[1] BIBA – Bremer Institut für Produktion und Logistik GmbH at the University of Bremen, Bremen, Germany
ptz@biba.uni-bremen.de

[2] Faculty of Production Engineering, University of Bremen, Bremen, Germany

Abstract. The demand for customized products increases, leading to smaller product volumes and batch sizes, down to batch size one. The necessary flexibility and variety places high demands on assembly and increases the complexity. Therefore, the automation of manual assembly processes is often not cost-effective. To cope with these basic conditions, workers in the manual assembly should be supported cognitively by informational assistance systems. In addition to the typical product- and process-related aspects, adaptable human-centered functionalities must be considered, aiming to improve productivity, quality, workers' health, and motivation. Thus, this paper examines the assistance functionalities that future assistance systems should provide for manual assembly processes and presents approaches for their implementation. Design Science Research is the framework for our research activities. The starting point is the analysis of existing assembly assistance systems and a determination of process optimization potentials. Through interviews with experts and the modeling of a manual assembly process, we determine the support dimensions and required functionalities for future assistance systems. Subsequently, the overall system architecture and the subsystems are designed and implemented. Intelligent image processing and deep learning algorithms are the basis for process progress recognition and analysis of the ergonomic situation. Gamification and augmented reality are further methods used. The processual changes resulting from the application of the presented novel assistance system are modeled in a case study, and the optimized aspects and implications for both workers and companies are discussed.

Keywords: Assistance systems · Manual assembly · Human-Machine interaction · Operator 4.0 · Ergonomics · Incentive-based assistance · Gamification · Process monitoring · Industry 4.0

1 Introduction

The trends of increasing customization and individualization of products lead to wide product varieties and decreasing lot sizes resulting in the need for a flexible assembly

M. Freitag et al. (Eds.): S-BPM ONE 2020, CCIS 1278, pp. 88–109, 2020.
https://doi.org/10.1007/978-3-030-64351-5_7

[1–3]. For assembly products with small to medium product volumes, these conditions result in full automation to be not cost-effective [4]. Instead, the high assembly complexity induced through great product varieties is intended to be managed by the cognitive abilities of human workers [5, 6]. Therefore, manual or hybrid workstations are used. However, with increasing complexity and flexibility demands, cognitive support of workers at manual or hybrid assembly stations becomes necessary [7, 8]. For this, assistance systems are used that provide informational support of the worker by providing the right information at the right time in the desired form [9]. Existing assistance systems mainly focus on product- and process-related aspects of the assembly task. In contrast, human-centered aspects of the task, such as ergonomics, motivational support, and individualization of assistance, are barely considered [10]. This results in unused potentials, as system acceptance by the employees [11] and motivation of workers, resulting in a willingness to perform, are key factors for assembly systems. Also, the support of in-process ergonomics offers the potential to lead workers to fewer physical complaints and, from an enterprise point of view, to fewer days of health-related down-time. Therefore, the combination of human-centered assistance and product-process-related support was proposed in [10].

In this paper, we present general functionalities and implementations towards a novel human-centered assistance system for manual assembly processes that combines seven assistance fields, which are 'assembly instructions', 'assembly progress recognition', 'assembly quality control', 'automatic configuration and calibration', 'ergonomics support', 'support individualization', and 'motivational support'.

The paper is structured as follows: In Sect. 2, we present our study design and research methodology. Section 3 discusses the related work on human-centered assistance systems by investigation of the state of the art assembly assistance systems and by analysis of fundamentals regarding ergonomic support dimensions at manual workstations. Then, we define in Sect. 4 assistance dimensions and functionalities for informational, human-centered assistance systems for manual assembly. Building on this holistic functionality definition, Sect. 5 presents the architecture for a novel assistance system and its implementation, focusing on three components, which are ergonomics analysis, motivational support, and assembly process recognition. We demonstrate in Sect. 6 the process optimizations resulting from the use of the presented assistance systems and discuss how both workers and companies could benefit from such assistance systems. Finally, Sect. 7 summarizes the outline future process optimizations and discuss further possibilities for human-centered worker support technologies that become available in the context of Industry 4.0.

2   Research Design and Methodology

The research activities presented in this paper are based on Design Science Research (DSR) framework [12, 13] and follow the DSR process model proposed by [13]. Figure 1 shows the subjects covered by this paper along the DSR process and the methodology used, which we detail in the following. Process observations and literature research on ergonomics are performed to gain a detailed knowledge of the considered manual assembly processes as well as the crucial aspects of ergonomics in manual assembly.

Further, the requirements for assistance systems for manual assembly as well as existing systems are investigated based on the results published in [10]. The definition of objectives for the novel assistance system builds on process models of manual assembly processes, which we modeled based on process observations by means of business process model and notation (BPMN) 2.0 [14] to identify potentials for process optimization. The identified weaknesses of the present process are combined with the results of conducted expert interviews to define the required functions of future assistance systems for manual assembly. From the set of functionalities needed, we derive the design of the architecture for a novel human-centered assistance system and implement the respective subsystems. For demonstrating the potential of the novel system to solve the identified process weaknesses, the assistance system is theoretically applied in a case study, and the resulting process change is modeled using BPMN 2.0. The final evaluation of the system to investigate effectiveness, efficiency, and worker acceptance is carried out through field tests and a user study. However, this is future work and is not covered by the scope of this paper.

DSR process	Subject	Methodology	Section
Problem identification & motivation	• Acquisition of detailed knowledge in manual assembly & ergonomics • Investigation of existing assistance systems and approaches	• Process observation • Literature research on ergonomics • Analysis of assistance systems based on overview table in [10]	1 & 3
Definition of objectives	• Development of process models • Investigation of potentials for assembly assistance systems • Identification of required functions	• BPMN 2.0 process models • Expert interviews • Derive functionalities from process weaknesses & identified potentials	4
Design & development	• Design and implementation of human-centered assistance system for support of manual assembly processes	• Development of overall concept derived from required functions • Implementation of the subsystems	5
Demonstration	• (Theoretical) application of novel assistance system in case study • Identification of optimized aspects • Discussion of implications	• Modeling of assembly process with presented assistance system in BPMN 2.0	6
Evaluation	• Investigation and observation of effectiveness, efficiency and acceptance	• Field tests • User study	7
Communication			

Fig. 1. Research approach following the Design Science Research process model from [13].

3   Related Work on Human-Centered Assistance Systems

Complexity in manual assembly processes increases as the number of product variants and assembly components increases [15]. To ensure quality and avoid errors, assistance systems are introduced by industrial companies with assembly processes [6]. Accordingly, a large number of assistance systems exist on the market [16]. In [10], informational assistance systems from both industry and research are analyzed with respect to various assistance functionalities. As described in the introduction, assistance mainly focuses on product- and process-related aspects of the assembly task [10]. Most often, besides general provision of instructions and guidance through the process, support for picking via pick-by-light systems and, partially, automated quality checks as well as automatic assembly progress recognition, are offered by such systems. However, the human-related aspects of the assembly task leading to system acceptance, intrinsically motivated workers, and enhancing ergonomic conditions, are barely considered [10].

In the following, ergonomics support dimensions and implications are discussed. Ergonomically designed workplaces offer the potential to reduce health-related downtime and thus provide long-term saving potential for companies [17]. Further, optimizing motion sequences can reduce process times, with movement distances and vertical height of objects having the most significant influence on process duration [18]. Ergonomic problems can be the cause of quality problems in assembly processes. According to [19–21], time pressure as a psychological strain and physical strain due to both suboptimal postures and suboptimal motion sequences are identified as the main reasons for quality problems. In addition to increased production output and quality improvements, ergonomic adaptations of the workplace positively influence the well-being of the employees [22] and employees' satisfaction [23]. In general, to minimize the level of effort, the workstation should be designed in the way of helping workers to use the neutral posture of their joints most of the time [24].

Ergonomic adaptation possibilities can be achieved by equipping assembly workstations with technical equipment, following ergonomics construction principles from standards and norms [25]. Based on [26] and the study of technical requirements conducted in [10], this involves, in particular, the following technical systems and equipment: height-adjustable work tables (depending on the user and the task to be performed); an optimized arrangement of production equipment to minimize movement distances around the work center [26]; installation of auxiliary devices and tools to avoid and minimize heavy loads and torsional movements; and suitable, adaptable lighting [27]. These aspects and technical components for ergonomic support in manual assembly processes are summarized in Fig. 2, together with the relevant norms and standards. The aforementioned ergonomic support dimensions are achieved by technical hardware equipment and, except for adaptive lighting, typically have a static effect on the ergonomic workstation setup before the start of the process. In contrast, informational assistance systems offer the potential to support ergonomics during the assembly process in two ways: Firstly, by providing information material in the peripheral field of vision and, secondly, by analyzing body posture and hand movements, triggering a respective warning in case of unfavorable ergonomics. We have therefore added a fifth aspect to the overview of technical systems supporting ergonomics in manual assembly shown in Fig. 2, namely adaptive information material managed by informational assistance systems.

Based on the overview table of state of the art assistance systems for manual assembly presented in [10], we investigated the functionalities of systems that implement human-centered assistance functionalities more closely. Focusing on ergonomics support, assistance individualization and incentive systems, we consider the following systems or, respectively, research projects, to be most relevant: *Ergonomic Assembly 4.0* [28], *motionEAP* [29], *XTEND* [30], *Arkite HMI* [31]. According to [10], ergonomics

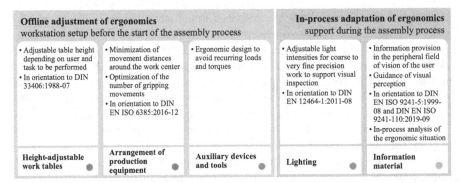

Offline adjustment of ergonomics workstation setup before the start of the assembly process			In-process adaptation of ergonomics support during the assembly process	
• Adjustable table height depending on user and task to be performed • In orientation to DIN 33406:1988-07	• Minimization of movement distances around the work center • Optimization of the number of gripping movements • In orientation to DIN EN ISO 6385:2016-12	• Ergonomic design to avoid recurring loads and torques	• Adjustable light intensities for coarse to very fine precision work to support visual inspection • In orientation to DIN EN 12464-1:2011-08	• Information provision in the peripheral field of vision of the user • Guidance of visual perception • In orientation to DIN EN ISO 9241-5:1999-08 and DIN EN ISO 9241-110:2019-09 • In-process analysis of the ergonomic situation
Height-adjustable work tables ●	**Arrangement of production equipment** ●	**Auxiliary devices and tools** ●	**Lighting** ●	**Information material** ●

Fig. 2. Overview of technical equipment and aspects for support of ergonomics in manual assembly processes. In this paper, we focus on the informational, ergonomic assistance during the process (highlighted in green) with regard to the ergonomics support dimension. (Color figure online)

support is only offered by a single assistance system for manual assembly, namely *Ergonomic Assembly 4.0* [28], which senses the anthropometry of the worker and automatically adjusts the height of the table. However, although this assistance system provides a user-adapted setup for a physically ergonomic workplace, it only affects the ergonomic situation before starting assembly work and does not consider the actual ergonomic situation during assembly.

To analyze the individual ergonomic situation of assembly workers during the process, online measurement of a natural posture with particular regard to a straight spine (c.f. [26]), body symmetry, and torsion of the upper body (c.f. [32]) is necessary. In the related work on assistance system for manual assembly, however, this has not yet been implemented. Moreover, all related assembly assistance systems, even those that integrate individual human-related assistance functionalities, do not comprehensively combine product- and process-related assembly support with human-centered assistance. This leads to our research-guiding questions:

- What optimization potentials with regard to cognitive, informational support of the worker as well as automatic execution of non-value-adding tasks, exist in typical manual assembly processes that are already supported by conventional assistance systems?
- And what assistance functionalities can be derived from this for future assistance systems for manual assembly?

4   Functionalities of Human-Centered Assistance Systems

In this section, we identify and discuss, based on expert interviews and process optimization potentials, the main functionalities that novel assistance systems should provide.

4.1 Process Modeling and Identification of Support Dimensions

We model the process for the manual assembly of a fuel pump using BPMN 2.0 [14], as proposed in [10], and accordingly determine the optimization potentials for the process by identifying value-adding and non-value-adding activities (Fig. 3). Similar to the findings in the case study carried out in [10], it results that all (non-value-adding) controlling and auxiliary steps could be replaced by an intelligent information-based assistance system and that all other activities could be supported cognitively.

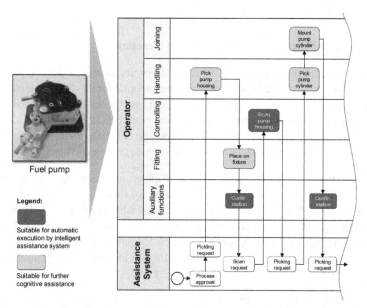

Fig. 3. Potentials of intelligent assistance system illustrated by a modeled process flow for the assembly of a fuel pump. Process steps highlighted in blue are suitable for automatic execution by an intelligent assistance system. Process steps in yellow can be supported with further cognitive assistance (illustration and identification of the assistance potentials according to [10]). (Color figure online)

To obtain a more comprehensive insight and knowledge, we conducted expert interviews with a total of four experts. The experts are composed of two persons from practice with competences in industrial assembly and experience in the practical use of incentive systems as well as two scientists from the field of assembly assistance or gamification, respectively. As a result of the optimization potentials identified above, the expert interviews and the technical, process-related, organizational and motivational requirements for incentive-based assistance systems defined in [10], we follow that both, human-centered assistance as well as product- and process-related assistance features are to be integrated and combined in human-centered assistance systems for manual assembly. From the findings, the support dimensions for human-centered assistance systems for manual assembly are derived. Figure 4 shows these assistance dimensions, which we subsequently discuss in this section.

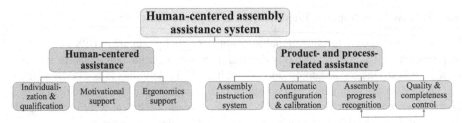

Fig. 4. Support dimensions of informational, human-centered assistance systems for manual assembly.

4.2 Product- and Process-Related Assistance Functions

Product- and process-related assistance functionalities are already widely implemented in the state of the art assistance systems and are fundamental for ensuring product quality and process reliability, resulting in appropriate system performance. As these are highly important aspects of assembly assistance systems, developers should consider these functions. Based on the interviews with experts from the field of assembly, the processual needs for these systems and the data required in each case are explained.

Assembly Instruction System. According to the expert interview, the most fundamental functionality of informational assistance systems for manual assembly is to provide assembly instructions. With these detailed instructions, which are typically displayed on a frontal screen, the worker is guided through all steps of the assembly process. To ensure process reliability, the employee has to confirm each conducted step, which are mostly alternating picking (handling) and mounting (fitting or joining) steps. Sometimes, the worker is asked for additional controlling steps (c.f. [10]).

Various studies show that both process times and system acceptance are improved by projecting assembly instructions onto the worktop instead of displaying information on a frontal screen only [33, 34]. Therefore, for our novel assistance system, we intend to provide both frontal screen instructions and worktop-projected instructions. With the help of this projection of instructions onto the worktop, which represents a means of device-less augmented reality, we offer short instructions at the process-relevant positions. However, the assistance system also allows less-experienced workers to obtain additional and more detailed information via the front-mounted screen.

Assembly Quality and Completeness Control. The quality of assembled products is the essential requirement of industrial companies to satisfy customers [35]. Therefore, efficient quality control procedures are crucial. Quality checks are either performed by human operators or by automatic quality control functions. In addition to quality control functions after finishing the assembly of a product, continuous supervision of assembly step completeness can be applied to increase process reliability and ensure the assembly of even hidden components. However, the classical end-of-line check could be performed either directly at the assembly station through industrial image processing methods, potentially with a freely movable camera system, or separated at a dedicated control station, while continuous quality and completeness control systems need to be integrated into the workstation. Typically, such camera systems are mounted on top of the station, which requires robustness against covering the assembly product, for example, by the hands of the worker. Due to the benefits of controlling both assembly completeness and quality, we highlight that continuous control systems are preferable. Therefore, we implement these into the novel human-centered assistance system.

Assembly Progress Recognition. As a conclusion of the expert interviews, there is a clear desire to optimize the manual confirmation steps, i.e., auxiliary functions, described above by executing them automatically. For performing this, two main possibilities exist: either, recognizing the successful execution of specific steps or tracking the complete assembly process.

For the former case, e.g., some pick-by-light systems directly integrate a physical button beneath the light to confirm successful picking. However, this only puts the auxiliary function close to the relevant location but does not remove it. Other picking assistance systems add light barriers to assembly component boxes to automatically activate the next step as soon as the worker took a component from the box. Through torque-checking screwdrivers, also screwing steps could be confirmed automatically. However, all options are limited to confirmation of specific steps. Only when using assembly completeness control (detailed above) as the sole recognition system for process tracking, specific process step recognition could be sufficient to confirm the whole process automatically. In this case, the worker would only be asked to assemble a bunch of components, which the worker picks from any material supply box. Then, only the mounting of components to the assembly product is recognized using image processing technologies. Also, a combination of recognizing multiple specific steps are conceivable.

The second possibility is to track the movements of the worker continuously. Here, image processing algorithms are necessary to track the hands of the operator continuously. In addition to the possibility of checking the process times for later individualization of support, which in principle would also be possible by combining several partial recognition systems, this approach offers the possibility of reconfiguring the workplace in a process-optimized way by analyzing suboptimal movements. Also, only a single camera system is needed instead of numerous partial systems, which results in low-cost systems and short-term economy of the manual assembly assistance system. Therefore, our novel assistance system builds on such a low-cost camera system and a continuous hand-tracking approach, which we, however, combine with the recognition of specific steps to increase the robustness of detection.

Automated Configuration and Calibration. A typical assistance system requires to be configured for changed product variants (c.f. [36]). Also, when using camera-based image processing methods, the system needs to be calibrated for new or modified assembly stations. This requires trained specialist personnel or consulting of the system provider. To simplify configuration, industrial assembly instruction control systems already offer intuitive user interfaces to facilitate the setup procedure. For automatic calibration of camera systems, marker-driven approaches or algorithms that completely base on reference frames are feasible.

4.3 Human-Centered Assistance Functions

Even though the implementation of product- and process-related assistance functions leads to the successful fulfillment of some processual requirements, such as high quality with low error rate as well as high process reliability, it does not necessarily result in optimal system performance with respect to output rate. The missing consideration of human-centered requirements (see technical and motivational requirements suggested in [10]), results in insufficient or at least a non-optimal satisfaction of system acceptance, healthy work conditions, and intrinsic motivation. Besides, by not implementing the requirement of individualized assistance, either experienced employees are annoyed by superfluous information or less-qualified employees need personal supervisors during training phases (c.f. [10]). Therefore, in the following, we present assistance functionalities that focus on three important human-centered aspects of the manual assembly work, i.e., ergonomics support, individualization of assistance, and motivational support.

Ergonomics Support. From the related work on ergonomics in manual assembly, one fundamental aspect of ergonomics in manual assembly is an appropriate configuration of the workstation. Several guidelines [25, 27, 37] exist to support industrial companies in designing assembly workstations. However, especially for industrial assembly lines with multi-shift operation, personalization of the workstation is hardly feasible, even with adjustable worktops. In the course of the working day, this often results in suboptimal ergonomic postures of workers [38] leading to back problems and, eventually, not negligible days of health-related down-time [39].

Here, in-process analysis of ergonomic situations offers the potential to advise assembly workers regarding suboptimal postures. From the study of the essential ergonomics characteristics, we deduce four aspects:

- vertical inclination of the upper body;
- symmetrical, upright posture with regard to hip and shoulder axis without twisting;
- arm, wrist, and forearm positions; and
- duration and frequency of physical strain.

For human-centered assistance systems, we propose the measurement of these aspects either by active, respectively passive markers or by external camera technology, in each case in conjunction with algorithms for criteria evaluation.

Further elaborated, this even enables in-process adjustments of workstation for both personalization as well as product- and process-optimal arrangement of tools and materials.

Individualization of Assistance and Worker Qualification. As stated above, to adapt an assistance system to the needs of the respective worker, individualization of assistance is important to provide only relevant instructions and information. A straightforward approach is to offer multiple assembly instructions with various degrees of detail regarding both granularity, i.e., number of instructions, and comprehensiveness of additional information. Then, before starting the program, either the respective assembly officer or the workers themselves would decide for a suitable detailing of instructions. This can be realized through identification tags storing the workers' qualification level. However, instead of manually deciding on appropriate detailing of instructions, assistance systems can make this decision automatically, or at least support the decision making, by measuring appropriate indicators and calculating a corresponding qualification score based on these. We highlight that the evaluation of these criteria should consider not only typical performance values but also the adherence of a positive ergonomic posture. Further, the calculation of this qualification score should include both the current extent of these criteria and trend analysis. To calculate the qualification score, we propose three dimensions, which are:

- Product- and work quality, i.e., the correct assembly or error rate of complete components as well as individual components and errors during picking.
- The performance, precisely the average total throughput time for n assembly products and its variance, the speed of completion for individual process steps and its variation for different types of steps, as well as the time for searching of assembly parts and assembly locations.
- The ergonomic situation, which is composed of the aforementioned aspects that are measured by various criteria detailed in Sect. 5.

Based on the qualification score, the assistance system can decide for a suitable level of information detailing, which facilitates training phases for new employees and the introduction of new product varieties or products.

Incentive-Based Motivational Support. As shown in [10], the motivation of the worker influences willingness to perform and thus task performance. By implementation of a sophisticated gamification approach, motivation can be achieved in a targeted and long-term manner [40]. As the benefits of gamification applications are not significantly affected by age [41], gamification offers a suitable means of addressing a broad group of assembly workers.

Even though provided at a less fine-granular differentiation, the qualification score discussed above and the related different detailing of assembly instructions already represent a simple game-design-element, especially supporting the training and learning phase of new employees. However, for the long-term motivation of assembly workers, more sophisticated game-design-elements are expedient [40]. In [42, 43], different game-design-elements are analyzed with respect to flow theory and self-determination theory with its basic needs for autonomy, social inclusion, and competence. The feeling of competence is usually already satisfied to a sufficient degree by experiencing one's own abilities, objectives, and received feedback. Therefore, elements that encourage a positive experience of autonomy and social inclusion should be specially selected [43]. According to [43], these are mainly narratives, levels, tasks, avatars, and badges, of which the latter four can be implemented with reasonable effort. Scores and performance graphs are also used to strengthen the competence feeling.

5   Implementation of a Novel Human-Centered Assistance System for Support of Manual Assembly Processes

Based on the defined target functionalities for human-centered assistance systems, we developed a concept for a novel assistance system for manual assembly, which implements all support dimensions shown in Fig. 4. Table 1 provides an overview of our implementation approach for each targeted assistance function, as proposed in the previous section. In this paper, we focus in the following on three aspects, which are assembly process recognition, ergonomics analysis and support, as well as motivational support through a gamified incentive system.

Table 1. Overview of target functionalities for future assistance systems for manual assembly and the implementation approach for the presented novel assistance system.

Assistance system functionality	Our implementation approach
Assembly instruction system	Frontal screen instructions and worktop-projected instructions
Quality and completeness control	Top-mounted depth-image camera with intelligent algorithms for continuous control of assembly product completeness and quality
Progress recognition	Top-mounted depth-image camera combining continuous hand-tracking (process monitoring) with ROI detection (robust recognition of component picking)
Automated configuration and calibration	User configuration interface and automatic camera system calibration
Ergonomics support	Front- and side-mounted camera technology in conjunction with intelligent algorithm for evaluation of human posture
Individualization of support and worker qualification	Qualification evaluation based on product quality, performance and ergonomics to adapt assistance instructions with varying granularity and level of detail
Incentive-based motivational support	Gamification application with levels, badges, tasks and an individualized avatar, taking into account quality, ergonomics, and productivity aspects

The general setup of the assembly station, which integrates the novel assistance system is shown in Fig. 5. Apart from boxes for the material supply and fixtures to facilitate product assembly, it consists of two front-mounted screens, one for displaying assembly instructions and the other presenting a user-interface for human-centered support. The latter screen visualizes the body posture with ergonomics analysis, shows current tasks and levels as well as a user-individualized avatar with badges, and offers the option to query current and historical performance indicators. Further, a communication platform for connection with other workers and supervisors, as well as means for suggesting improvements or reporting errors are planned. With this screen, we mainly account for the requirement of transparency (c.f. [10]) by providing interfaces for the operator to inform at any time about the data collected and the analyses performed on basis thereof.

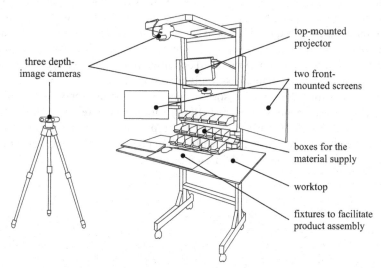

three depth-image cameras

top-mounted projector

two front-mounted screens

boxes for the material supply

worktop

fixtures to facilitate product assembly

Fig. 5. Setup of assembly station. Three low-cost cameras are used to provide input for the image processing and analyzing algorithms of the human-centered support system. The camera perspectives are utilized as follows: side view and front view for ergonomics analysis; top view for assembly process recognition, quality and completeness control, and measurement of process times for individualization of support.

In addition, a top-mounted projector for device-less augmented reality firstly projects green or red lights onto the assembly component boxes to implement the pick-by-light functionality. Secondly, in addition to screen-based visualization of assembly instructions, it enables the projection of additional instructions as well as mounting positions of components onto the worktop, to facilitate the search for assembly locations. And, thirdly, we utilize the projector to project simple game-design-elements, such as recently achieved badges onto the worktop.

For realizing the human-centered assistance functionalities, both tracking of human motions and data on process indicators are required. For the latter, we exploit data that is recorded by the assembly instruction control system already. However, for automatic confirmation of successfully performed assembly steps, and for human posture analysis and ergonomics evaluation, additional camera technology is required. As shown in Fig. 5, we utilize three depth-image cameras for this, mounted on top, frontally, and laterally. For a short-term economic efficiency of the novel human-centered assistance system for manual assembly, low-cost depth-image cameras are used, namely the Intel RealSense D435i.

Assembly Progress Recognition

From the possible options to recognize the assembly progress, detailed in Sect. 4.2, we decided to implement an automatic progress recognition without manual confirmation. For this, we combine the detection of specific steps with continuous hand tracking. With this approach, we ensure that certain steps, which are desired by many installation companies according to the expert interviews conducted, are reliably identified. Furthermore, by implementing continuous hand tracking, we enable the monitoring of the entire assembly process, which we use to increase the robustness of automatic progress confirmation, to calculate a qualification score for the implementation of assistance individualization, and to implement a motivational incentive system. The assembly progress recognition solely bases on the top-mounted depth-image camera (see Fig. 5) that could be easily mounted onto any manual assembly workstation.

The algorithm for recognition of specific steps bases on the depth frame only and compares user-defined regions of interest (ROIs) within a mean reference depth frame, which is calculated from 10 initial frames and representing the boxes for assembly components, with the respective ROIs within the current depth frame. The principle calculation procedure is schematically presented in Fig. 6.

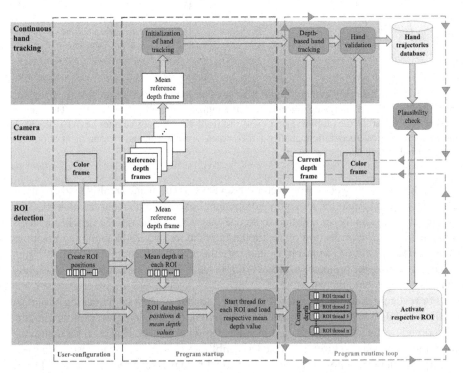

Fig. 6. Procedure for automatic assembly progress recognition, combining detection of specific regions of interest with continuous hand tracking.

Each ROI consists of four areas (see Fig. 7), and for each of these areas, the mean depth reference value is stored. During runtime, we run a separate thread for each ROI, which continuously compares its mean depth references values with the current depth stream. In order to be robust against depth defects, we activate the ROI, and thus the component removal, only after three consecutive images have detected a shallower depth in the ROI. With this approach, real-time detection can be even implemented on lower-cost hardware, which is beneficial in comparison to the application of sophisticated, computationally more expensive hole-filling algorithms. An intuitive user interface is provided for the configuration of ROIs, allowing the user to draw the boxes on the color image. Then, the depth values are automatically calculated and stored.

Fig. 7. User interface showing activation of ROIs for configured components boxes of the manual assembly station.

However, as the detection of ROIs with the explained straightforward approach is relatively simple, one cannot distinguish between arbitrary objects being inserted in the ROI and worker's hands taking assembly components from component boxes. Therefore, the ROI detection is combined with a continuous hand-tracking algorithm. The algorithm is intended to continuously track the center of the hand for both arms of the worker based on the depth frame and validated with the color image. Alternatively, existing open-source real-time hand detection algorithms based on depth images can be used. An overview of corresponding approaches is presented in [44]. Besides the use for improving the robustness of assembly progress recognition, the hand trajectories are stored and analyzed, building a data basis for individualization of assembly assistance.

Ergonomics Analysis and Support

For analysis of the ergonomic situation of assembly operators, we analyzed the characteristics identified in the related work on ergonomic fundamentals. From these, we deduced five specific measurement criteria to determine the individual ergonomic situation of the worker at the assembly station, which are summarized and visualized in Fig. 8 and detailed in the following.

The inclination of the back in the sagittal plane should not exceed a maximum angle of 20° in the forward direction [26] to ensure an optimal ergonomic position of the spine. The comfortable adjustment range for the elbow joint angle is between 85 and 110° [32]. In order to detect only significant deviations from this ideal position, a maximum permissible angular deviation of ±45° in relation to a right-angled forearm position is chosen here. However, this parameter is adjustable depending on the requirements of the workstation with respect to the type of activity and the weights to be handled

a)

b)

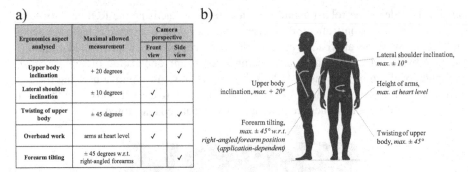

Ergonomics aspect analysed	Maximal allowed measurement	Camera perspective	
		Front view	Side view
Upper body inclination	+ 20 degrees		✓
Lateral shoulder inclination	± 10 degrees	✓	
Twisting of upper body	± 45 degrees	✓	✓
Overhead work	arms at heart level	✓	✓
Forearm tilting	± 45 degrees w.r.t. right-angled forearms		✓

Fig. 8. Ergonomics analysis of human posture. a) Analyzed ergonomics aspects with both relevant measurement criteria and required camera perspective for respective detection. b) Measurement criteria visualized on key points of the human body pose.

(c.f. [25]). During assembly, the load and motion distribution should be as symmetrical as possible to prevent spinal misalignment due to one-sided loading (c.f. [24, 26]). For robust detection of deviations from the comfortable, completely horizontal position [32], we define a maximum shoulder inclination of ±10° in the frontal plane as acceptable. Further, twisting the upper body about the waist is a typical awkward posture [24] and an indicator for the ergonomic disorganization of a workstation [18]. We aim at detecting critical rotations in the transverse plane and thus select a (configurable) angle of ±45° as the maximal allowable twisting value. Finally, we check for overhead work (above the heart level), which leads to muscle fatigue, upper limb discomfort, decreased efficiency, and contributes to shoulder disorders [45–47]. As mentioned above, to provide maximum flexibility and adaptability of the system to the tasks and the workstation, it offers the user the option to adapt all limits for a wide customization and individualization.

For calculating these measurement criteria, an algorithm based on an open-source deep-learning-based human pose estimation implementation was developed. Various 2D- [48, 49] and 3D- [50] approaches and implementations for human pose estimation are available. For the application of ergonomics analysis on manual assembly stations within our setup, fundamental requirements are real-time capability, compatibility with Intel RealSense depth camera, accuracy, and robust detection even in close distances. From these requirements, we identified the 2D pose estimation algorithm *AlphaPose* [51–53] as an appropriate implementation, especially as it is robust against small distances and partly covered body parts.

However, due to the 2D pose estimation approach, some ergonomics aspects are only detectable from either front or side view, as indicated in Fig. 8. Therefore, we use two cameras, each from one perspective (see Fig. 5), which serve as input to two parallel executions of the *AlphaPose* algorithm. The ergonomics analysis algorithm developed on top of *AlphaPose* is schematically shown in Fig. 9. Firstly, it extracts the coordinates of the detected keypoints 'left shoulder', 'right shoulder', 'left elbow', 'right elbow', 'left wrist', 'right wrist', 'left hip', 'right hip' and 'neck' in each case from the output of the two *AlphaPose* executions, whenever these points are detected in the corresponding input image with a user-defined confidence score. From these human body points, we calculate the upper body inclination, the lateral shoulder inclination, and the forearm tilting by calculating the respective distance between belonging points and applying trigonometric functions accordingly. To detect overhead work, we analyze if the vertical coordinate of the elbow is above that of the shoulder. Finally, from a set of experiments, we found that there is a relationship between the distance of shoulders and hips when rotating the body. Therefore, we calculate the Euclidean distance between the left and right shoulder as well as the Euclidean distance between the left and right hip. We then calculate the ratio of the distance of shoulder to distance of hip and detect twisting of the upper body when the ratio exceeds a threshold, which is user-dependent calibrated for both camera perspectives.

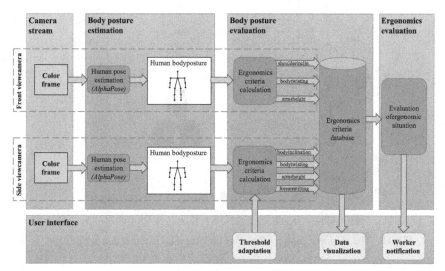

Fig. 9. Procedure for detection of the ergonomic situation of the worker at the manual assembly station.

The results of the ergonomics analysis are saved and continuously analyzed, respecting both current and historical data. Whenever a non-ergonomic working situation is detected by the algorithm for either a longer period of time or repeated regularly, the worker is informed using a worktop projection. Additionally, the user interface offers the worker options to study trend analyses on the user-screen constituting both transparency and systems acceptance.

Motivational Support

Based on the process for integration of gamification into industrial processes proposed in [40], we developed a gamification application for the novel human-centered assistance system for manual assembly. We designed the gamification application to address a wide range of aspects of manual assembly work, which are productivity, work quality, and ergonomics. For this, the following game-design-elements are applied: a customizable avatar, badges in several achievable stages, score-based levels, and additional tasks. These tasks also make it easy to provide new content for the gamification application at certain intervals, which is important for motivating users over a longer period of time [40]. Accordingly, all data acquired by the different sensing systems, i.e., body posture criteria, output performance, error rate, picking times, and throughput times are evaluated over hours up to a whole week. The overall principle design of the gamification application is presented in Fig. 10.

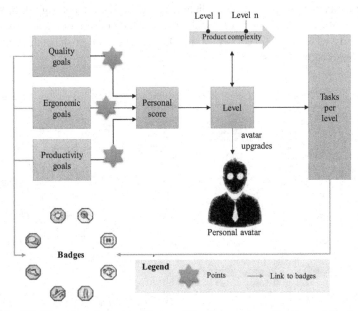

Fig. 10. The principle design scheme of the proposed gamification application.

Levels are based on a score calculated proportionally from the mentioned criteria with points, and also consider the product complexity. By achieving a higher level, the personal avatar can be upgraded (e.g., sunglasses, hair cut). With these two game-design-elements, we indirectly offer best-lists, as avatars and levels can be compared between work colleagues, but without the negative effects of classical best-lists. Besides, the user can achieve different badges by achieving defined quality, ergonomic, and productivity goals or by fulfilling specific tasks. Eventually, we offer the possibility to apply additional level-specific tasks to get score-boosts and achieve extra-badges.

6   Discussion

After the detailing of the design and development of the novel assistance system, we apply the system to the case study described in Sect. 4.1 on a theoretical basis to identify both the impact on the process and optimized process steps.

Figure 11 shows the new assembly process when using the novel assistance system, modeled with BPMN 2.0. It follows that the majority of the non-value-adding process steps are performed by the assistance system, while the value-adding tasks are carried out by the worker. At a closer look, all auxiliary functions are performed by the assistance system in an automated way. The remaining steps (fitting, handling, and joining) are supported cognitively by various assistance functionalities. In this case study, the controlling step of pump house scanning remains an activity to be performed manually using an external scanning device. However, other controlling steps, such as checking the completeness or correct orientation of assembled components, are automatically performed by the novel assistance system. In addition to these product- and process-related aspects, the human-centered assistance functionalities, namely ergonomics support, motivational support as well as qualification and individualization, accompany the entire assembly process, which has a positive mid- to long-term effect on the process in terms of health-related downtime, worker performance, and training phases and thus improves the company's profitability (c.f. [10]).

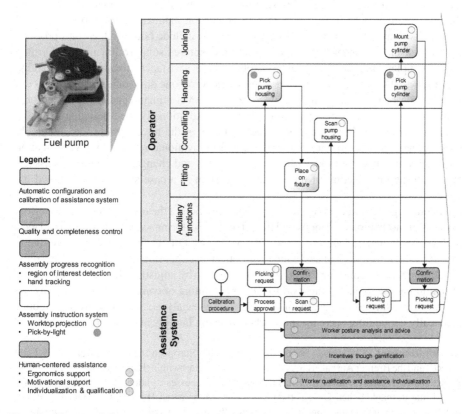

Fig. 11. Change of the assembly process of the fuel pump when using the presented novel assistance system.

All in all, by introducing such informational assistance systems, which provide human-centered aspects as well as product- and process-related support at future manual assembly workplaces, we postulate that both assembly workers and companies could benefit from all effects: higher productivity and quality, better integration of differently qualified people, and healthier and more motivating work conditions. However, the evaluation of the extent of these expected effects remains future work.

It would also be interesting to evaluate the implications of either merging the subsystems for assembly progress detection with assembly completeness verification or relying on only one of the systems. Then, the process itself would be controlled in a less fine-granular way, e.g., only at fitting and joining steps, which would lead to a more significant process responsibility taken by the assistance systems.

7   Conclusion and Outlook

This paper proposes targeted support functionalities that future informational assistance systems for manual assembly should implement. These were identified based on the investigation of optimization potentials in current manual assembly processes and the results of expert interviews. The functionalities include both product- and process-related assistance dimensions as well as human-centered support dimensions. Further, various implementation approaches enabling these assistance functionalities are discussed. Based on these considerations, we decided on one approach in each case constituting the general setup and architecture for a novel human-centered informational assistance system for manual assembly processes. Additionally, we detailed our specific implementation for three assistance functionalities of the novel system, i.e., assembly progress recognition, ergonomics support, and motivational support by a gamification application. Finally, we modeled the improvements and changes to the process associated with the introduction of the assistance system in a case study and discussed the effects.

In our ongoing research, we focus on the evaluation of the user acceptance, the effectiveness of motivational support, and the effects on performance and quality in field tests with assembly workers and, respectively, companies. For our future research, we intend to extend the informational assistance with physical support regarding two dimensions: Firstly, we plan to continue the ergonomics support by adjusting the workstation setup in relation to the height of the worktop and positioning of component boxes during the process according to the results of our ergonomics analysis. Secondly, we will reduce physically demanding tasks for the worker by using intelligent collaborative robots.

Acknowledgment. The authors would like to thank the European Regional Development Fund (EFRE) and the Bremer Aufbau-Bank (BAB) for their support within the project AxIoM - Gamified AI assistance system for support of manual assembly processes (funding code: FUE0619B). We would like to thank Jichen Guo, Fabian Siekmann, Muhammad Husnain Ul Abdeen, and Joel Egharevba for their valuable contributions to literature research and algorithm implementation.

References

1. ElMaraghy, H., et al.: Product variety management. CIRP Ann – Manuf. Technol. **62**, 629–652 (2013). https://doi.org/10.1016/j.cirp.2013.05.007

2. Scholz-Reiter, B., Freitag, M.: Autonomous processes in assembly systems. CIRP Ann. **56**, 712–729 (2007). https://doi.org/10.1016/j.cirp.2007.10.002

3. Harari, N.S., Fundin, A., Carlsson, A.L.: Components of the design process of flexible and reconfigurable assembly systems. Procedia Manuf. **25**, 549–556 (2018). https://doi.org/10.1016/j.promfg.2018.06.118

4. Müller, R., Vette-Steinkamp, M., Hörauf, L., Speicher, C., Bashir, A.: Worker centered cognitive assistance for dynamically created repairing jobs in rework area. Procedia CIRP **72**, 141–146 (2018). https://doi.org/10.1016/j.procir.2018.03.137

5. Andrianakos, G., et al.: An approach for monitoring the execution human based assembly operations using machine learning. Procedia CIRP **86**, 198–203 (2020). https://doi.org/10.1016/j.procir.2020.01.040

6. Faccio, M., Ferrari, E., Galizia, F.G., Gamberi, M., Pilati, F.: Real-time assistance to manual assembly through depth camera and visual feedback. Procedia CIRP **81**, 1254–1259 (2019). https://doi.org/10.1016/j.procir.2019.03.303

7. Keller, T., Bayer, C., Bausch, P., Metternich, J.: Benefit evaluation of digital assistance systems for assembly workstations. Procedia CIRP **81**, 441–446 (2019). https://doi.org/10.1016/j.procir.2019.03.076

8. Lampen, E., Teuber, J., Gaisbauer, F., Bär, T., Pfeiffer, T., Wachsmuth, S.: Combining simulation and augmented reality methods for enhanced worker assistance in manual assembly. Procedia CIRP **81**, 588–659 (2019). https://doi.org/10.1016/j.procir.2019.03.160

9. Hinrichsen, S., Bendzioch, S.: How digital assistance systems improve work productivity in assembly. In: Nunes, I.L. (ed.) AHFE 2018. AISC, vol. 781, pp. 332–342. Springer, Cham (2019). https://doi.org/10.1007/978-3-319-94334-3_33

10. Petzoldt, C., Keiser, D., Beinke, T., Freitag, M.: Requirements for an incentive-based assistance system for manual assembly. In: Freitag, M., Haasis, H.-D., Kotzab, H., Pannek, J. (eds.) LDIC 2020. LNL, pp. 541–553. Springer, Cham (2020). https://doi.org/10.1007/978-3-030-44783-0_50

11. Sochor, R., Kraus, L., Merkel, L., Braunreuther, S., Reinhart, G.: Approach to increase worker acceptance of cognitive assistance systems in manual assembly. Procedia CIRP **81**, 926–931 (2019). https://doi.org/10.1016/j.procir.2019.03.229

12. Hevner, A.R., March, S.T., Park, J., Ram, S.: Design science in information systems research. Manag. Inf. Syst. Q. (MIS Q.) **28**, 75–105 (2004). https://doi.org/10.2307/25148625

13. Peffers, K., Tuunanen, T., Rothenberger, M.A., Chatterjee, S.: A design science research methodology for information systems research. J. Manag. Inf. Syst. **24**, 45–77 (2007). https://doi.org/10.2753/mis0742-1222240302

14. Chinosi, M., Trombetta, A.: BPMN: an introduction to the standard. Comput. Stand Interfaces **34**, 124–134 (2012). https://doi.org/10.1016/j.csi.2011.06.002

15. Asadi, N., Jackson, M., Fundin, A.: Drivers of complexity in a flexible assembly system- a case study. Procedia CIRP **41**, 189–194 (2016). https://doi.org/10.1016/j.procir.2015.12.082

16. VDMA Maschinen- und Anlagenbau Kompetenzmatrix der Assistenzsysteme (2018). https://www.vdma.org/v2viewer/-/v2article/render/26008848. Accessed 20 Feb 2020

17. Bundesministerium für Gesundheit Betriebliche Gesundheitsförderung – Vorteile (2019). https://www.bundesgesundheitsministerium.de/themen/praevention/betriebliche-gesundheitsfoerderung/vorteile.html. Accessed 30 Sep 2019

18. Resnick, M.L., Zanotti, A.: Using ergonomics to target productivity improvements. Comput. Ind. Eng. **33**, 185–188 (1997). https://doi.org/10.1016/s0360-8352(97)00070-3

19. Eklund, J.A.E.: Relationships between ergonomics and quality in assembly work. Appl. Ergon. **26**, 15–22 (1995). https://doi.org/10.1016/0003-6870(95)95747-n

20. Lin, L., Drury, C.G., Kim, S.W.: Ergonomics and quality in paced assembly lines. Hum. Factors Ergon. Manuf. **11**, 377–382 (2001). https://doi.org/10.1002/hfm.1020

21. Bornewasser, M., Bläsing, D., Hinrichsen, S.: Informatorische Assistenzsysteme in der manuellen Montage: Ein nützliches Werkzeug zur Reduktion mentaler Beanspruchung? Zeitschrift für Arbeitswissenschaft **72**(4), 264–275 (2018). https://doi.org/10.1007/s41449-018-0123-x
22. Hemphälä, H., Eklund, J.: A visual ergonomics intervention in mail sorting facilities: effects on eyes, muscles and productivity. Appl. Ergon. **43**, 217–229 (2012). https://doi.org/10.1016/j.apergo.2011.05.006
23. Carlopio, J.R., Gardner, D.: Direct and interactive effects of the physical work environment on attitudes. Environ. Behav. **24**, 579–601 (1992)
24. Moore, S.M., Torma-Krajewski, J., Steiner, L.J.: Practical demonstrations of ergonomic principles. Rep. Invest. **9684**(2011–191), 1–57 (2011)
25. DIN EN ISO 6385. Ergonomics principles in the design of work systems (ISO 6385:2016); German version EN ISO 6385:2016 (2016)
26. Daub, U., Gawlick, S., Blab, F.: Ergonomische Arbeitsplatzgestaltung: Prinzipien aus Trainings-, Sport- und Arbeitswissenschaft zur Entlastung des Bewegungsapparates. Stuttgart (2018)
27. DIN EN 12464-1. Light and lighting - Lighting of work places - Part 1: Indoor work places; German version EN 12464-1:2011 (2011)
28. Fraunhofer, I.P.A., Daub, U.: Ergonomic Assembly 4.0 (2017)
29. Funk, M., Kosch, T., Kettner, R., Korn, O., Schmidt, A.: motionEAP: an overview of 4 years of combining industrial assembly with augmented reality for industry 4.0. In: Proceedings of 16th International Conference Knowledge Technologies and Data-driven Business, pp. 2–5 (2016)
30. Fraunhofer IOSB-INA, Röcker C: XTEND Assistance System (2018)
31. Arkite, B.V.: ARKITE Human Interface Mate (2016). https://www.arkite.be/him/. Accessed 24 Feb 2020
32. Lange, W., Windel, A.: Kleine Ergonomische Datensammlung, 16th edn. TÜV Media GmbH, Dortmund (2017)
33. Claeys, A., Hoedt, S., Van Landeghem, H., Cottyn, J.: Generic model for managing context-aware assembly instructions. IFAC-PapersOnLine **49**, 1181–1186 (2016). https://doi.org/10.1016/j.ifacol.2016.07.666
34. Mattsson, S., Fast-Berglund, L.D.: Evaluation of guidelines for assembly instructions. IFAC-PapersOnLine **49**, 209–214 (2016). https://doi.org/10.1016/j.ifacol.2016.07.598
35. Korn, O.: Context-Aware Assistive Systems for Augmented Work . A Framework Using Gamification and Projection. Universität Stuttgart (2014)
36. Hinrichsen, D., Riediger, D., Unrau, A.: Assistance systems in manual assembly. In: Production Engineering and Management. 6th International Conference. OWL University of Applied Sciences, Lemgo, pp. 3–14 (2016)
37. DIN 33402-2. Ergonomics - Human body dimensions - Part 2: Values, Corrigenda to DIN 33402-2:2005-12 (2007)
38. Zare, M., Bodin, J., Cercier, E., Brunet, R., Roquelaure, Y.: Evaluation of ergonomic approach and musculoskeletal disorders in two different organizations in a truck assembly plant. Int. J. Ind. Ergon. **50**, 34–42 (2015). https://doi.org/10.1016/j.ergon.2015.09.009
39. Romero, D., et al.: Towards an operator 4.0 typology: a human-centric perspective on the fourth industrial revolution technologies. In: International Conference on Computers & Industrial Engineering (CIE46), Tianjin, China, pp. 1–11 (2016)
40. Schuldt, J., Friedemann, S.: The challenges of gamification in the age of industry 4.0: focusing on man in future machine-driven working environments. In: IEEE Global Engineering Education Conference, EDUCON, pp 1622–1630. IEEE Computer Society (2017)
41. Koivisto, J., Hamari, J.: Demographic differences in perceived benefits from gamification. Comput. Hum. Behav. **35**, 179–188 (2014). https://doi.org/10.1016/j.chb.2014.03.007

42. Beinke, T., Freitag, M., Schamann, A., Feldmann, K.: Beruflich-betriebliche Weiterbildung 4.0 - Gamification im E-Learning in Verbindung mit individueller Spieleapplikation für die mitarbeiterorientierte Weiterbildung der Zukunft. Ind. 4.0 Manag. **35**, 13–17 (2019). https://doi.org/10.1016/j.enavi.2017.05.006

43. Keiser, D., Petzoldt, C., Beinke, T., Freitag, M.: Einsatz von Gamification zur Motivationssteigerung in manuellen Montageassistenzsystemen - Methodik zur Auswahl geeigneter Spiel-Design-Elemente. Ind. 4.0 Manag. **38**, 49–52 (2020)

44. Karbasi, M., et al.: Real-Time Hand detection by depth images: a survey. J. Teknol. **78** (2016). https://doi.org/10.11113/jt.v78.5292

45. Kinali, G., Kara, S., Yıldırım, M.S.: Electromyographic analysis of an ergonomic risk factor: overhead work. J. Phys. Ther. Sci. **28**, 1924–1927 (2016). https://doi.org/10.1589/jpts.28.1924

46. Lowe, B.D., et al.: Evaluation of a workplace exercise program for control of shoulder disorders in overhead assembly work. J. Occup. Environ. Med. **59**, 563–570 (2017). https://doi.org/10.1097/jom.0000000000001030

47. Sood, D., Nussbaum, M.A., Hager, K.: Fatigue during prolonged intermittent overhead work: reliability of measures and effects of working height. Ergonomics **50**, 497–513 (2007). https://doi.org/10.1080/00140130601133800

48. Khan, N.U., Wan, W.: A review of human pose estimation from single image. In: ICALIP 2018 - 6th International Conference on Audio, Language and Image Processing. Institute of Electrical and Electronics Engineers Inc., pp. 230–236 (2018)

49. Dang, Q., Yin, J., Wang, B., Zheng, W.: Deep learning based 2D human pose estimation: a survey. Tsinghua Sci. Technol. **24**, 663–676 (2019). https://doi.org/10.26599/tst.2018.9010100

50. Sarafianos, N., Boteanu, B., Ionescu, B., Kakadiaris, I.A.: 3D Human pose estimation: a review of the literature and analysis of covariates. Comput. Vis. Image Underst. **152**, 1–20 (2016). https://doi.org/10.1016/j.cviu.2016.09.002

51. Fang, H.S., Xie, S., Tai, Y.W., Lu, C.: RMPE: regional multi-person pose estimation. In: ICCV (2017)

52. Li, J., et al.: CrowdPose: efficient crowded scenes pose estimation and a new benchmark. In: Proceedings of IEEE Computer Society of Conference on Computer Vision and Pattern Recognition, June 2019, pp. 10855–10864 (2018)

53. Xiu, Y., Li, J., Wang, H., Fang, Y., Lu, C.: Pose flow: efficient online pose tracking. In: British Machine Vision Conference, BMVC 2018 (2018)

Process Mining and the Internet of Actors and Behaviors

The Internet-of-Behavior as Organizational Transformation Space with Choreographic Intelligence

Christian Stary[(⊠)] [iD]

Business Informatics, Johannes Kepler University Linz, Linz, Austria
Christian.Stary@jku.at

Abstract. The next generation Internet-of-Things (IoT) is touted Internet-of-Behavior (IoB). Its topping quality is the dynamic generation of behavior (prescriptions), based on extensive data analytics. Although this can be of benefit for timely adaptation, it requires qualified representation and informed design capabilities to understand its impact on individuals and the embodiment in organizational structures. This paper instantiates the concept of IoB as continuous transformation space. Its baseline are behavior encapsulations representing organizational intelligence through choreographic interactions. Transformation is based on describing role- or task-specific behavior as part of mutual interaction patterns to achieve a common objective. Refinements of behavior encapsulations and interactions to executable processes follow value-based analysis of interactions. The selected level of granularity determines the extent to which the operational intelligence of an organization can be de- or reconstructed and enriched with further intelligence. The presented design-science model could be institutionalized for continuous transformation due to its design-integrated engineering nature.

Keywords: Internet-of-Things · Behavior-Driven software development · (digital) transformation · Subject orientation · Value engineering · Design-integrated engineering · Design science

1 Introduction

Organizations increasingly shift to agile forms of work, pushing for fully digitized workplaces. 'The average work day is becoming filled with employee-facing technologies that are transforming how work gets done. Organizations that help their employees become more agile, inclusive and engaged are in an excellent position to use emerging technologies to drive competitive advantage. Competitive advantage for 30% of organizations will come from the workforce's ability to creatively exploit emerging technologies.' ([9], p. 1).

Recognizing the engagement of operational stakeholders as nucleus of continuous change and evolution means to push them into the role of (re-)designers and development engineers, once emerging technologies, such as the Internet of Things (IoT), algorithmic decision making, and deep learning become integral part of their work. Binding

© Springer Nature Switzerland AG 2020
M. Freitag et al. (Eds.): S-BPM ONE 2020, CCIS 1278, pp. 113–132, 2020.
https://doi.org/10.1007/978-3-030-64351-5_8

individual activities increasingly to digital actions through these technologies leads to an "Internet of Behavior" (IoB) ([28], p. 1) as follow-up to the Internet-of-Things (IoT) ([21], p. 2). Consequently, behavior data direct activities of socio-technical systems in real time, encouraging or discouraging human behavior. For instance, a home healthcare support system can adapt its behavior to the situation at hand based on received sensor data, and trigger specific actuator behavior based on algorithmic processing and data analytics. This trigger could lead to adjustments of human behavior, e.g., taking care of a certain order of using healthcare appliances (cf. [35]).

Hence, the design of IoB systems based on behavior (specifications) is a moving target. As such, it is an immanent and pervasive engineering task. It requires technical and technological capabilities, when 'by 2023, 40% of professional workers will orchestrate their business application experiences and capabilities like they do their music streaming services' ([28], p. 4). Due to their cyber-physical nature – they are based on the IoT – IoB systems require a model representation (termed digital twin) as baseline for continuous design-integrated engineering (cf. [25]). This paper aims to define and design such a scheme. It should enable the dynamic arrangement of networked behavior encapsulations, and thus, represent an operational framework of informed and continuous transformation. Thereby, transformation should be able to utilize IoB data for predictive analytics. Recent results indicate for specific domains the utility of algorithmic data analytics (cf. [38]). However, we rather target opportunistic IoB system behavior (cf. [17]), building on mutual actor awareness (cf. [15]) and value-based co-creation (cf. [30]), than unidirectional control of stakeholder behavior (cf. [31]).

Section 2 provides the methodological background of the study. Design Science-based Research has been used to generate the findings in this paper. Section 3 provides fundamentals of IoB system design and thus leads to the requirements to be met by the choreographic transformation scheme. Section 4 introduces the scheme from a methodological and representational perspective. Intelligence for transformation is identified through a value-stream analysis, and followed by subject-oriented refining and adapting of Behavior-encapsulating Entities and their mutual interaction. The approach is exemplified through a field study of home healthcare, involving various stakeholders and IoT devices. Section 5 concludes the paper.

2 Methodology

In this section, the Design-Based Research procedure is explained, detailing the steps of the presented work. Design Science has attracted attention increasingly for the last decade (cf. [6, 19]). Its dual while iterative nature with respect to design artifacts and design theory equally supports practical development and conceptual understanding.

The Relevance Cycle (Fig. 1) applied to the objective of this work connects the environment of the IoB implementation project with its core development activities. The Rigor Cycle relates these activities to a knowledge base informing the project. The Design Cycle iterates between the core development activities (building and evaluating artifacts). This intermediate position ensures on one hand that artifact development remains in the context the process started, and on the other hand, that each development cycle is informed by scientific theories and domain-specific practice, and the results can be documented in a structured form. Each design cycle result can be traced back to its starting point and related to previous design cycles. In this way, each step in developing the IoB transformation space becomes transparent.

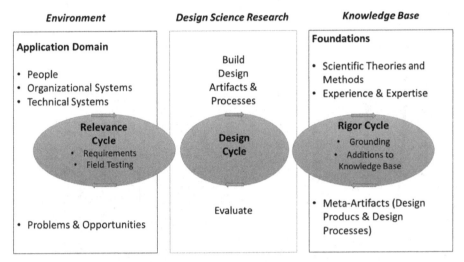

Fig. 1. Design cycles embodied in pragmatic and methodological context (according to [19]).

The original Design Science framework has been operationalized by Peffers et al. [29]. It captures the development stages as shown in Fig. 2: (i) identification of the problem, (ii) definition of objectives for a solution, (iii) design and development of artifact, (iv) demonstration of artifact use to solve the problem, (v) evaluation of the solution, (vi) communication of achievements:

1. *Identification of object and motivation*: The research problem needs to be identified and the value of a solution needs to be justified. So far, the concept of IoB has been specified and promoted by strategic foresight rather than elaborated development requirements. For structuring development, IoB value drivers and properties need to be elaborated. Since the IoB is based on the IoT that are part of Cyber-Physical Systems, digital models ('twins'), and thus modeling needs to be addressed. They serve as baseline for organizational transformation, in particular through dynamic adaptation and predictive analytics.

2. *Definition of objectives for a solution*: The solution needs to facilitate dynamic transformation of organizations through informed IoB developments supporting business operation. Developers can design digital models ('twins') in the course of transformation, and utilize them for execution (operation), dynamic adaptation and behavior prediction. Particularities of industrial developments, such as Industry4.0 (https://www.plattform-i40.de/) and related system architectures, e.g., of Cyber-Physical Production Systems, need to be recognized and taken into account.

3. *Demonstration*: Each Design Science cycle uses the current version of the artifact to exemplify whether and how the addressed problem is solved in practice. In our case,

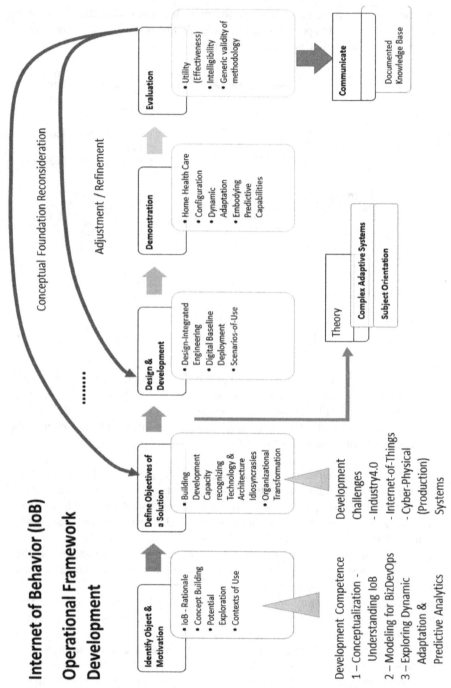

Fig. 2. Design-science based approach to IoB implementation as transformation space

a home healthcare scenario is selected due to its technological and organizational IoB fit, and existing findings with respect to the applied solution concepts (see Complex Adaptive Systems and subject orientation related to the transition between Definition of Objectives of a Solution and Design & Development in Fig. 2).

4. *Evaluation:* In each of the Design Science cycles the current solution is evaluated, based on the objectives and the requirements developed so far. It is checked whether the results from the use of the artifact in the demonstration case meets the requirements. As the directed backward links from Evaluation indicate, either the artifact requires further refinement and/or adjustment, or the objectives need to be reconsidered in terms of revisiting the conceptual foundation of the approach, before a new design cycle can be started.

5. *Communication* of all collected information and achievements, including the problem, the artifact, its utility and effectiveness to other researches and practitioners. It feeds to the Knowledge Base (see Fig. 1), and enables a complete picture of findings through the Rigor Cycle. Both, conceptual and experiential findings, are captured, allowing for reflecting on the process of finding a solution (i.e. meta-findings).

The result of the Design Science cycles is always a purposeful artifact. In our case it is an operational framework, i.e. a procedure involving IoT technology and methodological support (tools) to achieve an effective IoB implementation through organizational transformation. Like many Design Science projects the endeavor finally focuses on social systems and their members. The outcome of this work will be used by individuals applying IoB-concepts for organizations. Focus of their work is the interaction between people and technological products, and the representation of working IoB systems featuring human understanding and intelligibility. Human design activities are integrated with engineering ones, leading to a design-integrated IoB engineering approach to developing a solution. Whenever evaluation is performed, (previous) experiences, needs/requirements, conventions, and standards form the basis of reflection and further design.

In the following section, the requirements for a design-integrated engineering solution are detailed revealing the addressed socio-technical nature of IoB systems. It documents the results achieved in step 1 and 2 of the Design Science framework. Section 4 provides the result of running several Design Science cycles (step 3–5) to define the operational IoB framework, i.e. how to establish an organizational transformation space based on behavior specifications.

3 IoB Solution Requirements

When aiming to identify meaningful behavior patterns, the IoB, analogous to the IoT, provides an Internet address for behavior patterns. It enables accessing systems or addressing individuals engaged with a specific behavior. Such a connection can be used in various ways and directions, for data delivery, joint processing, or taking control. Like for IoT, the power of IoB is the scale that matters. Several billions of systems and/or actors and thus, behavior patterns populate the network and represent a unique source of collecting data and passing it on for processing, controlling, and thus, influencing behavior through generated information.

Figure 3 aims to categorize the technological advancements that are characteristics of IoB developments on the left side, and to develop a corresponding behavior perspective on the right side. After introducing IoT on an elementary or syntactic level, system components have been captured by semantic technologies which enabled contextual process design. Turning passive actors to active ones, and adding intelligence to system components has led to self-organizing actors, which allowed the emergence of novel system behavior [16] referring to the self and future developments.

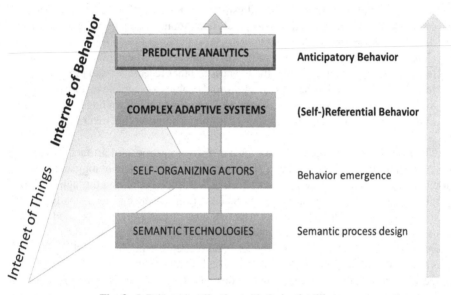

Fig. 3. IoB conceptualization with design intelligence

Complex Adaptive Systems [20] focus on the interdependence of behaviors. The concept raises awareness for the consequences of individual acting on other actors or system components, as individual acting influences the activities of other actors in the system. In this way, self-referential interaction loops develop in a specific system. Understanding such a system mechanism helps in the development of predictive analytics, since behavior can be anticipated based on the history of individual action and received inputs from other actors driven by those actions.

From this conceptualization two requirements for operational organizational transformation can be derived:

- (REQ 1) Design elements need to encapsulate behavior. They need to be considered the fundamental unit of design and engineering.
- (REQ 2) IoT fundamental to IoB requires a socio-technical approach, thus taking into account the interaction between behavior entities. Exchange (i.e. bi-directional) relations enable to capture the impact certain behavior of a single entity can have on a system (cf. Complex Adaptive Systems).

From an operational perspective, IoB systems are based on Internet-based connected technologies. Thereby, the IoT architecture serves as baseline and is represented traditionally as a stack (see Fig. 4). IoT-based architectures facilitate interaction and data exchange between systems, their components, and users. They take into account the business perspective as well as the environment of an IoB system influencing its use and the behavioral integration of its components. Comprehensive architectures frame data management and runtime issues, including access regulations and flow of control for developers.

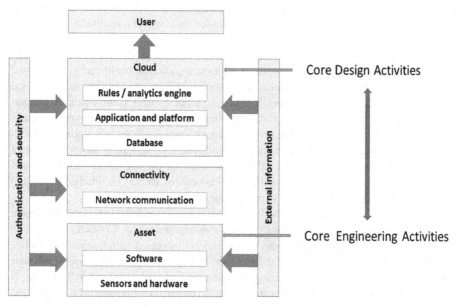

Fig. 4. The IoT stack (according to [23]) as baseline to design-integrated engineering

The core elements of IoT systems are positioned on the bottom of the stacked architecture. It comprises the sensor components and the software managing them (Asset part) as integrating software and hardware allows for embedded system design. Architecture components connected with the Asset are Internet components to share all kinds of collected data. They ensure connectivity of networked assets and the exchange of data. The logic to manage collected data and their transmission for processing is operated in the Cloud. Cloud computing services allow omnipresent and scalable access and distribution of system features. They comprise storing data in a database, applications and platforms to run services, rule engines to enforce (business) regulations, and analytics to generate decision-relevant information. Finally, all elements need to be related to the context of an application. It contains all relevant information for design and operation (termed external information in the stacked architecture). Another frame of the stack components is composed of overarching performance-relevant topics, in particular authentication and security. Both affect the interactive and automated use of architecture components, and thus, running the overall system.

It is the upper part of the stacked architecture injected by external information that is crucial for design-integrated engineering (see Fig. 4). At some point in time, stakeholders acting in specific roles need to access the IoT system, triggering data collections or interpreting the results of analysis. They also need to know the involved component for developing and maintaining the IoT technologies, either directly or via a corresponding model (digital twin). Consequently, the following requirements need to be met:

- (REQ 3) IoB designers (including operational workforce) model IoT components the same way as their work tasks or business processes.
- (REQ 4) For design-integrated engineering, models should be executable, in order to provide direct feedback to stakeholders in their role as system designers.

The ongoing proliferation of connected system components drives current application development and propagation in large domains, such as healthcare (cf. [8]), and production industry (cf. [13]). Large capabilities for intelligent system design are enabled by autonomous data collection through sensor systems, as well as the dynamic adaptation and remote control of devices through actuators. When using the Internet as basis of so-called smart services (cf. [7]), physical objects, such as shoes, are augmented with Internet-based functions, extending their capabilities, e.g., signaling the possibility of exhaustion. The provision of such services is based on the recording of sensors and operational data, the transmission via digital networks, as well as the interpretation and delivery of analysis results, e.g., via smartphone apps.

When products originally designed for a specific use get enriched in scope, the design process needs to take into account further services and processes. Consider clients of a home healthcare appliance with smart shoes who are provided with health intelligence according to their individual use of the product. Design tasks need to encounter further components for interpretation, leading to (dynamic) adaptation of an IoB system. It enables novel relationships between stakeholders (in particular between producers and consumers) and components, intermingling their role through operation and utilization (cf. [24]). Hence, design-integrated engineering should take into consideration dynamic adaptation, such as

- Use case or even business model development based on an enriched use of IoB systems, services, or collected data, e.g., [4]
- Revisiting product lifecycles, e.g., [14]
- 'Smartification' of traditional industrial products, e.g., [32]

Although these efforts contribute to the overall goal of higher market and customer orientation, there is only fragmented knowledge on how to systematically inform designers when developing IoT-based systems (cf. [18, 36]). Besides indications that design-integrated engineering could profit from Software Engineering embedded system analysis and design (cf. [18]), design modeling has to meet the following requirement of dynamic adaptability of system behavior:

- (REQ 5) Adaptation capabilities need to be captured in a generic, however, context-sensitive form.

The following section demonstrates how the specified requirements of a solution can be met by utilizing existing concepts stemming from Value Network Analysis [3] and Subject-oriented Business Process Management [10].

4 Transformation Space Design

This section provides the results of iterating several Design Science cycles (see step 3–5 in Fig. 2) to define the operational IoB framework as subject-oriented transformation space. As methodological entry point, IoB systems are considered as Complex Adaptive Systems and analyzed according to value streams between Behavior-encapsulating Entities as described in the first sub section. The resulting map can be refined from a function and communication behavior perspective. Thereby, Subject-oriented Business Process Management (S-BPM) and its choreographic representation schema play a crucial role: Enriched S-BPM models form the baseline for design-integrated engineering, as shown in sub Sect. 4.2, following the value stream analyses presented in sub Sect. 4.1. The resulting models can be enhanced for dynamic adaptation and prediction of behavior, utilizing existing S-BPM features (see sub Sect. 4.3).

4.1 Value Stream Representation and Analysis

This section reports on the results for meeting REQ 1 and REQ 2, looking for artifacts based on behavior entities and their interaction. This type of entity constitutes the design space for transformation, engineered for putting IoB applications to operation, and for linking them to predictive analytics:

- Design elements encapsulate behavior. They represent the fundamental unit of design and engineering (cf. REQ 1).
- IoB is a socio-technical system design approach due to the underlying IoT. It takes into account the interaction between behavior entities. Exchange (i.e. bi-directional) relations refer to the impact a certain behavior of an entity has on system behavior (according to Complex Adaptive Systems theory) (cf. REQ 2).

Methodological intervention is based on operational business knowledge and its structured representation of value streams between involved stakeholders, and between support systems and the stakeholders (cf. [5]). Recognizing support systems as design elements equal to stakeholder roles the approach enriches Value Network Analysis (VNA) originally introduced by Allee [3]. However, the exchange of deliverables as patterns of acting and receiving feedback is still at the focus of transformation. VNA is meant to be a development instrument beyond engineering, as it aims to understand organizational dynamics, and thus to manage structural knowledge from a value-seeking perspective, for individual stakeholders and the organization as a whole. However, it is based on several fundamental principles and assumptions of Complex Adaptive Systems that are shared in the proposed transformation space design as value network [1–3]:

- Network nodes (IoB elements) encapsulate legitimized behavior, i.e. human, digital, semi-digital, or trans-human actors, process information and contribute values to the network, and thus to an organization.
- A value contribution is a transaction meaningful in relation to the system as a whole, even though it occurs between two nodes.
- Network nodes, and thus an organization operates in a highly dynamic and complex setting. In their socio-technical nature they are self-regulating and self-managing entities.

For self-organization to happen, stakeholders need to have an understanding of the organization, and its behavior as a whole. Since the behavior of autonomous stakeholders cannot be predicted fully, organizations need design representations and design support to guide behavior management according to the understanding of stakeholders and their capabilities to change their behavior (cf. [27, 34]).

The proposed VNA-variant builds upon patterns of interaction as design elements for analysis and refinement to operation. An organization is a value stream network represented as self-adapting complex system, which is modeled by identifying patterns of interactions representing relations between behavior-encapsulating entities (BeE) as nodes of the network. Each BeE in a certain organizational role produces and delivers assets along acts of exchange (transactions).

Since transactions denote organizational task accomplishment through exchanges of goods or information, they encode the currently available organizational intelligence (determining the current economic success). They can be modeled in concept maps [26], according to the following guidelines:

- Each nodes represents a BeE, i.e. an organizational role of an IoB element.
- BeEs send or extend deliverables to other BeEs. One-directional arrows represent the direction in which the deliverables are moving in the course of a specific transaction. The label on the arrow denotes the deliverable.

Each transaction is represented by an arrow that originates with one BeE and ends with another. The arrow represents the transmission and denotes the direction of addressing a BeE. Deliverables are those entities that move from one BeE to another. A deliverable can have some physical appearance, such as a document or a tangible product, or be of digital nature, such as a message or request for information.

The concept of exchange is considered a bi-directional value stream: An exchange occurs when a transaction results in a particular deliverable coming back to the originator either directly or indirectly. It ranges from feedback on a BeE deliverable to a new request 'for more of the same', or to a change of behavior. Exchanges reveal patterns typical of organizational relationships, e.g., goods and money.

In the following we exemplify a BeE map for home- and healthcare involving a service company providing innovative instruments (methods and technologies) for customers with specific healthcare needs. The IoB system should help tracking a person's blood pressure, sleep patterns, the diet, blood sugar levels. It should alert relevant stakeholders to adverse situations and suggest behavior modifications to them towards a different outcome, such as reducing blood pressure through a different diet, or reducing the dose of pills for the sake of daytime agility. Moreover, the system should provide every-day convenience, in particular alerting for timely healthcare and medical supply.

The BeE map helps scoping the design and transformation space and leverages potential changes for each BeE. Accurate service provision for wellbeing of a customer in home- and healthcare is the overall goal of the exemplified IoB system. It monitors health- and living conditions to continuously improve service provision.

The first step designers need to consider in the modeling process is the set of organizational tasks, roles, or units, as well as functional technology components and systems that are considered of relevance for service provision. They represent BeEs, and include the IoT devices Blood Pressure Measurement, Sleep Pattern Monitoring, Diet Handler, Medication Handler, and the Personal Scheduler, as well external medical services. Each of the identified roles or functional task represents a node in the BeE network which is partially shown in Fig. 5.

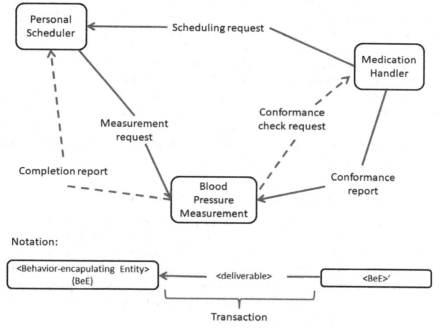

Fig. 5. Part of a BeE-map scoping and structuring the transformation space

According to Verna Allee [2, 3], analyzing the capabilities of a value-driven network and developing opportunities for constructive transformation requires an initial assessment of the structure and transactions of the represented system as a whole. Designers need to perform an exchange analysis targeting (i) the overall objective of the organization in terms of value streams, and (ii) the question: What is the overall pattern of exchanges in the represented system?

In the course of this analysis, designers investigate the overall pattern of interactions addressing a variety of structural issues. When starting to identify missing relations for operating the business or links requiring a rationale, potential breakdowns in flow that can be critical for the business can be determined. In that context, the coherence of relations and resulting flows of how value is generated in the network can be evaluated. For successful operation, an end-to-end value stream (i.e. a set of adjacent transactions) should be identified representing how the organizational objective is met. For instance, for home healthcare, the value stream should contain sequences of transactions that contribute to the well-being of clients in term of preventing adverse conditions.

The overall pattern of reciprocity reveals involvement data of the BeEs (as perceived by the respective modeler). Extensive sources and sinks of interactions should be noted as potentials for optimizing the entire network, avoiding specific BeE benefitting at the expense of others.

In the BeE map in Fig. 5, a specific pattern can be noticed. The Medication Handler triggers Blood Pressure Measurement, involving the Personal Scheduler to start in time. In the network without dotted transactions, Blood Pressure Management is a sink of information. Hence, in order for information not to result in "dead ends", information on blood measurement needs to be passed on explicitly to the Medication Handler and Personal Scheduler. In this way significant knowledge can be exchanged and further action can be designed in case of adverse conditions.

At this stage of design, exchange relations can be added, as indicated by the dotted transactions in Fig. 5. In the simple example, Blood Pressure Measurement should be in exchange relations to the Medication Handler and Personal Scheduler, as the medication could be adapted optimized according to time and current condition of the client. It needs to be noted, that this is a semantically grounded supplement requiring systemic domain knowledge and human intervention, in contrast to syntactically checking whether each BeE interacts with all others in the network.

4.2 Subject-Oriented Refinement and Runtime Completion

In this section we proceed with refining design representations, such as the BeE map, towards digital models of IoB systems serving as baseline for engineering. The presented approach refines BeE maps from a function and communication behavior perspective, utilizing the choreographic representation and engineering scheme from Subject-oriented Business Process Management. It enables embodying BeE maps and refines the involved (socio-technical) components, thereby generating digital twins. In this way REQ 3 and REQ 4 (see Sect. 3) are addressed:

- IoB designers (including operational workforce) are able to model IoT components the same way as their work task or business processes (REQ 3).
- For design-integrated engineering, models can be refined until being executable, in order to provide operational feedback to designers (REQ 4).

Subject-oriented modeling and execution capabilities (cf. [10, 12]) view systems as sets of interacting subjects. Subjects are defined as behavior encapsulation. As they address tasks, machine operations, organizational units, or roles people have in business, they correspond to the Behavior-encapsulating Entities (BeEs) defined for analyzing value streams in the previous section. From an operational perspective, subjects operate in parallel. Thereby, they exchange messages asynchronously or synchronously. Consequently, the transactions forming value streams can be interpreted as transmissions of messages between subjects.

IoB systems specified in subject-oriented models operate as autonomous, concurrent behavior entities representing distributed (IoB) elements. Each entity (subject) is capable to performing (local) actions that do not involve interacting with other subjects, e.g., calculating a threshold value of blood pressure for a measurement device in medical care. Subjects also perform communicative actions that concern transmission of messages to other subjects, namely sending and receiving messages.

Subjects as behavior encapsulations are specified in adjacent diagrams types: Subject Interaction Diagrams (SIDs) and Subject Behavior Diagrams (SBDs). They address different levels of behavior abstraction: SIDs a more abstract one, denoting behavior entities and an accumulated view on message transmissions, and SBDs refining the behavior of each subject of a SID by and revealing the sequence of sending and receiving messages as well as its local actions (i.e. functional behavior).

SIDs provide an integrated view of an IoB system, comprising the subjects involved and the messages they exchange. A part of the SID of the already introduced home- and healthcare support system is shown in Fig. 6. According to the BeEs in Sect. 3, it comprises several subjects involved in IoT communication. In the figure the messages to be exchanged between the subjects are represented along the links between the subjects as rectangles, already including the supplemented ones from the value stream analysis:

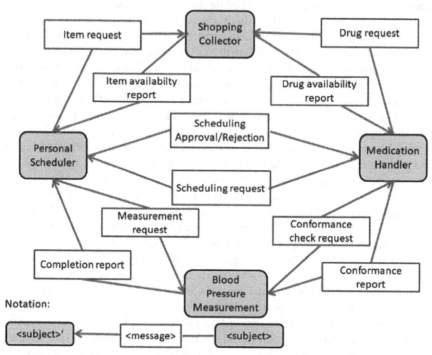

Fig. 6. Sample Subject Interaction Diagram representing a home healthcare appliance

- The Personal Scheduler (subject) coordinates all activities wherever a client is located (traditionally available on a mobile device).
- The Medication Handler takes care of providing the correct medication at any time and location.
- The Blood Pressure Measurement subject enables sensing the blood pressure of the client.
- The Shopping Collector contains all items to be purchased to ensure continuous quality in home health care.

The client handles the measurement device and needs to know, when to activate it and whether further measurements need to be taken. The Shopping Collector receives requests from both, the Medication Handler when drugs are required from the pharmacy, physician, or hospital, and the Personal Scheduler, in case further medicine for the client is required.

State transitions are represented as arrows, with labels indicating the outcome of the preceding state. The part shown in Fig. 7 represents a scheduling request to the Personal Scheduler subject sent by the Medication Handler subject, in order to demonstrate the choreographic synchronization of behavior abstractions (cf. [37]). The figure reveals the parallel operating nature of the 2 subjects involved in the interaction. Once the need for (re)scheduling – modelled as send activity – is recognized by the Medication Handler, a corresponding message is delivered to the Personal Scheduler. When the Personal Scheduler has received that message, the request can be processed, either recognizing a conflict or fixing an entry into the schedule. In both cases, the result is delivered by 'send reaction' to the Medication Scheduler. The subject that has initiated the interaction can now process the results, i.e. the Medication Handler processes the reaction of the Personal Scheduler (modelled by the function of the respective SBD).

Each subject has a so-called input pool as a mailbox for receiving messages (including transmitted data through messaging that are termed business objects). Messages sent to a subject are kept in that input pool together with their name, a time stamp of their arrival, the data they transport and the name of the subject they come from. The designer can define how many messages of which type and/or from which sender can be deposited. The modeler can also define a reaction, if messaging restrictions are violated, e.g., to delete arriving messages, to replace older messages in the input pool. Hence, the type of synchronization through messaging can be specified individually.

Internal functions of subjects process (the transmitted) data. In our example the subject Blood Pressure Measurement has a counter for each application. An internal maintenance function increases the counter by one when the client activates the device. The function can either end with the result "sufficient energy" or "change battery".

Once a Subject Behavior Diagram, e.g., for the Blood Pressure Measurement subject is instantiated, it has to be decided (i) whether a human or a digital device (organizational implementation) and (ii) which actual device is assigned to the subject, acting as technical subject carrier (technological implementation). Validation of SBDs is sufficient for interactive process experience and testing process completion. Besides academic engines, e.g., UeberFlow [22], commercial solutions, such as Metasonic (www.metaso nic.de) and actnconnect (www.actnconnect.de), can be used. Since neither the input pool nor the business objects are part of the modeling notation, it depends on the environment

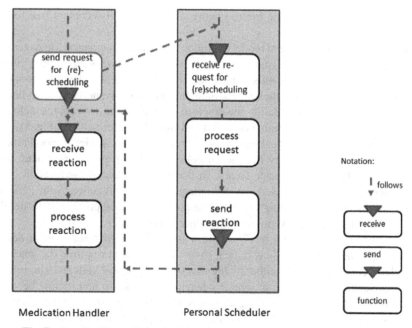

Fig. 7. Sample Subject Behavior Diagrams and message exchange upon request

and runtime engine used for development, at which point in time and in which form data structures and business logic determining the communication on the subject instance level can be specified for pragmatic process support.

4.3 Dynamic Adaptation and Predictive Analysis

After refining BeEs from a function and communication behavior perspective by means of Subject-oriented Business Process Management and its choreographic representation scheme, for organizational transformation, dynamic adaptation and prediction of behavior can be tackled as addressed in this section. The design scheme is enriched with modeling the dynamic adaptability of system behavior, thus aiming to meet REQ 5:

- Adaptation is captured in a generic, however, context-sensitive form (REQ 5).

Dynamic adaptation is based on a trigger, such as a result from performing a function or a sensor signal, which requires special behavior specification. It can be handled according to S-BPM's concept of event processing, thus allowing to capture variants of organizational behavior at design time (cf. [11]). The trigger to dynamic adaptation independent to its implementation can carry some data as payload. For instance, with the trigger "blood pressure above threshold" some information can be tagged to the physical device. Like an event, a data object representing a trigger can carry three types of information: Header, payload and plain content. The header consists of meta-information about the trigger like name, arrival time, priorities, etc. The payload contains specific information about the triggering event. Finally, a trigger can also contain free format content.

With respect to operation and model execution, triggers are messages. Messages of a S-BPM model represent event types. Once a process instance is created and messages are sent, these messages become events. If messages are sent and kept in the input pool they get a time stamp documenting their arrival time. Instantaneous events can be handled by Message Guards. They are modeling constructs to represent behavior variants including the conditions when which variant is relevant and should be executed (see Fig. 8).

For instance, the message "call emergency service" from the subject Blood Pressure Measurement can arrive at any time when delivering data from measurement. This message is handled by a Message Guard. In that Message Guard the reaction of an instantaneous message is specified, e.g., the emergency service is called by the Personal Scheduler subject, since reaching a certain threshold of the blood pressure indicates the need for medical expert intervention for the concerned client.

Message Guards as shown in Fig. 8 allow handling adaptive behavior at design time. The specification shows how critical cases are handled at run time (i.e. once the subject has been instantiated), either by humans or technological systems. The general pattern reveals that jumping from routine behavior (left side) to non-routine behavior is based on flagging functions serving a triggers and (re-)entry points. In the addressed home healthcare example the Message Guard can be applied when a threshold of Blood Pressure has been reached. Once the flag is raised at runtime, either

- either substitutive procedures, returning to the regular SBD sequence – see left side of Message Guard, or
- complementary behavior, leaving the originally executed SBD – see right side of Message Guard in Fig. 8 – is triggered.

Message Guards can be flagged in a process in various behavior states of subjects. The receipt of certain messages, e.g., to abort the process, always results in the same processing pattern. Hence, this pattern should be modeled for each state in which it is relevant. The design decision that has to be taken concerns the way how the adaptation occurs, either extending an existing behavior, or replacing it from a certain state on.

In the home healthcare example, returning to the original sequence (regular SBD sequence), is given when the called emergency service in case of high blood pressure does not require any further intervention of medical experts. Replacement of the regular procedure, however, is required, in case the Medication Handler subject, and as a follow-up, the Personal Scheduler subject (referring to the time of medication), have to be modified.

Once the organizational transformation includes predictive analytics, its integration needs to be structured according to its context (cf. [33]). Figure 9 shows an organizational approach for embodying predictive analytics. The developed pattern is based on a Monitor subject that is triggered by a function in an idle loop observing an IoB system. The monitored data needs to be evaluated to identify the need of adaptation. For algorithmic decision making, a (business) rule base could be of benefit.

Recognizing the need of adaptation requires business intelligence stemming from a Predictive Analytics subject. According to the behavior data available and the calculation

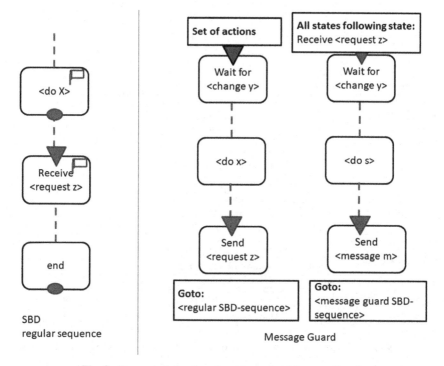

Fig. 8. Dynamic behavior adaptation using Message Guards

model to either predict the behavior of the acting, or the behavior of other interacting subjects, a proposal is generated. In order to avoid re-iterating certain behavior patterns, the adaptation request is stored, together with the newly generated proposal. The latter will be evaluated for effectiveness and efficiency.

With respect to our home healthcare case, organizing the setting could be challenged on whether medical experts need to be contacted once the blood pressure is higher than a specific threshold by predicting that an additional data analysis (e.g., diet patterns) could help avoiding triggering emergency services. Implementing such a proposal requires extending the SID with a Diet Handler subject that can deliver timely data on the diet behavior of the client. It would need to interact with all other subjects, as its functional behavior to provide the requested data leads to novel patterns of interaction.

Given this path of exploratory growth of networked behavior entities, the design science-based framework sketched in Sect. 2 supports their iterative while structured development. Each enrichment can be iteratively tested along design-evaluation iterations of various granularity. Consequently, whenever the transformation space is to be enhanced with choreographic intelligence, the resulting additional requirements for a solution can be exemplarily met by (re-)designing the artefact, demonstrating and evaluating the envisioned enhancement. In this way even variants of system intelligence can be explored and checked for viability.

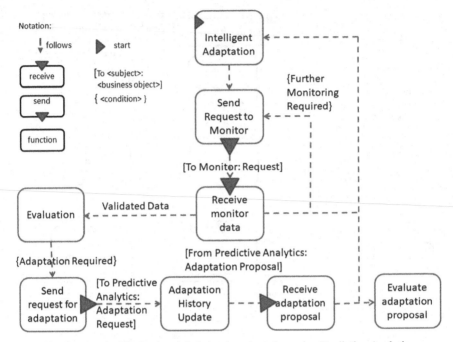

Fig. 9. Sample SID for dynamic behavior adaptation using Predictive Analytics

5   Conclusion

The Internet-of-Behavior (IoB) is built upon IoT and leading towards dynamics adaptation and generation of behavior. Due to its networked nature data analytics can be used for timely adaptation and manipulation of behavior. The resulting system complexity can be handled by representation and access capabilities. The presented approach follows a well-structured and consecutive development approach stemming from design science. It targets organizational structures that can be developed to IoB transformation spaces due to the choreographic behavior encapsulation of functional entities.

The transformation process starts with describing the individually perceived role- or task-specific behavior as part of mutual interaction patterns that are challenged with a specific objective. In a further step, the identified behavior encapsulations and inter-action patterns are refined to executable process models. In this way organizations can experiment with IoB system solutions, and structure analytical intelligence development according to their needs.

References

1. Allee, V.: The Knowledge Evolution: Expanding Organizational Intelligence. Butterworth-Heinemann, Amsterdam (1997)
2. Allee, V.: The Future of Knowledge: Increasing Prosperity Through Value Networks. Butterworth-Heinemann, Amsterdam (2003)

3. Allee, V.: Value network analysis and value conversion of tangible and intangible assets. J. Intellect. Capital **9**(1), 5–24 (2008)
4. Arnold, C., Kiel, D., Voigt, K.I.: How the industrial internet of things changes business models in different manufacturing industries. Int. J. Innov. Manag. **20**(08), 1640015 (2016)
5. Augl, M., Stary, C.: Adjusting capabilities rather than deeds in computer-supported daily workforce planning. In: Ackerman, M.S., Goggins, S.P., Herrmann, T., Prilla, M., Stary, C. (eds.) Designing Healthcare that Works. A Sociotechnical Approach, pp. 175–188. Academic Press/Elsevier, Cambridge (2017)
6. Baskerville, R., Baiyere, A., Gregor, S., Hevner, A., Rossi, M.: Design science research contributions: finding a balance between artifact and theory. J. Assoc. Inf. Syst. **19**(5), 358–376 (2018)
7. Bertino, E., Choo, K.K.R., Georgakopolous, D., Nepal, S.: Internet of things (IoT): smart and secure service delivery. ACM Trans. Internet Technol. (TOIT) **16**(4), 22 (2016)
8. Bhatt, C., Dey, N., Ashour, A.S. (eds.): Internet of Things and Big Data Technologies for Next Generation Healthcare. Springer, Cham (2017). https://doi.org/10.1007/978-3-319-497 36-5
9. Costello, K.: How artificial intelligence, smart workspaces and talent markets will boost employee digital dexterity in future digital workplaces, Gartner Top Technology and Trends driving the Digital Workplaces (2019). https://www.gartner.com/smarterwithgartner/top-10-technologies-driving-the-digital-workplace. Accessed 10 Feb 2020
10. Fleischmann, A., Schmidt, W., Stary, C., Obermeier, S., Börger, E.: Subject-Oriented Business Process Management. Springer, Heidelberg (2012). https://doi.org/10.1007/978-3-642-323 92-8
11. Fleischmann, A., Schmidt, W., Stary, C., Strecker, F.: Nondeterministic Events In Business Processes. In: La Rosa, M., Soffer, P. (eds.) BPM 2012. LNBIP, vol. 132, pp. 364–377. Springer, Heidelberg (2013). https://doi.org/10.1007/978-3-642-36285-9_40
12. Fleischmann, A., Schmidt, W., Stary, C. (eds.): S-BPM in the Wild: Practical Value Creation. Springer, Cham (2015). https://doi.org/10.1007/978-3-319-17542-3
13. Gilchrist, A.: Industry 4.0: The Industrial Internet of Things. Apress, New York (2016)
14. Goto, S., Yoshie, O., Fujimura, S., Tamaki, K.: Preliminary study on workshop facilitation for IoT innovation as industry-university collaboration PLM program for small and medium sized enterprises. In: Ríos, J., Bernard, A., Bouras, A., Foufou, S. (eds.) PLM 2017. IAICT, vol. 517, pp. 285–296. Springer, Cham (2017). https://doi.org/10.1007/978-3-319-72905-3_26
15. Gross, T., Stary, C., Totter, A.: User-centered awareness in computer-supported cooperative work-systems: Structured embedding of findings from social sciences. Int. J. Hum. Comput. Interact. **18**(3), 323–360 (2005)
16. Guo, B., Zhang, D., Wang, Z.: Living with internet of things: the emergence of embedded intelligence. In: International Conference on Internet of Things and 4th International Conference on Cyber, Physical and Social Computing, pp. 297–304. IEEE, New York (2011)
17. Guo, B., Zhang, D., Wang, Z., Yu, Z., Zhou, X.: Opportunistic IoT: exploring the harmonious interaction between human and the internet of things. J. Netw. Comput. Appl. **36**(6), 1531–1539 (2013)
18. He, J., Lo, D.C.T., Xie, Y., Lartigue, J.: Integrating internet of things (IoT) into STEM undergraduate education: case study of a modern technology infused courseware for embedded system course. In: 2016 IEEE Frontiers in Education Conference (FIE), pp. 1–9 (2016)
19. Hevner, A.R.: A three cycle view of design science research. Scand. J. Inf. Syst. **19**(2), 87–92 (2007)
20. Holland, J.H.: Complex Adaptive Systems. Daedalus **121**, 17–30 (1992)
21. Kidd, C.: What is the Internet-of-Behavior. IoB Explained, The Business of IT Blog, BMC (2019). https://www.bmc.com/blogs/iob-internet-of-behavior/. Accessed 10 Feb 2020

22. Krenn, F., Stary, C.: Exploring the potential of dynamic perspective taking on business processes. Complex Syst. Inf. Model. Q. **8**, 15–27 (2016)

23. Kwon, D., Hodkiewicz, M.R., Fan, J., Shibutani, T., Pecht, M.G.: IoT-based prognostics and systems health management for industrial applications. IEEE Access **4**, 3659–3670 (2016)

24. Larivière, B., et al.: "Service Encounter 2.0": an investigation into the roles of technology, employees and customers. J. Bus. Res. **79**, 238–246 (2017)

25. Lee, E.A.: Cyber physical systems: design challenges. In: 11th IEEE International Symposium on Object and Component-Oriented Real-Time Distributed Computing (ISORC), pp. 363–369. IEEE (2008)

26. Novak, J.D., Cañas, A.J.: The origins of the concept mapping tool and the continuing evolution of the tool. Inf. Vis. **5**(3), 175–184 (2006)

27. Oppl, S., Stary, C.: Facilitating shared understanding of work situations using a tangible tabletop interface. Behav. Inf. Technol. **33**(6), 619–635 (2014)

28. Panetta, K.: Gartner top strategic predictions for 2020 and beyond (2019). https://www.gartner.com/smarterwithgartner/gartner-top-strategic-predictions-for-2020-and-beyond/. Accessed 10 Feb 2020

29. Peffers, K., et al.: The design science research process: a model for producing and presenting information systems research. In: Design Science Research in Information Systems and Technology (DESRIST 2006), pp. 83–106, February 2006. https://doi.org/10.2753/MIS0742-122 2240302

30. Pera, R., Occhiocupo, N., Clarke, J.: Motives and resources for value co-creation in a multi-stakeholder ecosystem: a managerial perspective. J. Bus. Res. **69**(10), 4033–4041 (2016)

31. Savitha, J., Akhilesh, K.B.: Conceptualizing the potential role of IoT-enabled monitoring system in deterring counterproductive work behavior. In: Akhilesh, K.B., Möller, D.P.F. (eds.) Smart Technologies, pp. 111–120. Springer, Singapore (2020). https://doi.org/10.1007/978-981-13-7139-4_8

32. Schuh, G., Zeller, V., Hicking, J., Bernardy, A.: Introducing a methodology for smartification of products in manufacturing industry. Procedia CIRP **81**, 228–233 (2019)

33. Sodero, A., Jin, Y.H., Barratt, M.: The social process of big data and predictive analytics use for logistics and supply chain management. Int. J. Phys. Distrib. Logistics Manag. **49**(7), 706–726 (2019). https://doi.org/10.1108/IJPDLM-01-2018-0041

34. Stary, C.: Non-disruptive knowledge and business processing in knowledge life cycles – aligning value network analysis to process management. J. Knowl. Manag. **18**(4), 651–686 (2014)

35. Tan, V., Varghese, S.A.: IoT-enabled health promotion. In: Proceedings of the First Workshop on IoT-Enabled Healthcare and Wellness Technologies and Systems, pp. 17–18 (2016)

36. Isakovic, H., et al.: CPS/IoT ecosystem: a platform for research and education. In: Chamberlain, R., Taha, W., Törngren, M. (eds.) CyPhy/WESE -2018. LNCS, vol. 11615, pp. 206–213. Springer, Cham (2019). https://doi.org/10.1007/978-3-030-23703-5_12

37. Wen, Z., Yang, R., Garraghan, P., Lin, T., Xu, J., Rovatsos, M.: Fog orchestration for internet of things services. IEEE Internet Comput. **21**(2), 16–24 (2017)

38. Zhiyuan, J.L., Jung, J., Goel, S., Skeem, J.: The limits of human predictions of recidivism. Sci. Adv. **6**(7), eaaz0652 (2020). https://doi.org/10.1126/sciadv.aaz0652

Security and Safety by Design in the Internet of Actors: An Architectural Approach

Giovanni Paolo Sellitto[1]([⊠]), Helder Aranha[2], Massimiliano Masi[3],
and Tanja Pavleska[4]

[1] Rome, Italy
gogiampaolo@gmail.com
[2] Lisbon, Portugal
hmspider@gmail.com
[3] Grapevine World GmbH, Vienna, Austria
massimiliano.masi@grapevineworld.com
[4] Jozef Stefan Institute, Ljubljana, Slovenia
atanja@e5.ijs.si

Abstract. The Internet of Actors (IoA) provides a complete framework to attain interoperability by design in Subject-oriented Business Process Management (S-BPM). However, at present, some important architectural concerns remain out of focus. In this paper we lay the basis to ensure critical architectural qualities by adopting an Enterprise Architecture (EA) approach based on the Reference Model for Industry 4.0 (RAMI4.0) integrated with a goal oriented development methodology. This approach aims to facilitate the adoption of IoA in the workflow of regulated sectors like the Smart Grid, Industry 4.0 or e-Government, where other qualities must be ensured in addition to interoperability.

Keywords: Internet of Actors · IoT · Enterprise Architecture · Model checking

1 Introduction

The Internet of Actors (IoA) [1] provides a complete framework for agile Subject-Oriented Business Process Management (S-BPM) based on the concept of *Smart Actors*, which are self-coordinating Agents representing people or services. Smart Actors participate in *choreography* to fulfill complex business needs. An important aspect of the Internet of Actors is its conceptual foundations and the availability of a formal specification [2]. This allows borrowing ideas and models from similar contexts to address important architectural concerns. In particular, in the IoA framework important aspects such as governance, sustainability, security and safety are still neglected. In similar contexts (e.g. IoT and Industry

G. P. Sellitto and H. Aranha—Independent Scholar.

M. Freitag et al. (Eds.): S-BPM ONE 2020, CCIS 1278, pp. 133–142, 2020.
https://doi.org/10.1007/978-3-030-64351-5_9

4.0) the adoption of an *Architecture Development Method* (ADM) provides the means to address relevant architectural concerns straight from the early phases of system development, by default and by design [3]. Such an approach has the advantage to account for the solution of a problem people with both the expertise and the tools needed to devise mitigation and solutions, relieving the adopters of the solutions from the need to have technical skills and knowledge for securing the systems against threats or to solve other concerns, like safety, privacy and sustainability. In the Smart Grids domain, this "security-by-design" approach relieves the so-called "prosumers" (producer-consumers) from the necessity to engage cybersecurity experts to connect their appliances to the Grid [4]. The IoA would benefit from the adoption of proven mechanisms, frameworks and tools to support the achievement of multiple and possibly conflicting architectural goal from the initial stages of the architectural design.

The IoA framework relies on the European Interoperability Framework (EIF) [5] to provide a *Business Architecture* and lay down the bases of the *Solution Architecture*, a set of technical building blocks containing the agent's implementation and operation details. Highly regulated sectors such as Critical Infrastructures, Smart Grid, and Industry 4.0 adopt a similar approach, based on the definition of a *Reference Architecture* (RA) that serves as a canvas for the development of solution architectures. The Smart Grid Architectural Model (SGAM [6]) and the Reference Architectural Model for Industry 4.0 (RAMI 4.0 [7]) are examples of RAs. Both models rely on a multidimensional architecture, where the use case is mapped from its lower level (e.g., the field device) up to the business capability to conduct the whole project.

By employing an ADM, we can enrich the IoA with important architectural properties (e.g., security and safety by design), while maintaining the high level of interoperability provided by the IoA. In this paper we will provide guidance on how to *dissect* IoA artifacts, made up of composable Agents, their behavior and the Choreography over a multi-layer Architecture Model, which can be used to enable the adoption of IoA in Industry 4.0-based projects [8]. In addition, we will propose a goal-based ADM that can apply both to the development of Smart Agents and Choreography and to their evaluation.

The rest of this paper is divided as follows: Sect. 2 briefly introduces and contextualizes the IoA architecture, Sect. 3 describes how it can be mapped onto the RAMI 4.0 model to produce a specific profile of RAMI 4.0 for Smart Actors, Sect. 4 integrates the conceptual model with a goal-based methodology to achieve architectural objectives (in the specific case, cybersecurity) by design in the context of IoA and Smart Actors. Section 5 presents the application of the mapping and of the methodology applied to a simple use case of IoA in an highly regulated domain, where some legal requirements must be taken into account in addition to interoperability. Finally, Sect. 6 concludes and touches upon future work.

2   Architectural Viewpoint for the Internet of Actors

IoA fosters interoperability and collaboration between *Smart Actors*. A Smart Actor's role is to participate in *choreography* to form complex socio-technical systems and fulfill complex business needs. A choreography is modeled by a network of Smart Actors, where the links represent message exchanges. The interfaces of the Actors are named *Role Based Interfaces* (RBI). RBIs are specific graphs containing information about message synchronization and the process behaviour [9]. Actors are determined by their *observable behaviour* and the communication among them is possible only when their RBI match. When actors are composed, the resulting observable behaviour is given by the RBI of the composed PASS graph. Based on these premises, the IoA Architecture builds on modular Building Blocks (*the Smart Actors*) that can be composed into complex structures (*the Choreography*), which in turn can be composed into an ever growing dynamic network of Choreography that form a Socio-Technical System. The behaviour of the Actors can be specified as a *Parallel Activities Specification Scheme* (PASS) graph, which lends itself for a formal verification of properties through *model checking*, as described in [1,9]. PASS graphs can be further interconnected to compose more complex PASS graphs.

The Smart Actors can be devised as the Building Blocks for a flexible S-BPM. Following the approach described in TOGAF[1], we will use a goal based ADM to provide guidance in the fulfillment of specific business or regulatory (legal) goal when designing the choreography.

3   Mapping IoA onto RAMI 4.0

In order to facilitate the cross-fertilization between different sectors, in the this paragraph we will map the IoA concepts onto the RAMI 4.0 conceptual space (Fig. 1) providing a RAMI 4.0 profile for Smart Actors (RAMI 4.0-SA profile). The RAMI 4.0-SA model (Fig. 2) can be considered as the IoA architecture filtered through RAMI 4.0 conceptual space, where each slice in this new RAMI 4.0-SA profile is mapped to the relevant IoA Building Blocks (or part of the IoA BBs). The RAMI 4.0-SA model provides a tool for a finer classification of the IoA artefacts in a conceptual space which is the same used for the RAMI 4.0 systems. We choose RAMI 4.0 as it provides a sound conceptual framework for the design of IoT systems and solutions, expressly conceived for the architectural development of complex systems, i.e. Systems of Systems. The overall goal of IoA is to facilitate the composition of Smart Actors into service networks, which are systems of systems, thus the model seems to fit perfectly. A similar procedure can be used to map IoA onto other conceptual spaces, like for example the Smart Grid Architectural Model (SGAM).

The RAMI 4.0 reference cube defines a conceptual space structured along three dimension spanning respectively:

- Z) the different *architectural layers*, spanning different levels of abstraction of the system, from the physical entities and assets (e.g., IoT, OT, actuators, IT hardware) up to the immaterial business cases producing value;

---

[1] TOGAF® is The Open Group Architecture Framework is an open framework for the development of Enterprise Architectures https://www.opengroup.org/togaf.

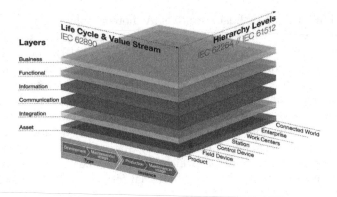

Fig. 1. The RAMI 4.0 architectural model

- X) the *system life-cycle/the value stream* (the "Vita" axis);
- Y) the *hierarchy of the system levels*, from simple constituents to the connected world. The "connected world" concept, which describes the interoperability of each layer with the external context, can be considered as the equivalent of the Actorsphere in IoA.

This reference space defines a system of coordinates where we can place the different entities that are part of the system under consideration. In order to tailor the conceptual space of RAMI 4.0 to the Internet of Actors and the Smart Agents, we proceed dissecting and mapping the IoA essential building blocks over the layers and renaming the landmarks of the RAMI 4.0 conceptual space with the related IoA concepts. We will conduct this operation proceeding layer by layer (Z axis) and considering for each layer the lifecycle (X axis) of progressively more complex entities (Y axis), borrowing the methodology shown in [7], inspired by the mixed-up approach in [8]. The resulting 3D model will consider the IoA systems from the point of view of their *lifecycle stages* and their *scope*, spanning over six architectural layers which are *interoperability layers*, since interoperability is the main architectural concern of IoA:

- Z') The *Interoperability layers* address different architectural levels of IoA, from the physical assets up to immaterial choreography and legal framework,
- X') The *Life-cycle stages* dimension represents the Smart Actors' life-cycle, supporting participation in dynamic, volatile and complex contexts,
- Y') The *Scope* dimension represents the extension of the Choreography of Smart Agents, from the behavior of a single actor or of a constellation of actors, up to the outside world.

In detail, the six *interoperability layers* in the vertical dimension are:

- *Legal* (depicting the legal and regulatory concerns, like GDPR or eIDAS[2]),

---

[2] See the two EU regulations, GDPR (EU) 2016/679, and eIDAS (EU) 910/2014 respectively.

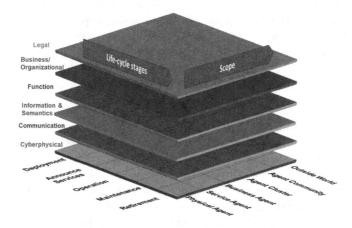

Fig. 2. The RAMI 4.0-SA profile for IoA

- *Business/organizational* (normalized business processes executed by the actor, as part of a more general business choreography),
- *Functional* (capabilities necessary to execute the business processes),
- *Information & semantics* (information model/formats of messages)
- *Communication* (data transmission protocol and communication channels),
- *Cyberphysical* (interface with physical objects/Administration Shell).

The above levels are derived from RAMI 4.0 and the LOST (Legal, Organizational, Semantic, Technical) approach to interoperability used in EIF, enriched with the Functional and the Communication layers, which are typical of IoA. Functional interoperability refers to the concept of RBIs exposed by the Smart Agents, while the Communication layer conceptualizes the PASS graphs. The *Life-cycle* dimension is comprised of the following stages[3]:

- *Deployment* (the Actor becomes active in some infrastructure),
- *Announcement* (the Actor publishes its services, e.g. an URI),
- *Service* (the Actor is ready to perform its announced services),
- *Operation* (the Actor is actually put into service),
- *Maintenance* (the Actor signaled it is not ready to perform its services)
- *Retirement* (the Actor has signaled it will terminate to provide services),

The *Scope* dimension classifies the systems of Smart Actors from the point of view of their increasing organizational complexity and it corresponds to the definitions given in [1]:

- *Physical actor* (objects, sensors or machines),
- *Service actor* (digital assistants for business or physical actors),

---

[3] The perspective here is that of the S-BPM designers, which have little power on the actors' design - we focus instead on the choreography of actors. This is reflected in structure of the RAMI 4.0-SA LC axis.

- *Business actor* (users on a topic, process or business process actors),
- *Agent cluster* (sets of actors having or sharing the same function),
- *Agent community* (set of actors which share the same policy - this could be an organizational policy, hence the community would correspond to an organization. Actors can belong to several communities);
- *Outside world* (agents which do not fit in any of the previous classifications or considered as black-boxes).

Such a reference architectural model can serve for the dissection of complex systems into smaller conceptual and technical components.

In general, an ABB may stem from the composition of several re-usable ABBs and it can address multiple concerns at different interoperability levels, therefore a single ABB can be projected onto several interoperability layers in the model. As an example, if we take a simple choreography in IoA, we can note that the definition of the RBIs is relevant both for the communication and the integration layer of the assets (the hardware on which the actors are running), while exchanged information is represented by the specific messages among the various actors, which are placed in the information and semantics layer. The functional layer contains the description of the functionalities implemented by the actors. In addition, the model represents a conceptual space to organize generic and reusable pieces of information addressed to the various stakeholders, like standards, techniques and the knowledge relevant for a specific architectural layer, in a given phase of the system life cycle and for some level of aggregation of the components: given an important architectural characteristic, we can associate to the goal the relevant *measures*[4], depending on the layer, the life cycle phase and the level of aggregation. In the field of cybersecurity, the identified and documented threats and the respective countermeasures can be placed in their location (architecture layer, life cycle phase, level of aggregation) with reference to RAMI 4.0. This point will be discussed further in the next paragraph.

4   A Goal-Based ADM for the IoA

The RAMI 4.0-SA profile provides a common conceptual space for the contextualization of IoA artifacts in the Industry 4.0 environments, but it does not include a methodology to ensure the attainment of architectural properties by design. However, we can complement the (static) conceptual model with a (dynamic) Architecture Development Methodology to attain a robust framework that can support the IoA system designer in the construction of a well-behaved choreography based on Smart Agents. With the expression "well-behaved" we refer to a choreography which is aware of other concerns in addition to interoperability. For the sake of simplicity and usability, our proposal relies on the application of the Reference Model for Information Assurance and Security, RMIAS [10] (Fig. 3). The model is generic and lends itself to be used in different sectors

---

[4] A *measure* is a technological, social and/or organizational solution that supports the attainment of the objective and reduce risk or counteract threats.

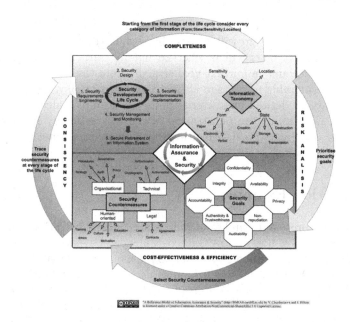

Fig. 3. The Reference Model for Information Assurance and Security, RMIAS [10]

and in conjunction with any software development life cycle, there comprised the possibility of composing the systems "on the fly" using Smart Actors. The methodology is goal-based, since it starts from the definition of the objectives in terms of architectural qualities that the target system must deliver. In the case of our RAMI 4.0-SA model, the objectives can be evaluated performing a risk analysis and a cost-benefit evaluation - the level of granularity of the analysis will depend on the layer under evaluation and on the phase of the lifecycle we are in. For example, the goal of *confidentiality* can have different countermeasures at different layers, such as *access control* at the Function layer and *encryption* at the Communication layer. The four steps of the adopted model are illustrated in Fig. 3. In the first step the information assets are categorised through a taxonomy quadruple, identifying each asset's level of *sensitivity* (e.g., restricted, public), *form* (e.g., electronic, verbal), *state* (e.g., creation, decommission), and *location* (e.g., the security zone). The ADM proceeds as follows: *for each* RAMI 4.0-SA layer, *for each* taxonomy quadruple, *select* the security goal, and *evaluate* the security countermeasures. At the end of the process, a full list of security controls that must be applied will be available, mapped over the information layers (defense-in-depth) and the identified assets. In [11], an algorithm was introduced that, taken a BB can "elicit" security countermeasures out of a risk analysis carried out by business people with no deep cybersecurity expertise - the usability of goal based methods is valuable also for IoA, since the designers of the choreography are business experts and they have plenty of knowledge of *what* to protect (the "assets") but little knowledge of *how* to protect them. The prevalence in the context of IoA of the S-BPM composition phase over the Actor's design will have an impact on the preferred usage of the RMIAS, since the artefacts will be checked mainly during composition. However, taking into account important goal straight from the design of the agents will bring a considerable advantage also in the choreography. In addition, the possibility to attain desired characteristics as for example safety and security "by-design" would favour the penetration of the IoA in highly regulated contexts, like e.g. the Smart Grid, eHealth pervasive environments, eGovernment services.

5   Application Example

In this section we present a simple and well documented scenario[5] in a highly regulated domain, to show how an IoA Choreography can be mapped onto RAMI4.0 using the methodology defined above and how some security goal can be derived by the mapping. An essential description of use case is the following: *A hospital uses mobile devices providing measurements to follow-up on the recovery of discharged patients. Each measurement is submitted to an Hub in the hospital data center and possibly shared via the regional eHealth infrastructure with other cross-border organizations.*[6]

From an IoA perspective we can identify two Smart Actors: *Sensor Device* (the medical device) and *Hub/Gatherer* (managing the hospital data centre) and an *Infrastructure* agent (the eHealth infrastructure). The business choreography inferred from the use case is modeled by a diagram in the RAMI 4.0-SA **Business/organizational layer**, depicting the following narrative: (a) the Sensor Device exchanges *Readings* and *Monitoring Alerts* with the Hub which adds them to the patient's medical record; (b) the Hub distributes *medical records* internally and externally; (c) the Infrastructure agent shares records received from the Hub through the regional infrastructure. Regarding the **Scope dimension**, the Sensor Devices are considered Physical Agents. The Hub/Gatherer is placed in the Agent Cluster, the Infrastructure Actor in the Outside World. Proceeding to the **Functional layer**, the Sensor Device provides *Read/process data* and *Send alert* functions; the Hub provides functions *Gather data* and *Make Medical records available*; the Infrastructure actor provides a *Share Medical records cross-border* function. Regarding the **Information & Semantics layer**, the Sensor Device and Hub exchange *structured clinical data*; Hub translates the data into structured *medical records* with different formats, as required internally to the hospital group (Agent Community dimension) or for standard cross-border exchanges (Outside world dimension). The resulting records are made available internally and to external organizations through communication

---

[5] This scenario is defined by the IHE Mobile Access to Health Document scenario https://wiki.ihe.net/index.php/Mobile_access_to_Health_Documents_(MHD) and it is loosely based on a previous similar work of the authors [11].

[6] The use of IHE specifications to achieve interoperability is not new in the ecosystem of the IoA [2].

mechanisms modeled in **Communications layer**. As for the **Cyberphysical layer** the Sensor Device is to *read & process physical sensor input, detect abnormal signal patterns* and *run self-diagnostics*.

Having covered all interoperability layers, we will now address cybersecurity concerns by applying the RMIAS model. Following a goal-based approach for security management, it accounts for the nature of the information assets to be protected, acknowledges the organizational risk trade-offs in handling said assets, and develops countermeasures to address the risks and vulnerabilities of the IT system. Looking at the specifications, it is important to note that in the **Legal layer** we find a requirement to *authenticate the patients* when *assigning* them a mobile Sensor Device. The provision of the services of this type in Europe is subject to the eIDAS regulation[7]. The process of device assignment/de-assignment will be supported by a Service Agent assisting the human (hospital clerk) responsible for the process. The authentication process identified in the Legal layer, together with the *gathering, transmission, translation, storage* and *access* of patient data must conform to GDPR[8] and other applicable legal provisions to guarantee patient rights to data [*Privacy, Confidentiality, Integrity*]: our first set of architectural goal. Those must be attained for all information assets, across all architectural layers, LC stages and agent aggregation levels. Goal may require different countermeasures at different layers. The countermeasures must apply to the relevant information assets, like *medical records, structured clinical data*, alerts and messages. In the case of *confidentiality* we must adopt *access control* at the Function layer and *encryption* at the Communication layer, while lower-level transactions *Provide Documents* and *Retrieve Documents* require mandatory *Secure Communication* channels. Additional goal may be selected as result of further risk analysis. One must analyze the candidate solutions (spanning both agents and message exchanges in the choreography), checking for missing countermeasures, eventually adding them and repeat the ADM cycle until all goal are satisfied by design, in every zone of the RAMI 4.0-SA cube.

6   Conclusion

Although this work is not the first one to devise the possibility to apply a flexible workflow based on the IoA in the context of Industry 4.0 and IoT, the conceptual and methodological tools presented here are intended to foster the adoption of IoA in critical infrastructures such as the Smart Grid, or Industry 4.0-based supply chains where other architectural concerns such as security-by-design must be considered in addition to interoperability and flexibility.

The adoption of a goal-based methodology as an Architecture Development Method is intended to foster usability of the whole framework, in line with the original IoA proposal - this method can be further refined and applied in a pretty generic version to any other important architectural concern or to achieve complex objectives. Moreover, it can be used to support Model Checking as a

---

[7] See European Regulation 910/2014.
[8] See European Regulation 2016/679.

design tool, and this is a possible evolution of the present paper. The authors have implemented a model-based solver that can be applied to S-BPM simple choreography to check the attainment of the objectives and eventually to revise them[9]. As a future work, we plan to formalize this proposal by defining the process algebra to further enhance the Internet of Actors with the properties necessary for practical implementation in safety-critical systems.

References

1. Strecker, F., Gniza, R.: The internet of actors - a peer-to-peer agile value creation network. In: Proceedings of the WS@S-BPM ONE 2019, Sevilla, Spain, 26–28 June 2019. http://ceur-ws.org/Vol-2388/paper2.pdf
2. Gniza, F., Strecker, F.: Interoperability network - the internet of actors. In: Proceedings of the WS@S-BPM ONE 2019, Sevilla, Spain, 26–28 June 2019. http://ceur-ws.org/Vol-2388/paper1.pdf
3. Pavleska, T., Aranha, H., Masi, M., Grandry, E., Sellitto, G.P.: Cybersecurity evaluation of enterprise architectures: the e-SENS case. In: Gordijn, J., Guédria, W., Proper, H.A. (eds.) PoEM 2019. LNBIP, vol. 369, pp. 226–241. Springer, Cham (2019). https://doi.org/10.1007/978-3-030-35151-9_15
4. Aranha, H., Masi, M., Pavleska, T., Sellitto, G.P.: Enabling security-by-design in smart grids: an architecture-based approach. In: 15th European Dependable Computing Conference, EDCC 2019, Naples, Italy, 17–20 September 2019, pp. 177–179. IEEE (2019)
5. Wimmer, M.A., Boneva, R., di Giacomo, D.: Interoperability governance: a definition and insights from case studies in Europe. In: Proceedings of the 19th Annual International Conference on Digital Government Research: Governance in the Data Age, dg.o 2018. Association for Computing Machinery, New York (2018)
6. CEN-CENELEC-ETSI Smart Grid Coordination Group: Smart grid reference architecture (2012)
7. Heidel, R., Hoffmeister, M., Hankel, M., Doebrich, U.: Industrie 4.0, The Reference Architecture Model RAMI 4.0 and the Industrie 4.0 Component. VDE Verlag, Berlin (2019)
8. Gottschalk, M., Uslar, M., Delfs, C.: The Use Case and Smart Grid Architecture Model Approach. SE. Springer, Cham (2017). https://doi.org/10.1007/978-3-319-49229-2
9. Fleischmann, A.: Distributed Systems. Springer, Heidelberg (1994). https://doi.org/10.1007/978-3-642-78612-9
10. Cherdantseva, Y., Hilton, J.: A reference model of information assurance and security. In: 2013 International Conference on Availability, Reliability and Security, pp. 546–555, September 2013
11. Aranha, H., Masi, M., Pavleska, T., Sellitto, G.P.: Securing mobile e-health environments by design: a holistic architectural approach. In: 2019 International Conference on Wireless and Mobile Computing, Networking and Communications, WiMob 2019, Barcelona, Spain, 21–23 October 2019, pp. 1–6. IEEE (2019)

---

[9] See https://github.com/mascanc/mosa2.

Process Discovery Method in Dynamic Manufacturing and Logistics Environments

Wacharawan Intayoad[1,3(✉)], Till Becker[2], and Otthein Herzog[1,3]

[1] International Graduate School for Dynamics in Logistics, University of Bremen,
Bremen, Germany
`int@biba.uni-bremen.de, Otthein.herzog@uni-bremen.de`
[2] Faculty of Business Studies, University of Applied Science Emden/Leer,
Emden, Germany
`till.becker@hs-emden-leer.de`
[3] Department of Mathematics/Informatics, University of Bremen, Bremen, Germany

Abstract. Process mining is a promising way to extract insight knowledge on business processes in manufacturing and logistics. However, implementing process mining is challenging in dynamic and complex environments as the discovered process models may not reach the aspired quality. As a result, current process mining solutions do not hold in practical situations effectively in the domain of manufacturing and logistics. In this paper, we propose a sequence clustering methodology based on Markov Chains and Expectation-Maximization. We propose two approaches to improve the existing method of sequence clustering which provide improvement of finding the main behavior and its variants for each process cluster. We evaluate the proposed methodology with real-world data sets by measuring model quality dimensions. The results demonstrate that the proposed methodology is capable to improve process discovery when confronted with dynamic and complex business processes. The resulting models present the main behavior of business processes miming and process variants with a satisfying process model quality.

Keywords: Process discovery · Process mining · Sequence clustering · Manufacturing · Logistics

1 Introduction

The business processes in the manufacturing and logistics domain are considered as a dynamic environment. They are frequently changed and expanded to achieve optimal results. For several years a great effort has been devoted to the improvement of business process performance in manufacturing and logistics. To improve processes, insight and comprehensive knowledge of actual and variant behaviors of business processes are crucial for decision making, problem-solving,

© Springer Nature Switzerland AG 2020
M. Freitag et al. (Eds.): S-BPM ONE 2020, CCIS 1278, pp. 143–163, 2020.
https://doi.org/10.1007/978-3-030-64351-5_10

and enhancing productivity [10]. The effective way to automatically extract such valuable knowledge from data is process mining. Process mining analyzes the data generated during the real operations, the so-called 'event log'. An event log is the collection of data that relates to products, processes, machines, planning, and logistics performance, which can be used to explore and discover valuable information and knowledge [7]. Process mining has been successfully deployed in various domains such as health-care, education, software implementation, telecommunication, and logistics s [5, 14, 18–21].

Process discovery is an essential application of process mining. However, process discovery algorithms encounter problems when they are used to analyze the event logs from high dynamic environments. The business processes are frequently changed and such changes cause process variants. The business processes which have a high degree of flexibility cause the diversity of the business behaviors which can give rise to a number of task nodes and relations in process models. A large number of task nodes and relations impact the discovered process models and render them unstructured, a so-called 'spaghetti-like' process [24]. As a result, the discovered process models are difficult to comprehend and thus are not useful for a subsequent process improvement. Moreover, a high degree of flexibility generates a wide range of process variants and ad-hoc processes in the industrial event logs. These types of process variants are significant for analysis in the area of process improvement. However, they might be hidden and might not be presented in the discovered models.

As a result, process mining is not practical when coping with data from dynamic environments. It has not been applied widely and systematically in the manufacturing and logistics domain, even though a large amount of data is typically generated in this industry during operation. Several studies have applied clustering methods [6, 8, 11, 15, 25] to reduce the complexity of the event logs. However, these methods cannot work effectively when they deal with the event logs from the focused domain. For example, the clustering methods that are based on a vector space can cluster event data into a group that has similar characteristics, but this type of methods often neglects the sequence of activities which is important in the control-flow process models. Another approach is a sequence clustering. It can maintain the sequence of events by grouping similar types of sequences into the same cluster [25]. These types of methods often focus on the directed follow relation between a pair of activities and do not allow for a sequence with a disjoint activity grouped into the same cluster. For example, trace $\{A, B, C, D, F\}$ and trace $\{A, B, C, E, F\}$ have D and E as disjoint activities. With the existing sequence clustering approach, these two traces are considered as dissimilar. In real-world situations, the disjoint activity might be derived from the diversity of the process behavior or noise in the event log [28]. Moreover, the existing techniques of clustering applied in process mining consider only the quality of clusters, but process model accuracy and quality are neglected [9].

Therefore, in this work, we propose a methodology that can fill the gaps encountered for event logs in the manufacturing and logistics domains. Our proposed methodology satisfies the following requirements;

i The clustering method improves the resulting models of process discovery. They can present the main behavior of the business process and also its variations.
ii The sequence of activities in the business process is taken into account for the clustering feature.
iii The resulting clusters and models provide a satisfying quality.

The proposed methodology is called "sequence clustering methodology" which is based on a probabilistic model, Markov Chains, and Expectation-Maximization (EM). Moreover, we introduce two novel approaches to be included in the methodology to cope with the event longs from dynamic environments. The first approach is used for initializing cluster centroids from repeated patterns as a pre-clustering step to improve clustering results. The second approach is used to calculate the associated probabilities between cluster centroids and traces in the event logs by using the minimum transition probability from centroid Markov chains. In this way, traces that represent disjoint activities can possibly be assigned to the same group of similar traces. We evaluate the proposed methodology using both perspectives; clustering quality and process model quality. For the clustering quality, we rely on established performance indicators by determining the summed-up distance between the centroid probability matrix and the member probability matrices. For the model quality, the established process mining performance indicator 'replay fitness' and 'precision' are applied. We validate the proposed methodology by real-life event logs from three different companies in manufacturing and logistics.

This paper is organized as follows: The next section introduces the concept of process discovery, its objective, and its limitations. Then we discuss the related works that use clustering methods to reduce the complexity of the event logs and highlight the advantages and drawbacks of existing solutions. The section also points out the existing gaps and issues in the related works. Section 3 introduces the proposed approaches to close the gaps related to the requirements of the manufacturing and logistics domains. Section 4 describes our proposed methodology based on the sequence clustering approach. Section 5 discusses the experiments and their results. In Sect. 6, we discuss our findings. Finally, Sect. 7 concludes with remarks on future work.

2   Related Works

This section introduces the concept of process discovery and related works. Section 2.1 describes the input of the process discovery, process models (output), the challenge of dynamic environments, and process model quality. Section 2.2 addresses the related works of process clustering and also presents the advantages, drawbacks, and the gaps in our requirements.

2.1   Process Discovery

The process discovery objective is to recognize patterns from the observed event logs. It automatically constructs actual process models from the behavior observed in the event logs. Event data is recorded by information systems, applications, and other systems. The data in the event logs is a set of process executions capturing business process activities [23]. They generally report the state change of an activity [13]. An activity may contain information such as resources, start time, and end time [23]. The case identifier (case ID) is used to specify activities and events that belong to the same process instance. Additional information may be derived from event logs, e.g., a number of events per case, a unique path, the similarity among process instances, process variants, and the performance of different activities. From Table 1, we can derive two traces corresponding to case ID 1 and 2. The first trace of the process instance, case ID 1, is A, B, D and the second one, case ID 2, is A, B, C, E. The length of case ID 1 and 2 are three and four, respectively.

Table 1. An example fragment of an event log

Case ID	Activity	Start time	End time
1	A	8:00 am	9:00 am
1	B	9:30 am	10:00 am
1	D	10:00 am	11:00 am
2	A	9:00 am	10:00 am
2	B	10:00 am	10:30 am
2	C	10:40 am	11:00 am
2	E	10:40 am	11:00 am

Process discovery analyzes and interprets the event data as process models. A resulting process model is the representation of the behavior seen in the event log. For example, if the data in Table 1 is a sufficient example of event data, the resulting model from process discovery should present the control-flow perspective of the observed behaviors in the event log. The discovered process model can replay traces from Case ID 1 and 2.

However, real-life data is not a simple event log as it is unstructured and contains noise. Noise in the context of process discovery means exceptional and infrequent behavior. It refers to activities or patterns that are rare. Noise can be removed by preprocessing an event log or by the discovery algorithms [23]. Many discovery algorithms address the issue of noise and exclude it from the process models. Nevertheless, discovering infrequent behaviors is also important as it may represent valuable information,e.g., in the case that we want to detect fraud in the process: The deviation can be used to detect irregular patterns. Therefore, selecting the appropriate algorithm is crucial for the objective of the analysis and the quality of the resulting model.

When evaluating the quality of the resulting models, a good balance between underfitting and overfitting has to be considered. The resulting process models should be able to present the general behavior of business processes and also their variations. The underfitting model fails to relate the models to the data. This means that the process models should not be over-generalized and unrelated behaviors should not present in a model. On the other hand, it should be aware of overfitting models that only allow for the observed behaviors. For example, the overfitting model can represent the behavior from a particular event log, but could not replay other sample event logs that originate from the same process.

To evaluate the quality of process models, the measurement of replay fitness and precision can be used. A model that has a good replay fitness means that the model can replay traces or the behaviors which have been seen in the event log. In a dynamic environment, a high score of fitness replay may result in a process model with a large number of nodes and relations which leads to a complex or an unstructured model ('spaghetti-like'). Therefore, there is a trade-off for the precision value. Precision means that a process model does not allow too many behaviors different from the observed behaviors. A poor precision model is determined as an overfitting model. There are many methods to calculate the value of replay fitness and precision. In this work, we use the method for calculating fitness replay and precision from the work of Adriansyah et al. [1] and Adriansyah et al. [2], respectively. As these methods exhibit a robust analysis and are widely used to evaluate the process model quality. Moreover, these methods have been deployed in ProM 6 which is the open-source framework for process mining [26]. The details of the methods are described in Sect. 4.2.

There are several existing methods for process discovery. This research selects heuristic mining [27] as a discovery algorithm. The method is a practical application mining algorithm as it can deal with noise and can represent the main behavior of business processes. The advantage of the algorithm is that it takes frequencies of the events and sequences into account when constructing process models. However, the algorithms do not guarantee that the discovered model can replay all traces.

2.2 Challenges in Related Works

Process discovery is the most challenging task when it has to deal with unstructured data and noise generated from a flexible, uncertain environment [24]. There are several studies which apply clustering methods for grouping similar traces to reduce the complexity. The resulting clusters correspond to a coherent set of cases that can improve the accuracy and the comprehensibility of resulting models [24]. We divided clustering approaches used in process mining as (i) vector space approach, (ii) context-aware approach, and (iii) model-based sequence approach.

The vector space approach transforms the features of the traces into a vector space model and then measures the distance between each pair of traces to find similarities between them. The similar traces in the event logs are then grouped into the same cluster, and traces that belong to different clusters are dissimilar.

Several methods are based on the vector space approach. Greco et al. [15] proposed the method to transfer event logs into a vector space model corresponding to the activity transition in the traces based on k-means clustering. Later, the approach has been extended and implemented as two plug-ins in the ProM software [8]. Song et al. [22] applied trace clustering based on an activity profile (counting the number of activities in a trace) and an originator profile (counting the number of originators in a trace). They applied different distance functions as well as clustering algorithms, i.e., Euclidean distance, Hamming distance, Jaccard distance, K-means clustering, and Hierarchical clustering. Based on the expert results, trace clustering can group different types of processes in health care systems. However, the vector-based clustering methods do not capture the dynamics of the process execution and the order of executed events [6].

The context-aware approach has been introduced to trace clustering. [6] proposed an approach that integrates context-awareness to trace clustering based on a generic edit distance. They refered context information as the order of executed activities in traces (event time, case and additional data don't refer to context-information). The proposed approach can preserve the sequence of activities, and the resulting models demonstrate that the approach outperforms the existing trace clustering approaches based on vector space in term of fitness score. However, their approach calculating the cost of distance is based on tri-grams. Working tri-grams results in a huge computation overhead, particularly with a large number of activities, e.g., for 100 activities, potentially 100^3 dimensions must be computed and then the frequency of occurrences corresponding to each tri-gram must be found. Therefore, this method is not suitable for the manufacturing and logistics domain as the number of activities can be very large. Furthermore, in our previous work, we have applied the concept of context-information to trace clustering [4]. The context information refers to the frequency of occurrences of a process and the stability of the cycle time of repeating processes. This study found out that using the most frequent processes in the event logs as the main processes returns the best results. Nevertheless, the clustering method cannot preserve the sequence of executed activities in the traces. And the study only focused on the quality of the clusters and did not mention the quality of the resulting models.

The model-based sequence approach is an approach that can potentially preserve the sequence of executed activities. This approach takes a set of sequences and groups similar types of sequences into the same cluster [25]. The sequence clustering approach is based on a probabilistic model; Markov Models and EM. The approach starts by identifying a number of the clusters and randomly initializes a cluster centroid for each cluster. A centroid cluster represents a sequence of activities interm of Markov Cain. Then the method assigns each trace in the event log to one of the clusters that have the highest associated probability (probability of membership.). The centroid of each cluster is recalculated by considering all traces in the cluster. The last two steps are repeated until the transition probabilities of all clusters converge. Ferreira et al. [11] proposed to use a mixture of first-order Markov Models and the EM algorithm to identify different tasks and compositions of element steps. Moreover, they also apply pre-processing steps before the sequence clustering such as grouping similar tasks to one task, eliminating duplicate tasks, and removing some infrequence tasks. In this way, the sequence clustering method can deliver better results with less deviations of the business processes. However, they do not provide an analysis of the resulting process models. Later on, a similar approach has been applied to business processes in healthcare analysis [20]. The proposed method focuses on the health care workflow. The number of clusters is first determined by the Microsoft SQL Server and then manually adjusted by experts. This methodology can be used to enhance the performance of the process discovery. The resulting models can be used to analyze process performance and social perspectives. However, they did not focus on the accuracy of the control-flow perspective, particularly on the aspect of replay fitness. Nor on evaluating the quality of clusters.

According to the related works, the vector space approach cannot observe the sequence of executed activities. Therefore, it is not suitable for our objective to focus on improving the accuracy of the process model based on replay fitness. For the context-aware approach, the proposed method by Bose and van der Aalst [6] can deal with the order of activities in the traces. However, as manufacturing and logistics processes have a high degree of diversity in terms of process deviation and activities, it would require a prohibitive computational effort to calculate the frequencies based on tri-grams.

The sequence clustering approach has performed better than other approaches [25] and successfully applied in a complex environment [11]. Also the sequence clustering approach can preserve the sequences of executed activities. Such that, the sequence clustering approach provides sufficient reasons justify to use in the domain of manufacturing and logistics. However, directly applying the approach to the event logs from the manufacturing and logistics domains may result in a bad quality model. A diversity of process behaviors affects the associated probability as a punishment for a disjoint activity between a trace and a cluster is too strong. For instance, if a Markov model of a trace has $P(B|A) > 0$, where $P(\cdot|\cdot)$ is a transition probability and a centroid Markov model has $P(B|A) = 0$, the associated probability between the trace and the cluster is punished to be 0. Hence, the trace is considered as dissimilarity to the other traces in the cluster. Moreover, randomly initializing Markov models in the first step is not an effective way as the quality of the clusters is depended on the initial seeds [3,17]. Different initial seeds may result in different clusters. Therefore, the strong penalization of disjoint activity and poor choice of initial seeds might cause an extremely small cluster or even become empty during the clustering process since no data point is assigned to them.

Another requirement, the quality of process models and the quality of clusters. The previous works only evaluated one of the quality perspectives, neither the quality of process models nor the quality of clusters. We evaluate our results from both perspectives. For assessing cluster quality, we apply one evaluation method based on internal information in the clusters. These methods can be used to measure intra-cluster cohesion (how near the data point in the same cluster) and inter-cluster separation (how different between the cluster centroids). Any distance function can be used for these purpose [17]. Also the choice of a number of clusters must take into account to provide the most desirable result, as the low number of clusters may be composed of from different behaviors in each cluster. These different behaviors in one cluster may create many relations between activities and may result in complex process models. In contrast, a large number of clusters cause similar variants to be spread across several clusters with relatively low support. The detail of how to calculate the summed distance is described in Sect. 4.1. However, only evaluating the quality of clusters is not sufficient in process mining as clustering methods are used to support the main task in the process discovery. We use replay fitness and precision to evaluate the quality of the process model. The detail of both quality dimensions are described in Sect. 4.2 and Sect. 4.2.

3   Approach for Process Mining for Dynamic Environments

This section proposes two approaches in order to cope with the issues of sequence clustering when dealing with manufacturing and logistics processes. The study is based on sequence clustering which is similar to the work of Ferreira et al. [11], who apply Markov Chains and EM.

The novel approaches are key to our proposed methodology which is described in Sect. 4. The first approach handles the process of initializing cluster centroids to improve the quality of clusters. The second one handles how to penalize disjoint activities. The new penalizing approach allows the traces that have similar behavior as a disjoint activity have an opportunity to be grouped into the same cluster. With the proposed approaches, the sequence clustering method performs effectively with business processes in flexible manufacturing and logistics environments which allows for a high diversity of potential behaviors. Then good quality clusters from sequence clustering can be determined, and these clusters provide the improvement of the resulting models from the process discovery.

3.1   Initializing Cluster Centroids with Main Processes

Sequence clustering can be interpreted as unsupervised learning. The data used for learning is unlabeled and there are no pre-defined classes. The learning algorithm must discover the hidden structures or patterns in the data. Therefore, sequence clustering based on a probabilistic model is sensitive to initial seeds, which are typically randomly selected. Consequently, different initial seeds may result in different clusters [17]. Moreover, poor initial seeds may lead to empty clusters and unassigned data points.

To deal with these problems, we choose to set 'main processes' as the initial centroids for clusters. These main processes are determined by the frequency of repeated patterns where a repeated pattern is identified when any traces (1) have the same length, (2) have a same set of activities, and (3) do not have disjoint activities. For example, trace (A, B, C, D, E) and trace (A, C, D, B, E) are considered as repeated patterns, while trace (A, B, C, D, F) is considered as an unrepeated pattern as there is a disjoint activity F. Also, trace (A, B, C, D, D) is considered as an unrepeated pattern since it misses an activity E in the trace.

3.2 Penalizing Disjoint Activity with a Minimum Transition Probability Penalty

Based on the probabilistic model, each unassigned trace will be assigned to the cluster which has the highest associated probability. However, with the existing algorithms, this approach often causes unassigned traces and empty clusters. As a result, we introduce a minimum transition probability min_{prob}, where $min_{prob} > 0$. It is derived from the lowest transition probability from the centroid cluster transition matrices. Instead of using the actual value of 0 when the value of transition probability from state x_{i-1} to state x_i in centroid cluster c_k is 0, $p(x_i|x_{i-1}, c_k) = 0$, we set $min_{prob} > 0$ as the transition probability. Therefore, the probability that a trace is associated with cluster c_k can be expressed as:

$$p(x|c_k) = \begin{cases} p(x_0, c_k) \times \prod_{i=1}^{i=L-2} p(x_i|x_{i-1}, c_k) \times p(x_L, c_k) & if\, p(x_i|x_{i-1}, c_k) > 0 \\ p(x_0, c_k) \times \prod_{i=1}^{i=L-2} p(x_i|x_{i-1}, c_k) \times p(x_L, c_k) & if\, p(x_i|x_{i-1}, c_k) = 0 \\ \qquad\qquad\qquad p(x_i|x_{i-1}, c_k) = min_{prob} \end{cases} \quad (1)$$

where $x = x_0, x_1, x_2, \ldots, x_L$ is a sequence of length L, the start state is x_0 and the end state is x_L. x_0 and x_L are introduced to simplify the probability equation, where $p(x_0, c_k) = 1$ is the transition probability of the state x_0 associated with the class c_k and $p(x_L, c_k) = 1$ is the transition probability of the state x_L associated with the class c_k. $\prod_{i=1}^{i=L-2} p(x_i|x_{i-1}, c_k)$ is the transition probability from state x_{i-1} to x_i associated with the class c_k

In this way all traces in the event logs can be assigned to the cluster with the highest probability, even if they miss a few transition probabilities when comparing with the centroid. For example, let trace $x = \{x_0, A, B, C, E, x_L\}$, $min_{prob} = 0.1$, and Fig. 1 be a Markov chain of a cluster C_k.

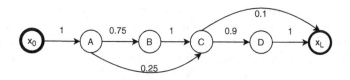

Fig. 1. Markov chain of cluster c_k

Then $p(x|c_k) = p(x_0, c_k) \times p(A|x_0, c_k) \times p(B|A, c_k) \times p(C|B, c_k) \times p(E|C, c_k) \times p(x_L|E, c_k) \times p(x_L, c_k) = 1 \times 1 \times 0.75 \times 1 \times 0.1 \times 0.1 \times 1 = 0.0075$. We can see that $p(E|C, c_k) = 0$ and $p(x_L|E, c_k) = 0$. Instead of applying 0 to the equation, we use min_{prob} instead. By this way, the process variants will have a chance to be assigned to a cluster of a similar process.

4 Methodology

This section presents the proposed methodology. The framework is composed of two main parts: (1) sequence clustering and (2) process discovery. In the sequence clustering step, the proposed approaches in Sect. 3 are applied in EM steps. And in the process discovery step, each cluster is used as input for process discovery algorithms. The research methodology framework is depicted in Fig. 2.

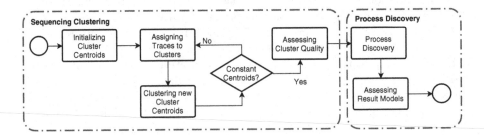

Fig. 2. Overview of the methodology

4.1 Sequence Clustering

The objective of this part is to reduce the complexity by grouping traces with similar behaviors and patterns from event logs into the same cluster. The sequence clustering method of the proposed methodology is based on Markov Chains. EM is applied as a framework to find the highest likelihood of an assignment to a cluster in the Markov Chains since they are unknown in the beginning. The algorithm is an iterative refinement to find parameter estimates. It assigns each trace to a cluster based on the associated probability. The centroid Markov Chains are updated by the cluster member. This part consists of four steps:

Initialization Step. In the first phase, the centroids Markov chains or transition probabilistic matrices of each clsuters are unknown. Instead of randomly creating Markov chains as centroids for clusters, we apply the approach of initializing cluster centroids with main processes as described in the previous section. The trace that has the highest number of repeated patterns is initiated as the centroid for each cluster. Hence, we can ensure that none of the clusters is empty since at least the traces which are considered as repeated patterns of the centroid are assigned to the same cluster. In this way, the initial centroids perform a pre-clustering for unstructured data, which are unlabeled and have an unknown number of classes.

Consequently, all the traces in the event logs are transformed into the transition probability matrices. The matrices are $n \times n$ matrices, where n is the number of states. For example, let x be the a sequence in an event log, $x = \{start, A, A, A, A, B, C, end\}$. The probability of $start \rightarrow A$ is 1. The probability of $A \rightarrow A$ happens in 3 of 4 times and $A \rightarrow B$ happens in 1 of 4 times.

As a result, the probability of $A \rightarrow A$ is $3/4 = 0.75$ and $A \rightarrow B$ is $1/4 = 0.25$. The transition probability matrix derived from sequence x is a square matrix as displayed in Fig. 3.

$$
\begin{array}{c c}
 & \begin{array}{ccccc} start & A & B & C & end \end{array} \\
\begin{array}{c} start \\ A \\ B \\ C \\ end \end{array} &
\left(\begin{array}{ccccc}
0 & 1 & 0 & 0 & 0 \\
0 & 0.75 & 0.25 & 0 & 0 \\
0 & 0 & 0 & 1 & 0 \\
0 & 0 & 0 & 0 & 1 \\
0 & 0 & 0 & 0 & 0
\end{array} \right)
\end{array}
$$

Fig. 3. Example of a transition probability matrix

Assigning Traces to Clusters (Expectation Sep). Given the centroid transition matrices, each trace in the event log can be assigned to the cluster with the highest associated probability. In this step, the approach of minimum transition probability, which is described in Eq. 1, is deployed for calculating the associated probability. For instance, given the cluster centroids as Fig. 4, and the sequence $x = \{start, A, A, A, A, B, C, end\}$ from the above example, the associated probability between cluster 1 and x is $p(A|start, c_{k=1}) \times p(A|A, c_{k=1}) \times p(A|A, c_{k=1}) \times p(B|A, c_{k=1}) \times p(C|B, c_{k=1}) \times p(end|C, c_{k=1}) = 1 \times 0.1 \times 0.1 \times 0.1 \times 1 \times 0.1 = 0.0001$, and for cluster 2 with a associated probability $1 \times 0.8 \times 0.8 \times 0.8 \times 0.2 \times 0.5 \times 0.2 = 0.01024$. Therefore, x is assigned to cluster 2.

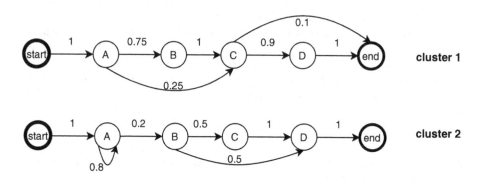

Fig. 4. Example of centriod Markov Chains

Calculate New Cluster Centroids (Maximization Step). After assigning all the traces to the clusters that have the highest associated probability, the centroid of each cluster is updated by the newly assigned members. Then, the algorithm compares the previous and new cluster centroids. If they are the same, the algorithm will execute the next step as the cluster centroids are convergent. Otherwise, the algorithm will repeat the Expectation and Maximization steps.

Evaluating cluster quality: summed distance calculation to the bias between cluster quality and resulting model quality, we evaluate the cluster quality by calculating the total distance between the centroid Markov Chain and each trace member of the cluster C_k to determine the similarity, while the resulting model quality is assessed by its replay fitness. In this phase, the method for calculating the summed-up distance is elaborated in Eq. 2. The total distance between cluster C_k and traces T_n, where n is the number of traces in the cluster C_k, is defined according to [12] as:

$$D(C_k, T_n) = \frac{1}{2} \sum_i \sum_j \left[P(S_i^{C_k} \times M_{ij}^{C_k}) - P(S_i^{T_n}) \times M_{ij}^{T_n} \right] \tag{2}$$

where $M_{ij}^{C_k}$ and $M_{ij}^{T_n}$ are the elements in the transition matrices of cluster C_k and trace T_n, respectively. $P(S_i^{C_k})$ and $P(S_i^{T_n})$ are the state-space distributions of each activity i of cluster C_k and trace T_n, respectively. The smaller $D(C_k, T_n)$, the more similar are the Markov chains. The probability of S_i in cluster C_k is given by:

$$P(S_i^{C_k}) = \frac{\sum S_i T_r}{\sum r |T_r|} \tag{3}$$

where S_i is the state-space of cluster C_k, $\#S_i$ is the number of occurrences of an element S_i in trace T_n, n is the number of traces in cluster C_k, and $|T_n|$ is the length of trace T_n.

Finding an optimal number of clusters is a fundamental issue in cluster analysis and there are several methods available. The goal is to find the minimum number of clusters that still have low summed-up distance. The Elbow method is selected for determining the optimal number of clusters in this study. The Elbow method is based on a k-means algorithm. It determines the total intra-cluster variation. In our case, we use $D(C_k, T_n)$, thus it should be as small as possible. The idea is that one should choose the number of clusters so that adding another cluster does not greatly improve the resulting model.

4.2   Process Discovery

The next step is to run the process discovery method. In this step, we deploy the heuristic mining algorithm.

Heuristic Mining Algorithm. Heuristic mining focuses on the control-flow perspective. It claims that the method is a practical application mining algorithm as it can deal with noise and can express the main behavior of business processes [27]. The heuristic mining applies the alpha-algorithm method. Therefore, the event logs are analyzed to find the casual dependency. Furthermore, unlike the alpha-algorithm which only focuses on the direct follow relationship, Heuristic mining takes skipping activities or long distance dependencies into account. It applies the frequency matrix and dependency matrix together with the thresholds on both matrices to construct process models. The threshold values of frequency and dependency are set in order to construct the model. The thresholds are used to exclude infrequent paths from the model.

Evaluating Process Model Quality. The resulting models should be able to present the actual behavior of the clusters. The models have to be assessed in terms of the accuracy that it can replay the traces in the clusters. Moreover, it should reduce the complexity of the model. In order to assess the process model quality, we use the fitness replay for evaluating the accuracy of the model and we use the precision for evaluating the complexity of the model.

Replay Fitness. Fitness replay is typically measured first, as it is considered as one of the most important dimensions. The fitness replay reflects how well the model can describe the actual process from the given event log. If the fitness value is low, it means that the process model does not contain much useful information from measuring conformance on other dimensions [1]. One aspect of our research requirement is to ensure that the resulting model is able to replay the event logs. We use the replay fitness measurement method in this paper which is inspired by Adriansyah et al. [1]. The measurement of a cost-based fitness metric determines how well resulting process models describe traces in the event logs. The idea of this metric is aligning an event log to a given process model. If there are any asynchronous moves (activities) between the model and the trace, then the skipping or inserting activities will be placed in the process model and will be penalized as cost. The advantage of this method is its ability to explore the optimal alignment or path with minimum cost. As a consequence, it allows for a flexible cost deviation behavior.

The fitness value is normalized between 0 and 1. A bigger value of fitness means a better alignment between model and log. The maximum moved model cost and moved log cost can happen when there are no synchronous moves. The detail of the method can be found in Adriansyah et al. [1].

Precision. Precision dimension is used to evaluate the discovered model that they do not allow too much behaviors that are unrelated to what we observe in the event logs. Precision penalizes a process model for allowing unrelated behavior from the observed behavior. There are many methods to calculate the precision. Our study uses the alignment-based precision checking from Adriansyah et al. [2]. The advantage of this method is that it can calculate the precision even a trace is not completely fit the model. The method ignores the non-simply part, such that this method is robust to real-life logs. Moreover, this method is implemented in the ProM framework. For the further detail on alignment-based precision can be found here Adriansyah et al. [2].

5   Evaluation and Results

This section illustrates the results of the experiments of our proposed method presented in Sect. 4. The proposed method is assessed with regard to two quality aspects: (1) cluster quality and (2) resulting model quality. The experiments are set up with three real-world event logs from different manufacturing and logistics companies.

The event logs contain information about the type of events and their time of execution. They are available in a format that process discovery techniques can directly use them. An example of the data is presented in Table 1. The terminology in manufacturing and in Process Mining can be matched as follows: A shop floor *operation* is an *event*, a *work order* (consisting of a number of operations) is a *case* or a *trace*, and a *machine* is an *activity type*.

We deploy three data sets A, B, and C for evaluation. The event log A has the largest number of events, cases, and activities which are 100,593 events, 24,157 cases, and 220 activities types, respectively. The second one is event log C, which has 118,782 events, 16,116 cases and 104 types of activities. Event log B has the smallest number of events. It contains 31,437 events, 3,366 cases, and 51 activity types. We can observe that the event logs, which are created from feedback information provided by manufacturing execution systems, exhibit a large variety of process behaviors. For example, one cluster may be composed of a wide range of activities and trace lengths.

In order to evaluate the proposed methods, we group the event logs by trace length, then select the largest groups of the partitions for clustering analysis. In this way, we can focus on assessing performance and get more insights into the behavior of the proposed methods, as the proposed methodology is based on Markov chains, which do not take the sequence length into account [16]. If the entire logs, which contain heterogeneous processes, are applied for clustering analysis, the resulting clusters will contain a wide range of trance lengths that will affect the resulting process model. Therefore, we divide the event logs by length and select the largest groups that have the largest number of traces for further analysis.

Table 2 presents the largest groups by trace length for each event log. For event log A, the traces with length 5 is the largest group, while the largest groups of event log B and C are 7 and 5, respectively.

Table 2. The largest groups by trace length

Event log	Length	No. of events	No. of cases	No. of activity types
A	5	11,450	2,290	144
B	7	1,519	217	41
C	5	10,495	2,099	104

5.1   Sequence Clustering

The first objective is to assess the quality of the clustering results. The proposed methodology is based on Markov Chains and EM. These methods are coherent with the proposed approaches of initializing cluster centroids from main processes and penalizing disjoint activities with the minimum transition probability.

By doing so, we aim to optimize underlying process models. It is a fundamental problem of clustering that a number of classes and labels remain undefined. Selecting frequently occurring processes as the initial centroids is an option to separate process instances based on main processes. Moreover, this approach will minimize the chance that the initial clusters will be empty. In addition, penalizing disjoint activities with the minimum transition probability provides a chance that process variants can be assigned to similar processes and solve the problem of unassigned traces.

We examine the clustering performance by varying the number of clusters $k = 10, 20, 30, 40, 50, 60$ and 70. After that, the summed-up distance (see Eq. 2) is used to evaluate the quality of the clusters. For example, we set the number of the cluster to $k = 10$, and calculate for each cluster the total distance between the centroid and its members. Then all the results from 10 clusters are summed up. Table 3 shows the summed-up distances for varying numbers of clusters. The first column presents the event log A, B, and C, respectively. The second to the seventh columns present the summed-up distance for each event log with the different number of cluster k from 10 to 70. Table 4 presents the summed-up distance of the largest group by length.

Table 3. Summed distance results

Event logs	$k = 10$	$k = 20$	$k = 30$	$k = 40$	$k = 50$	$k = 60$	$k = 70$
A	18,499.90	17,445.04	16,819.80	16,280.99	15,758.92	15,410.34	15,027.43
B	25,35.15	23,84.34	23,13.83	22,46.91	21,98.70	2,152.56	2,107.13
C	12,140.36	11,550.42	11,257.50	10,964.47	10,425.17	10,236.90	10,097.36

Table 4. Summed distance results for the largest group

Event logs	$k = 10$	$k = 20$	$k = 30$	$k = 40$	$k = 50$	$k = 60$	$k = 70$
A	1,580.98	1,368.91	1,256.57	1,157.53	1,091.06	1,014.01	962.00
B	123.56	99.56	86.43	75.47	65.93	59.44	54.65
C	1,248.27	1,047.35	942.31	900.35	857.37	814.03	782.997

To find the optimal number of clusters, we plot the graphs from data in Tables 3 and 4. Figure 5(a) depicts the summed-up distance of all event logs as presented in Table 3. The summed-up distances of event logs A and C decrease significantly with the number of clusters increasing from 10 to 50. Thus, an optimal number of clusters could be between 50 and 60. In event log B, the summed-up distance decreases constantly between the number of clusters going from 10 to 50. Then, the optimal number of clusters can be determined by the Elbow method as stated previously. In order to avoid the problem of small and empty clusters, $k = 50$ is selected for event log A and C, and $k = 40$ for event log B.

Figure 5(b) illustrates the summed-up distance from the largest group by length (as presented in Table 4). The results are better than the summed-up distance of the entire logs. However, the patterns of the summed distance from the largest groups are similar to patterns from the entire log. Therefore, the number of cluster k of event logs A, B, and C are at 50, 40, and 50, respectively. The selected clusters from the largest groups are the input in the next step for the resulting model quality.

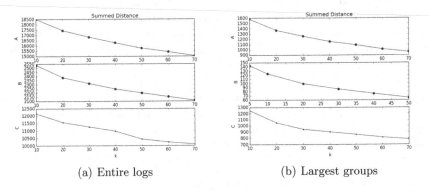

(a) Entire logs   (b) Largest groups

Fig. 5. Summed-up distance from (a) entire event logs, and (b) largest groups by the length of each event log.

5.2 Process Discovery

Once a set of clusters has been found, the next task is to perform process discovery to find the underlying process models from these clusters. In this step, we use the ProM 6.6 software to perform process discovery. The Heuristic Miner is applied to construct the process models. The standard parameter settings are used in both miners. Then, the outputs are translated into Petri nets by making use of the corresponding ProM plug-in.

Table 5 illustrates the result of the calculations of the cost-based fitness. The first column presents the event logs A, B, and C. The second and third columns present fitness from the resulting process models. The difference between the second and third columns is that the first one is the largest cluster and the second one is the result from the second largest. The second-largest groups are included in this step in order to evaluate the consistency of performance improvements of the resulting models. They are used to represent most of the remaining clusters excluding the largest one.

The event log B has the best results of fitness for both the largest and the second-largest groups as $fitness = 0.62$ and 0.88, respectively. It is considered as the smallest event log and it has also the smallest number of different activities. For event log A and C, the performance of process discovery is rather weak for the largest group as the resulting $fitness$ are 0.37 and 0.25, respectively. On the other hand, for the second-largest clusters, the quality measure of the process models is much higher as $fitness = 0.57$ and 0.82 for event log A and B, respectively. For the precision, the event log C have the best result in the largest group. For event log A and B, the precision is rather poor. And for the second group, all the event logs have high score of precision.

Table 5. Process Quality results

Log	Largest cluster		Second Large cluster	
	Fitness	*Precision*	*Fitness*	*Precision*
A	0.37	0.28	0.57	0.86
B	0.62	0.64	0.88	0.93
C	0.25	0.92	0.82	0.97

The reason that process discovery performs poorly for the largest clusters is caused by the difficulty of the proposed methodology to deal with infrequent behaviors. This is because the clusters are formed based on the main processes as the initial seeds. The largest clusters are likely created from the most repeating traces which tend to have a large number of members, which leads to a higher distribution of the transition probability. Together with the approach of penalizing disjoint activities with a minimum transition probability, the infrequent behaviors and noise are likely to be assigned to the largest clusters. On the other hand, the second largest clusters have an increased quality of the resulting models and less distribution of fitness. The details of the distribution of the cost-based fitness value are elaborated in Figs. 6 and 7.

Figure 6 illustrates the distribution of trace fitness for event logs A, B, and C. The largest cluster of event log A has 527 traces and 122 different activities. Figure 6(a) shows that 140 traces have $fitness \approx 0.8$, while there are 225 traces having $fitness \approx 0$. Event log B has 54 traces and 12 different activities. Figure 6(b) shows that 29 traces have $fitness \approx 0.67$, 17 traces have $fitness \approx 0.6$, 7 traces have $fitness \approx 0.53$, and 1 traces have $fitness \approx 0.45$. For event log C, there are 815 traces, and 83 different activities (see Fig. 6(c)). The majority of traces have $fitness \approx 0.25$.

For the second-largest clusters, fitness improves. For event log A, there are 167 traces and 33 activities. Figure 7(a) depicts that the majority of traces have $fitness \approx 0.67$. For event log B, there are 21 traces and 11 events. Figure 7(b)

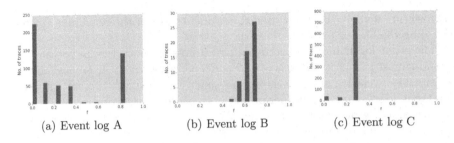

Fig. 6. Traces fitness of the largest clusters, (a) event log A, (b) event log B, and (c) event log C

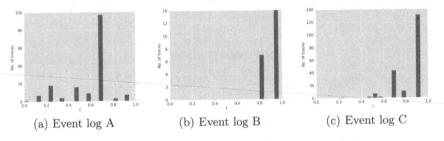

Fig. 7. Traces fitness of the second largest clusters, (a) event log A, (b) event log B, and (c) event log C

shows that the majority of the traces have *fitness* ≈ 0.93 and the rest has *fitness* ≈ 0.8. For event log C, there are 204 traces and 15 different activities (see Fig. 7(c)). The majority of traces are around 0.67 and the rests are distributed.

The largest clusters that have relatively low in replay fitness measurements require further analysis in order to investigate the real behavior of the business processes. In this case, we select the example from the largest cluster from event log A as it has the lowest replay fitness measurement among the three data sets.

To perform further analysis, we require additional methods or opinions from the process experts. In our case, we filter the high-frequency occurrence of the activities to demonstrate the main behavior of the clusters.

6   Discussion

Manufacturing and logistics processes are highly flexible and diverse as we can observe from the number of events and activities from three real-world event logs in this study. Applying our novel methodology provides clustering results with the optimal number of clusters without unassigned processes and empty clusters. The variant processes are assigned to the same group of similar processes. As a result, process discovery performs poorly for the largest clusters due to the difficulty of the proposed methodology to assign infrequent behaviors. We can notice that these clusters are larger than other clusters. They also contain a large number of traces and activity types. For example, the largest cluster of event log

A contains 527 traces and 122 different activities, which is many times larger than the second one which only contains 167 traces and 33 activities. Most infrequent behaviors are likely to be assigned to the largest clusters since they are generated from the most repeating traces. Therefore, the transition probability matrices from the largest clusters are often distributed. Consequently, when calculating the associated probability, the chance that these clusters will be penalized with the minimum transition probability is less than for other clusters. Infrequent processes and noise are often assigned to the largest clusters. As a consequence, the second-largest groups provide a satisfactory process model quality. The rest of the clusters tend to have a good resulting model quality as they have a similar structure as the second-largest cluster.

7   Conclusion

The objective of this research is to improve the result of process discovery in highly dynamic environments such as manufacturing and logistics. Existing process discovery methods tend to generate highly complex models that are difficult to understand when dealing with real-world data, which has a high amount of infrequent and ad-hoc behaviors. Therefore, this paper proposes a methodology for sequence clustering in order to improve the performance of process discovery. Our methodology is based on Markov Chains and Expectation Maximization. We introduce these approaches to solve the issue of unassigned traces and empty clusters of sequence clustering based on probabilistic models by selecting initial centroids from main processes. Moreover, this work introduces an approach for penalizing disjoint activities between traces by introducing a minimum transition probability. This approach makes it possible for variant processes to be grouped with similar processes. As in real-world processes, the sequence of activities can vary. We evaluate our methodology with three real-world data sets from manufacturing and logistics companies. The experimental results illustrate that the proposed methodology finds a good distribution in terms of finding the main processes. As a consequence, the resulting models by sequence clustering have a satisfactory model quality regarding the replay fitness dimension. However, the proposed methodology generates results of limited quality for the largest clusters.

Therefore, in our future work, we aim to enhance our proposed methodology to be more robust in respect to diverse business process types and behaviors, e.g., in the form of preprocessing data and using discovery algorithms. Furthermore, it will be an advantage to evaluate other types of process model quality measures. Also, we want to perform experiments with additional data sources, such as data form simulation, in order to compare the performance of existing methods and the proposed method in a variety of quality dimensions.

References

1. Adriansyah, A., van Dongen, B.F., van der Aalst, W.: Conformance checking using cost-based fitness analysis. In: 2011 15th IEEE International Enterprise Distributed Object Computing Conference (EDOC), pp. 55–64. IEEE (2011). ISBN 0-7695-4425-8
2. Adriansyah, A., Munoz-Gama, J., Carmona, J., van Dongen, B.F., van der Aalst, W.M.P.: Alignment based precision checking. In: La Rosa, M., Soffer, P. (eds.) BPM 2012. LNBIP, vol. 132, pp. 137–149. Springer, Heidelberg (2013). https://doi.org/10.1007/978-3-642-36285-9_15
3. Basu, S., Banerjee, A., Mooney, R.: Semi-supervised clustering by seeding. In: Proceedings of 19th International Conference on Machine Learning (ICML-2002. Citeseer (2002)
4. Becker, T., Intoyoad, W.: Context aware process mining in logistics. Procedia CIRP **63**, 557–562 (2017)
5. Becker, T., Lütjen, M., Porzel, R.: Process maintenance of heterogeneous logistic systems—a process mining approach. In: Freitag, M., Kotzab, H., Pannek, J. (eds.) Dynamics in Logistics. LNL, pp. 77–86. Springer, Cham (2017). https://doi.org/10.1007/978-3-319-45117-6_7
6. Jagadeesh Chandra Bose, R.P., van der Aalst, W.M.P.: Context aware trace clustering: towards improving process mining results. In: SDM, pp. 401–412. SIAM (2009)
7. Choudhary, A.K., Harding, J.A., Tiwari, M.K.: Data mining in manufacturing: a review based on the kind of knowledge. J. Intell. Manuf. **20**(5), 501–521 (2009)
8. de Medeiros, A.K.A., et al.: Process mining based on clustering: a quest for precision. In: ter Hofstede, A., Benatallah, B., Paik, H.-Y. (eds.) BPM 2007. LNCS, vol. 4928, pp. 17–29. Springer, Heidelberg (2008). https://doi.org/10.1007/978-3-540-78238-4_4
9. De Weerdt, J., van den Broucke, S., Vanthienen, J., Baesens, B.: Active trace clustering for improved process discovery. IEEE Trans. Knowl. Data Eng. **25**(12), 2708–2720 (2013)
10. Elovici, Y., Braha, D.: A decision-theoretic approach to data mining. IEEE Trans. Syst. **33**(1), 42–51 (2003)
11. Ferreira, D., Zacarias, M., Malheiros, M., Ferreira, P.: Approaching process mining with sequence clustering: experiments and findings. In: Alonso, G., Dadam, P., Rosemann, M. (eds.) BPM 2007. LNCS, vol. 4714, pp. 360–374. Springer, Heidelberg (2007). https://doi.org/10.1007/978-3-540-75183-0_26
12. Gillblad, D., Steinert, R., Ferreira, D.R.: Estimating the parameters of randomly interleaved Markov models. In: IEEE International Conference on Data Mining Workshops, 2009. ICDMW 2009, pp. 308–313. IEEE (2009). ISBN 1-4244-5384-4
13. Goedertier, S., Martens, D., Vanthienen, J., Baesens, B.: Robust process discovery with artificial negative events **10**, 1305–1340 (2009)
14. Goedertier, S., De Weerdt, J., Martens, D., Vanthienen, J., Baesens, B.: Process discovery in event logs: an application in the telecom industry. Appl. Soft Comput. **11**(2), 1697–1710 (2011)
15. Greco, G., Guzzo, A., Pontieri, L., Sacca, D.: Discovering expressive process models by clustering log traces. IEEE Trans. Knowl. Data Eng. **18**(8), 1010–1027 (2006)
16. Intayoad, W., Becker, T.: Applying process mining in manufacturing and logistic for large transaction data. In: Freitag, M., Kotzab, H., Pannek, J. (eds.) LDIC 2018. LNL, pp. 378–388. Springer, Cham (2018). https://doi.org/10.1007/978-3-319-74225-0_51

17. Liu, B.: Web Data Mining: Exploring Hyperlinks, Contents, and Usage Data. Springer, Heidelberg (2007). https://doi.org/10.1007/978-3-540-37882-2. ISBN 3-540-37881-2

18. Mans, R.S., Schonenberg, M.H., Song, M., van der Aalst, W.M.P., Bakker, P.J.M.: Application of process mining in healthcare – a case study in a dutch hospital. In: Fred, A., Filipe, J., Gamboa, H. (eds.) BIOSTEC 2008. CCIS, vol. 25, pp. 425–438. Springer, Heidelberg (2008). https://doi.org/10.1007/978-3-540-92219-3_32

19. Okoye, K., Tawil, A.-R.H., Naeem, U., Bashroush, R., Lamine, E.: A semantic rule-based approach supported by process mining for personalised adaptive learning **37**, 203–210 (2014). ISSN 1877–0509. https://doi.org/10.1016/j.procs.2014.08.031. https://www.sciencedirect.com/science/article/pii/S187705091400996X

20. Rebuge, Á., Ferreira, D.R.: Business process analysis in healthcare environments: a methodology based on process mining. Inf. Syst. **37**(2), 99–116 (2012)

21. Rubin, V., Günther, C.W., van der Aalst, W.M.P., Kindler, E., van Dongen, B.F., Schäfer, W.: Process mining framework for software processes. In: Wang, Q., Pfahl, D., Raffo, D.M. (eds.) ICSP 2007. LNCS, vol. 4470, pp. 169–181. Springer, Heidelberg (2007). https://doi.org/10.1007/978-3-540-72426-1_15

22. Song, M., Günther, C.W., van der Aalst, W.M.P.: Trace clustering in process mining. In: Ardagna, D., Mecella, M., Yang, J. (eds.) BPM 2008. LNBIP, vol. 17, pp. 109–120. Springer, Heidelberg (2009). https://doi.org/10.1007/978-3-642-00328-8_11

23. Van der Aalst, W.M.P.: Process Mining: Discovery, Conformance and Enhancement of Business Processes. Springer, Heidelberg (2008). https://doi.org/10.1007/978-3-642-19345-3

24. van der Aalst, W., et al.: Process mining manifesto. In: Daniel, F., Barkaoui, K., Dustdar, S. (eds.) BPM 2011. LNBIP, vol. 99, pp. 169–194. Springer, Heidelberg (2012). https://doi.org/10.1007/978-3-642-28108-2_19

25. Veiga, G.M., Ferreira, D.R.: Understanding spaghetti models with sequence clustering for ProM. In: Rinderle-Ma, S., Sadiq, S., Leymann, F. (eds.) BPM 2009. LNBIP, vol. 43, pp. 92–103. Springer, Heidelberg (2010). https://doi.org/10.1007/978-3-642-12186-9_10

26. Verbeek, H.M.W., Buijs, J.C.A.M., Van Dongen, B.F., van der Aalst, W.M.P.: Prom 6: the process mining toolkit, vol. 615, pp. 34–39 (2010)

27. Weijters, A.J.M.M., van Der Aalst, W.M.P., De Medeiros, A.K.A.: Process mining with the heuristics miner-algorithm **166**, 1–34 (2006)

28. Zhang, Y., Dudzic, M.S.: Online monitoring of steel casting processes using multivariate statistical technologies: from continuous to transitional operations. J. Process Control **16**(8), 819–829 (2006)

Industry 4.0

Interoperability of Logistics Artefacts in Industry 4.0-Driven IT Landscape

Marco Franke[1][✉], Karl A. Hribernik[1], and Klaus-Dieter Thoben[1,2]

[1] BIBA - Bremer Institut für Produktion und Logistik GmbH, Hochschulring 20, 28359 Bremen, Germany
{fma,hri,tho}@biba.uni-bremen.de
[2] Faculty of Production Engineering, University of Bremen, 28359 Bremen, Germany

Abstract. The heterogeneity of data in logistics processes is due to the use of different systems, standards and data repositories. The same information is codified differently making efforts to integrate data necessary. Information objects are typically used by different legacy systems and different standards may be applied in the global context of information flows. An information flow is a sequence in which each information exchange can be considered a bidirectional transformation of information between data formats, protocols and different rights & roles concepts of the different logistics artefacts. The high degree of heterogeneity means that implementing 1:1 interfaces for each logistics artefact is inefficient and not scalable. To solve this problem, a dynamic interoperability layer is proposed in this paper, with a wrapper component as part of each logistics artefact. The approach presented here is based on a conceptual level and a corresponding proof-of-concept is shown based on available technologies.

Keywords: Horizontal and vertical interoperability · Data-driven process transformation · Process-sensitive data transformation

1 Introduction

The customization of products by customers is a common feature of product related services. The provision of this feature directly influences the dynamics in logistics activities along the entire supply chain, ranging from the OEM to the customer and including all tier suppliers. The affected logistics processes are challenged by planning and implementing the transportation and storage of goods, taking into account time, quality and cost constraints [1]. Moreover, logistics is challenged by the growing popularity of online shopping and the desire of customers for transparency and same-day delivery. For example, the number of postal deliveries rose to over 3.5 billion in 2018 - this corresponds to almost 12 million postal deliveries per delivery day. The vast majority, around 84 percent, are parcels [2]. These trends affect the production and logistics processes.

© Springer Nature Switzerland AG 2020
M. Freitag et al. (Eds.): S-BPM ONE 2020, CCIS 1278, pp. 167–176, 2020.
https://doi.org/10.1007/978-3-030-64351-5_11

These trends lead to a reduction in delivery lot size and at the same time to an increase in the total amount of deliveries [3]. As a result, the growing delivery volumes place additional stress on urban transport and logistics systems caused by various criteria such as limited parking spaces, congestion, pollution and infrastructure deterioration [4].

Another relevant trend results from the massive and increasing networking of IT systems between the domains of Smart Manufacturing, Logistics and Smart Cities ranging from legacy systems like ERP (Smart Manufacturing) to new autonomous IoT (Smart City) and cyber-physical devices (Logistics) like cars or intelligent parking spots on a global level. The number of systems involved also increases due to modular production and cyber physical logistics systems that can interact with others through networked components predefined by their design intention. This also leads to a higher number of heterogeneous interfaces with respect to data formats and standards. Moreover, the interfaces of the mentioned IT systems are integrated within interlinked network topologies, which increases the effort required to integrate and control these systems [5].

The automatic support of these heterogeneous interfaces and complex network topologies in IT solutions are mandatory to enable data-driven process transformation without a continuous integration effort in logistics. In addition, the integration of a huge amount of data (Big Data) is necessary to support the process-sensitive data transformation.

The listed transformation aspects are already considered in the roadmap of Industry 4.0, especially by the reference architecture RAMI 4.0. The development of future RAMI 4.0 compliant production and logistics systems is supported by Cyber-Physical Systems (CPS) [6] which enable the autonomous and decentralized collaboration of systems in ubiquitous logistics [7]. The outcome is an Industry 4.0-driven IT landscape, in which legacy systems, IoT objects and CPS share the same working space and need to interact seamlessly with each other. In this landscape, the system borders are fluid, because autonomous transport vehicles or ad hoc sharing of logistics infrastructure are key elements [8]. Establishing interoperability on all levels is the precondition of an Industry 4.0-driven IT landscape, which have to be seamless and manageable for an open world logistics.

The challenge is that the interfaces between interwoven legacy systems and systems within logistics are currently implemented in a variety of already existing and upcoming IoT and Industry 4.0-related proprietary data formats and de facto standards for the cross-sectoral transmission of electronic business data. Apart from this heterogeneity, the essential logistics process of clearly identifying goods is currently also ensured by several standards in the scope of Auto-ID.

This article proposes an approach to address the heterogeneity of data formats and standards by exchanging information rather than data in heterogeneous data formats. For this purpose, the authors present the current state of interoperability gaps in logistics. Then an approach is presented to overcome the data integration conflicts in logistics. Finally, a summary and an outlook are given.

1.1 Current Situation for Interoperability in Logistics

As introduced above, the requirements towards interoperability in logistics include the ability to integrate heterogeneous IT systems that are distributed over stakeholders and spread over different IT networks to enable a flexible and adaptable information flow. An example of the hetero-geneity for the repre-sentation of the simple information *company* in current data formats is given in Fig. 1.

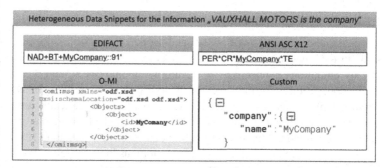

Fig. 1. Heterogeneous Data Sources

Apart from the data structures, countless traceability services are already available. The challenge is that there is no central service registry and the interaction is based on different APIs. Each of them offers a different REST service, and data formats. Examples are e.g. Omnitracs Scheduler API, Lufthansa Partner API, Expeditors Shipment Tracking API, Royal Mail Shipping API, and DHL API.

To achieve the interoperability for autonomous logistical services, each of them have to be identified manually and integrated manually by a specific adapter, which is not fea-sible in an open world, which is characterized by dynamic and not only predefined state changes. In the following, a detailed overview of relevant standards for data exchange in logistics is given.

1.1.1 Common Standards in Logistics

The legacy systems in logistics for inter- and intra-logistics like MES, ERP or PPS focus on the protocols IP and HTTP for the communication among each other. On the application level, there are standards, which define syntax and semantics of the applied terminology for sharing information snippets like parcel identification or parcel destination. The applied terminology contains both exchangeable commands as well as status information. In the following, the common set of standards and corresponding data formats is presented.

One of the most common standards, which is available in more than 80 countries, is EDIFACT EANCOM and covers commands as well as status information (see Fig. 1). The syntax and semantic of a command's payload define, e.g., the trade item, the place of manufacture, and the legal entity. The representation of such items is standardized, too. The standards Global Location Number (GLN), Global Trade Item Number (GTIN), Serial Shipping Container Code (SSCC), Global Identification Number for Consign-ment (GINC), etc. are examples for unambiguous identification of subjects and objects in logistics processes. The EDIFACT standard including identification standards cre-ates a common language and terminology to automate the communication processes.

Alternative standards are also available. Common combinations in the interaction among logistical systems are (EDIFACT <-> ANSI ASC X12), (GLN <-> ISO/IEC 6523) or (GTIN <-> ISO/IEC 15459). The interoperability, which is the precondition for data driven services like data-driven process transformation, is only given if logistical systems can interpret and translate these different standards in the right way.

1.1.2 IoT Related Technologies

IoT data monitors the state of objects and support responsible information-driven decisions in the smart city like traffic management. The current technology stack allows already ubiquitous connectivity and data-driven analysis around the world and offers tremendous features for improved connectivity, devices and data management via different IoT platforms (e.g. transport, energy, manufacturing, healthcare and city service providers) [9]. More than 250 IoT platforms are currently available, which are already heterogeneous and has led to a fragmentation of the IoT ecosystems [9]. This fragmentation has a direct impact on the targeted autonomous logistics relying on interoperability, because future logistics services require IoT data as well as company specific data as input to establish autonomous logistics processes. Relevant IoT data sources deliver e.g. environmental information like weather forecasts, congestion forecast or the current parking possibilities at the destination. These types of information are important for routing and just in time delivery. To close the information cycle, logistics systems have to communicate their action and state back to relevant IoT ecosystems. The above-mentioned heterogeneity does not only captures the heterogeneity of the data formats but also the heterogeneity across the entire OSI stack. An excerpt of the heterogeneity to be overcome is shown in Fig. 2.

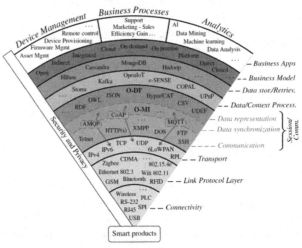

Fig. 2. IoT technologies and standards landscape, adapted from [10]

The interoperability of logistics artefacts has to handle this heterogeneity to enable seamless collaboration between legacy systems, IoT objects and CPS.

1.2 Problem Statement

An information exchange is the bidirectional transformation of information between data formats of the different logistics artefacts (see Fig. 1 and Fig. 2). Bellinger [11] defines information as "data that has been given meaning by way of relational connection".

The integration effort (see Fig. 3) within a supply chain increases with the number of stakeholders. The number of data transformations for 1:1 communication is defined by:

$$2 * \sum_{i=1}^{n-1} i, \text{ where n is the number of different types of stakeholders addressed.} \quad (1)$$

With respect to the amount of different IoT marketplaces (>250), the different parcel delivery services (>10) and the target tools for intra- and inter logistical planning to be supported by a logistics artefact, the amount of stakeholders is critical for a 1:1 communication. Furthermore, the approach of a direct transformation suffers from further drawbacks. For example, the adaption of a data format would result in an adaption process for all other stakeholders.

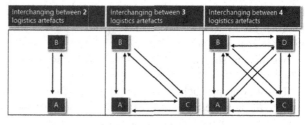

Fig. 3. Interoperability Effort

The same problem statement also applies to the communication and transportation layers. Accordingly, the programmatic implementation of 1: 1 interfaces between stakeholders is not a suitable solution with respect to the effort.

Apart from the amount of necessary supported syntax variants, the preservation of semantics is also a challenge in the interoperable communication for intermodal logistics. The different data formats apply different data schemas, which represents different amount of information. Existing stand-alone solutions [12, 13] have already demonstrated the **static** possibility to create and use uplifted heterogeneous data of different data sources to exchange information instead of data using fixed ontologies and predefined data sources. However, each of them only provides one **central** and **static interoperability layer** that is designed as a closed-world solution. Adding additional stakeholders, data schemas or data formats is not possible without manual development effort. As an outcome, there are a couple of isolated solutions. Therefore, they are not flexible enough to carry the-desired complete interoperability levels for Industry 4.0 driven IT landscape.

The data integration can result in faulty results in an open world. In a 1:1 transformation, information represented by the input format might not be able to be completely transferred to the target format, because the target syntax tree might not allow the representation of a specific information. In these cases, data integration conflicts like data type conflicts or aggregation conflicts occur which have to be resolved.

To reduce the amount of required transformations on the interface level, to reduce the required knowledge of all supported data formats and to have a sustainable data integration approach for an open world logistics, each logistics artefact needs a similar interoperability layer and Open API independent of its physical representation.

1.3 Approach

To enable a decentralized interoperability layer, one of the key challenges is to exchange information and not only data. The information shall be provided independently of the supported data formats. Moreover, all different information entities shall be representable also in the cases where the information cannot be represented in all data formats. For that purpose, an intermediate representation in the role of an interoperability model is applied that is shown in Fig. 4.

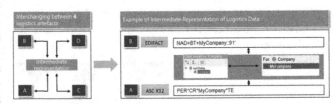

Fig. 4. Intermediated representation of Logistics artefacts' data view

The shown approach emphasizes the transformation of data from a source format first into the intermediate representation and then into the target format for communication. To enable these types of transformations, the focus is on a global as view (GAV) data integration approach. It defines a global information model over all data sources. While applying GAV and corresponding query mechanism, this approach supports the virtual (current data) as well as the physical data (Big Data) integration approach. In the following, the need to apply an intermediate model in the scope of logistics is given.

Each system should take the responsibility of providing information instead of data for any query request to achieve the interoperability. The step from the data to the information view is managed by the already motivated transformations.

The logistics artefact only maintains the applicable transformations from its data schema to the intermediate representation. It uses its own transformation rules to translate the data into the intermediate representation and vice versa. The data inside the data source is directly connected to the proprietary tool chain. The intention of the data inside the local intermediated representation is to provide the information for other stakeholders as well as added value services. This approach emphasizes using ontologies as intermediated representations. Moreover, an intermediate representation can furthermore enable discovery functions showing the currently available information of all connected devices. Thus, it does not define a fixed ontology describing all possible concepts and their relationships in logistics. Moreover, it does not emphasize using a single ontology but rather the loose coupling of existing domain ontologies. Relevant ontologies in logistics are e.g. GenCLOn for urban freight transport [14] or ontologies for logistical services [15]. The approach focusses on the creation of a network of ontologies based on the linked logistics artefacts. Each time a logistics artefact would like to initiate the communication, it automatically sends its local ontology for interfacing. Then, the local ontology is integrated loosely coupled into the overall GAV-based ontology and shared among the communication partners. After the synchronization of the shared GAV ontology, queries can be defined based on the shared terminology. With respect to the automatic ontology extension, pieces of the local ontology are ignored if the extension of the overall ontology violates the criterion of "monotonicity of entailment"[1]. The corresponding extended logistics artefact is shown in Fig. 5. A query is defined using a wrapper-specific query language like SPARQL or GraphQL and triggers the automatic transformation of the data into an Abox (part of ontology), which defines the requested data as ontology's individuals. For example, a query could request the company name (see Fig. 1 and Fig. 4).

The transformation module transforms, for example, the stored EDIFACT message into an individual of the concept company (see Fig. 4). The only needed manual transformation steps are the ongoing provision of the ontology and transformations rules belonging to the own data source.

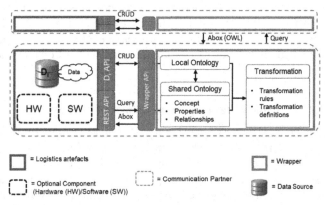

Fig. 5. Logistics artefact presented in [16]

1.4 Potential Implementation

In Fig. 5, the logistics artefact is an autonomous entity (blue rectangle) and is loosely coupled to an information layer (green rectangle). Together, they form a communication partner. The interlinkage of wrappers among each other enables the **dynamic interoperability layer**. For that purpose, the dynamic inclusion &exclusion of available local ontologies inside the shared GAV ontology **as intermediate representation is mandatory**. Based on the shared ontology, each wrapper offers a standardized query interface based on REST. Logistics artefacts do not communicate with each other directly, but via their wrapper's REST interface. Each incoming query to the wrapper triggers data acquisition at all linked and relevant (a map, in which the key is the information and the object is a list of wrapper ids) logistics artefacts and a data source-specific translation into an ontology (growing Abox in OWL over the different wrappers) based on predefined transformation rules. The transformation rules cover both directions of data access, i.e. read and write operations. The proposed wrapper concept has already been realized by some implementations. In the following, an Open Source solution of Semantic Web as well as of Social Media are presented as technology examples. Apart from concrete implementation frameworks, there are also initiatives like Industrial Data Space (IDS), which defines the overall proceeding and required capabilities for the secure exchange of data and the easy combination of data within value networks.

---

[1] https://scholar.harvard.edu/files/yxiang/files/ho7-entailment-monotonicity.pdf.

1.4.1   Virtual Data Integration Using a Semantic Mediator

A virtual data integration approach using a semantic mediator is presented based on SEMed. "It is a mature middleware layer for semantic, virtual interoperability and integration specifically of item-level product lifecycle data. It facilitates an ontological standard-based access to different kinds of common data sources like databases and file based repositories" [17]. Linking a logistics artefact in the role of an information consumer is possible by defining the query in the query language SPARQL for OWL/DL. It enables the creation of queries providing complex read and write transactions for intensional as well as extensional queries. Linking a logistics artefact in the role of a data source requires the selection of an already implemented wrapper and the assignment of a configuration. The configuration defines the local ontology as well as a XML based transformation rules.

1.4.2   Virtual Data Integration Using GRAPHQL

"GraphQL is a query language for APIs and a runtime for fulfilling those queries with your existing data. GraphQL provides a complete and understandable description of the data in your API" [18]. Linking a logistics artefact in the role of an information consumer is possible by defining the query in the query language GraphQL. It enables the definition of predefined queries and the later derivation of an API supporting the predefined queries. Linking a logistics artefact in the role of a data source requires the implementation of the wrapper as well as the implementation of the configuration. The configuration defines the global intermediate representation as well as the support of the predefined queries. The result is a JSON string.

1.4.3   Readiness of the Available Interoperability Solutions

The comparison of both solutions is shown in Table 1.

The solutions presented above provide the functions required for the flexible interoperability layer of logistics artefacts and enable the data integration over multiple heterogeneous data sources. SEMed focusses on a flexible approach in which the required transformation rules and the intermediate representation are configurable to achieve an open world data integration. In contrast, GraphQL focusses on the implementation of the transformation rules and intermediate representation in source code to have a static and fast data integration for fixed data schemas. Both solutions fit well to enable the proposed capabilities of the **flexible information layer** to integrate communication partners dynamically. The specific capabilities required to support specific supported data sources and privacy and security functions still need to be investigated. In addition, additional functionality required to enabling information-driven triggers for communication as well as process state changes have to investigated to enable data-driven process transformation and process-sensitive data transformation.

Table 1. Capabilities of GraphQL/SEMed

Property	SEMed	GraphQL
Persistence of data {Physical, Virtual}	Virtual	Virtual
Query approach {GAV, LAV}	GAV	GAV
Query language {Yes, No}	Yes, SPARQL	Yes, GraphQL
Capabilities of intermediated representation {Hypernym, Holonym, Troponym, Unions}	Yes for all	Yes for all
Type of Information Request {Unicast source, Multicast (multiple data sources}	Multicast	Multicast
Data aggregation over heterogeneous data sources {Yes, No}	Yes	Yes
Interface {REST, EVENTING}	REST	REST, EVENT
Global intermediated representation (data schema) {Fixed, Dynamic Extension}	Dynamic Extension	Fixed
Introspection of the global schema {Yes, No}	Yes	Yes
Capabilities of intermediated representation {Hypernym, Holonym, Troponym}	Yes for all	Yes
Transformation rules {Fixed, Extendable}	Extendable	Fixed
Type of Transformation rules	Declarative	Procedural

1.5 Summary and Outlook

The heterogeneity of data in logistics processes is due to the use of different systems, standards, and data repositories. Information objects are typically used by different legacy systems and different standards may be applied in the global context of information flows. In logistics processes, the amount of relevant standards will increase due to the trends in the areas of Internet of Things and Industry 4.0. To enable an interoperable information flow beyond the limits of the heterogeneous standards and static data integration solutions, the exchange of information and the corresponding dynamic transformation of data are needed. The approach presented is based on a conceptual level and a corresponding proof-of-concept is shown based on available technologies. The next steps are to examine the requirements for the required transformation functions at the specific interfaces to enable data-driven process transformations as well as process-sensitive data transformations. Moreover, linking interoperability layers of all logistics artefacts to each other has to be researched.

References

1. Kumar, A.: From mass customization to mass personalization: a strategic transformation. Int. J. Flex. Manuf. Syst. **19**, 533–547 (2007). https://doi.org/10.1007/s10696-008-9048-6
2. Statistika. https://de.statista.com/infografik/9992/in-deutschland-von-den-paket-und-kurier diensten-befoerderten-sendungen/. Accessed 21 Feb 2020

3. Ickert, L., Matthes, U., Rommerskirchen, S., Weyand, E., Schlesinger, M., Limbers, J.: Abschätzung der langfristigen Entwicklung des Güterverkehrs in Deutschland bis 2050 (Study for the German Ministry of Traffic, Construction and Urban Development). Prognosen und Strategieberatung für Transport und Verkehr (2007)

4. Müller, M., Görnert, S., Volkamer, A.: Güterverkehr in der Stadt - Ein unterschätztes Problem. Verkehrsclub Deutschland e.V (2006)

5. Becker, T., Weimer, D., Pannek, J.: Network structures and decentralized control in logistics: topology, interfaces, and dynamics. Int. J. Adv. Logist. **4**(1), 1–8 (2015). https://doi.org/10.1080/2287108X.2015.1012329

6. Veigt, M., Lappe, D., Hribernik, K.A., Scholz-Reiter, B.: Entwicklung eines Cyber-Physischen Logistiksystems. Industrie Management **29**(1), 15–18 (2013)

7. Wellsandt, S., Werthmann, D., Hribernik, K., Thoben, K.-D.: Ubiquitous logistics: a business and technology concept based on shared resources. In: Cunningham, P., Cunningham, M. (eds.) International Information Management Cooperation (IIMC), Proceedings of the eChallenges Conference (e-2013), Dublin, Ireland (2013). 8 p. ISBN 978-1-905824-40-3

8. Freitag, M., Becker, T., Duffie, N.A.: Dynamics of resource sharing in production networks. CIRP Ann. Manuf. Technol. **64**, 435–438 (2015)

9. bIoTope. https://st1.ning.com/topology/rest/1.0/file/get/1064966?profile=original. Accessed 21 Feb 2020

10. Vermesan, O., Friess, P.: Internet of Things – From Research and Innovation to Market Deployment. River Publishers, Aalborg (2014)

11. Data, information, knowledge, and wisdom. http://www.systems-thinking.org/dikw/dikw.htm. Accessed 23 Oct 2015

12. Casu, M., Cicala, G., Tacchella, A.: Ontology-based data access: an application to intermodal logistics. Inf. Syst. Front. **15**(5), 849–871 (2013). https://doi.org/10.1007/s10796-012-9395-4

13. Jinbing, H., Youna, W., Ying, J.: Logistics decision-making support system based on ontology. In: 2008 International Symposium on Computational Intelligence and Design, vol. 1, pp. 309–312. IEEE, October 2008

14. Anand, N., Yang, M., Van Duin, J.H.R., Tavasszy, L.: GenCLOn: an ontology for city logistics. Expert Syst. Appl. **39**(15), 11944–11960 (2012)

15. Scheuermann, A., Hoxha, J.: Ontologies for intelligent provision of logistics services. City (2012)

16. Franke, M., Becker, T., Gogolla, M., Hribernik, K., Thoben, K.-D.: Paper LDIC 2016: transformation mechanisms for the interoperability of logistics artifacts in a job-shop manufacturing environment (2016)

17. Semantic Mediator Front- end Backend (SEMed). https://www.fiware4industry.com/?portfolio=semantic-mediator-semed. Accessed 21 Feb 2020

18. GraphQL. https://graphql.org/. Accessed 21 Feb 2020

Tindustry: Matchmaking for I4.0 Components

Udo Kannengiesser[1,2(✉)], Florian Krenn[1], Christian Stary[2], and Pascal Höfler[1]

[1] Compunity GmbH, Linz, Austria
{udo.kannengiesser,florian.krenn,pascal.hoefler}@compunity.eu
[2] Institute of Business Informatics – Communications Engineering,
Johannes Kepler University Linz, Linz, Austria
{udo.kannengiesser,christian.stary}@jku.at

Abstract. The development of industry 4.0 (I4.0) systems is increasingly conceptualised as a configuration process during which components are selected and associated to compose a desired system. This paper presents an approach to configuring I4.0 systems in a distributed way involving the various stakeholders. It is termed Tindustry, as it is inspired by concepts from online dating using the app Tinder. In the approach, I4.0 components are "matched" by reciprocal agreement of the respective component owners. The matching of components is embedded in a metaphorical dating process that is aligned with the fundamental activities of configuration design. The Tindustry approach is illustrated using an I4.0 configuration example, demonstrating some of the benefits in a concrete scenario.

Keywords: Tinder · Industry 4.0 · Configuration design · S-BPM

1 Introduction

The large-scale, digital transformation of manufacturing towards industry 4.0 (I4.0) has been the goal of a number of initiatives driven by national governments, research organisations, industry associations and private companies. Their outcomes include reference models, standards and guidelines for I4.0 business models, maturity assessment, system architecture and interaction protocols [1]. What most of them have in common is their focus on the final result of the transformation: What types of functions should the I4.0 system provide, and how should its components interact? Providing uniform answers to these questions is the basis for developing standardised I4.0 components that can flexibly interoperate in a "plug-and-produce" manner, without being restricted to legacy solutions of particular vendors.

A detailed collection of I4.0 system specifications has been published by the initiative *Plattform Industrie 4.0* in Germany. One of them is the Reference Architecture Model Industrie 4.0 (RAMI 4.0) that is now becoming an international standard [2]. One conclusion that can be drawn from reviewing recent publications of *Plattform Industrie 4.0* is that the process of engineering an I4.0 system is increasingly viewed as an instance of configuration. In [1], a basic model of engineering I4.0 systems is described in which physical production assets are firstly selected and augmented with their digital twins. The digital twins include functionalities for information and communication management,

© Springer Nature Switzerland AG 2020
M. Freitag et al. (Eds.): S-BPM ONE 2020, CCIS 1278, pp. 177–194, 2020.
https://doi.org/10.1007/978-3-030-64351-5_12

resulting in standardised I4.0 components. These components are then "orchestrated" to produce the final I4.0 system. The basic idea of orchestrating or configuring systems based on standardised components is well aligned with increasing calls for incremental approaches in digital transformation [3–6]. Breaking down complex engineering tasks into smaller, manageable steps is also needed for continuous adaptation of existing I4.0 systems to new products and services, unexpected events and alterations in the technological or regulatory environment. Using a set of uniform components with standardised (and possibly certified) functionalities can facilitate the engineering process and increase overall system quality.

Although the ideas of configuration design and incremental transformation seem to gain traction in the I4.0 area, there is a scarcity of detailed methods and tools to support this engineering approach. The predominant methodology in production and mechatronic system engineering remains the Vee model [7] – representing the direct opposite approach based on big design up front rather than incremental changes. The lack of agile techniques in I4.0 engineering has been identified as a principal research issue from practitioners and researchers alike [8, 9]. Complexity in production systems has increased [10]. This rise in complexity is caused by the increasing number of components used, the heterogeneity of the components' interfaces (i.e. protocols, abstraction levels) and the complexity of the components themselves [9, 10]. Therefore, it is necessary that current best practices to handle complexity are transferred to the field of cyber-physical (production) systems [9].

This paper proposes an approach for configuring I4.0 systems based on an analogy with online dating. The approach is named "Tindustry 4.0" (or short: Tindustry), as it borrows concepts known from the popular dating app *Tinder*. Tindustry 4.0 provides a lightweight, intuitive tool for collaborative "matching" of components. An overall I4.0 system emerges from the bottom up as an increasing set of components find their interaction partners. Subject-oriented BPM (S-BPM) [11] is used for modelling and validating the interactions in the emerging I4.0 system. The paper presents the concepts of the approach and the current state of implementation.

The paper is structured as follows. Section 2 presents existing work on configuring I4.0 systems, identifying key challenges. Section 3 describes online dating with a focus on concepts used by Tinder, before mapping them onto the world of I4.0 components and developing the Tindustry approach. Section 4 illustrates how Tindustry may be used in a concrete configuration scenario, highlighting some of its benefits. Section 5 concludes the paper with a summary and a discussion of research issues for future work.

2   Configuring Industry 4.0 Systems: Related Work

Cyber-physical systems (CPS), which form the technological basis for I4.0 systems, are inherently distributed, heterogenous systems comprising interconnected components [9]. CPS blur the boundaries not only between the physical and the software world but also between automation and business processes. The heterogeneity of CPS also leads to a higher heterogeneity of the teams designing, implementing and operating these systems. Therefore, the collaboration of different domain experts with different backgrounds gains even more importance than in other engineering projects [9, 12–14]. Although several well-established standards and norms (e.g. IEC 61131, eCl@ss, AutomationML, OPC UA) exist, they are usually focused on particular domains and therefore cannot act as a *lingua franca* in the engineering process. Multiple domains and disciplines still require adjusting vocabularies and knowledge on how to structure data, software, and systems. Several principles should help avoiding inconsistencies throughout design, among them (cf. [15]):

- Service orientation of CPS, offered via the Internet, and based on a service-oriented reference architecture
- Data integration across disciplines, given highly standardized data models and modular engineering processes
- Self-organization, including the flexible adaptation and the ability of CPS to make decisions on their own (decentralization), and to connect systems and people

The latter can be considered most important for engineering. To keep the human in the loop requires understanding and working with digital representations of CPS on different levels of detail, and from different perspectives, including the engineering process and all relevant data. Human-related issues are still considered to be under-represented [16]. Once experts from different disciplines need to cooperate in engineering, not only their inputs need to be aligned, but also a common view of system engineering beyond their domain knowledge needs to be ensured [17, 18].

The distribution of expertise within the engineering team leads to a corresponding distribution of tasks in the engineering process. This aspect is further facilitated by the fine-grained, component-based structure of most I4.0 systems allowing for an easier task separation by encapsulating functions and features using components [12]. One of the proclaimed benefits of this modular engineering approach is the easy integration, reuse and (re-)configuration of separately developed components [19]. Although reconfiguring I4.0 systems has been recognized as a major benefit, it remains a demanding requirement [20]. Currently used engineering methods in this domain do not sufficiently support this reuse and reconfiguration possibility provided by the CPS architecture [9]. The challenges behind I4.0 (re-)configuration, are not only caused by the sheer number of components but also by their "cross-linking" diversity [12]: Interfaces of components can be difficult to understand or detect, which in turn complicates their combination and orchestration.

Configuring a system is a special kind of design process, where all the components needed are available and need to be put together. Traditionally, configuration is based on an inventory providing relevant components for a specific product design [21]. According to Brown [22], the process of configuring generally encompasses three classes of activities:

- *Selecting*: is concerned with choosing components.
- *Associating*: establishes relationships between the components. There are two subclasses of associating:

  - *Relating*: establishes abstract (or "logical") relationships (e.g. "next to", "touching" or "connected to").

– *Arranging*: establishes concrete relationships, by specifying more detailed attributes of the relationship.
• *Evaluating*: deals with compatibility testing and goal satisfaction testing.

Selecting and associating can also be found in the I4.0 configuration approach proposed in [1], where it is augmented with the additional step of digital twinning, leading to model as reference representation of cyber-physical systems. This I4.0 configuration process utilizes the concept of the asset administration shell (AAS) to represent an asset's information and interactions in a standardized and semantically adequate way. It should facilitate interoperability engineering and automated interaction through consistent vertical and horizontal integration [23]. Domain experts may generate a semantic description of plants, machines and components, by transforming an information model from OPC Unified Architecture (OPC UA) into an AAS [23].

At the core of I4.0 modelling are communication-enabled components of the shop floor, as they are the most important source of operational, condition and process data. Configuration needs to address information models as they represent aligned data. Transformed data for automated interaction have to take into account common industrial communication protocols and frameworks for application development. Since digital twins represent the points of reference for configuration, all components, including physical objects need to be part of I4.0 models. Their properties and capabilities need to be aligned and processed in digital support environments for I4.0 engineering.

Bauer et al. [24] addressed automated configuration requiring some evaluation. The proposed architecture follows RAMI 4.0 and enables I4.0 systems to be automatically configured from scratch and reconfigured based on self-orchestration and decision-making capabilities. The data foundation is the set of provided I4.0 component vendor functionalities that are filled into pre-structured configuration templates. These templates are processed by machine learning algorithms. The template information can be enriched with operational logic for component orchestration logic and agent behaviour.

Concluding, engineering methods and tools support the (re-)configuration in the industry 4.0 domain face three key challenges:

1. Technical barriers due to the complexity of configuration tasks (e.g. interface identification, interface interpretation, number of components)
2. Large decision space based on the high number of available and/or required components that may be selected for configuration
3. Distributed engineering process involving engineers from multiple domains with different (technical) backgrounds.

3   An Approach Inspired by Online Dating

In this section, we present how online dating can be used as a source of inspiration for dealing with the key challenges in I4.0 configuration identified in Sect. 2. Some of the key concepts of online dating in general, and the dating app *Tinder* in particular, are then transferred into the world of Industry 4.0 to form a matchmaking approach for I4.0 components.

3.1 What Can We Learn from Tinder?

Different meanings are associated with the notion of dating. Most commonly, dating refers to the trial period of a romantic relationship (before committing to a permanent relationship), or to a stage in someone's life in which romantic relationships with different people are actively pursued.[1] For the purposes of this paper, we view dating as a comprehensive process: from mingling with and selecting potential mates to engaging in a short- or long-term relationship.

Internet-based support for dating has been available for around 20 years. Its main functions include facilitating access to potential partners, supporting online communication and providing automated matching algorithms [25]. The popularity of online dating was boosted since the 2010s with the advent of smartphones. Numerous dating apps were developed, one of the first of which was Tinder[2]. Launched in 2012, it is today the most popular dating app in the United States[3] and presumably in many other parts of the world. Some of the distinguishing features of Tinder include:

- *Focus on physical appearance*: The most prominent visual element on users' profiles is their (portrait) photo, labelled with their name and age, as shown in Fig. 1. Free text can be added, which is often used for describing oneself and what one looks for in others. Users can also include links to a connected social media account.
- *Location awareness*: Users must specify a radius around their current location within which they want to search for mates. The profiles of other users can be viewed only if they are located within the desired distance range (besides being of the desired gender within a specified age bracket).
- *Dichotomous selection*: Users are prompted to take simple Yes/No decisions when being provided with the profile of a potential mate. The decision is effectuated using a simple "swiping" gesture on the touchscreen (right for "like", left for "nope") or, alternatively, corresponding buttons underneath the profile (see Fig. 1).
- *Distributed matching*: A "match" between two users is established when both of them mutually "like" each other – analogous to the logical AND operator.
- *Chatting follows matching*: Users can communicate with each other (via Tinder's chat messenger) only after they establish a match.

With Tinder, an overall dating process emerges that comprises the following steps:

1. *Mingling*: corresponds to accessing the online dating platform by creating a user profile, specifying a search radius and desired partner characteristics (age, gender).
2. *Matching*: establishes mutual interest in exploring a potential relationship. It is the starting point for getting in direct contact through chatting.
3. *Chatting*: allows getting to know each other, i.e. each other's interests, goals, biographies, characteristics etc. Chatting is done initially online on Tinder, and later in an offline environment (i.e., in the real world).

---

[1] https://en.wikipedia.org/wiki/Dating#Different_meanings_of_the_term.

[2] https://tinder.com/.

[3] https://www.statista.com/statistics/826778/most-popular-dating-apps-by-audience-size-usa/.

Fig. 1. Example of a Tinder user profile and the "swiping" motion (Source: https://en.wikipedia. org/wiki/Tinder_(app))

4. *Reality check*: allows potential partners to experience whether they are compatible in real life, by shifting from just talking about things towards doing things together.

These steps are consistent with those in Brown's [22] configuration process and its extension to I4.0 configuration described in [1]. Specifically, mingling (step 1) maps onto creating the digital twin, matching (step 2) maps onto selecting components and establishing abstract relationships between them (i.e., "relating"), chatting (step 3) maps onto establishing specific relationships (i.e., "arranging") between the components, and reality check (step 4) maps onto evaluating the configuration (i.e., compatibility testing and goal satisfaction testing).

Assuming that the dating process can be seen as an instance of I4.0 configuration design, we can examine how Tinder addresses the challenges identified in Sect. 2:

- *Technical barriers*: Tinder is very simple and can be used with the most basic IT skills. The swiping gesture is understood and routinely applied by millions of smartphone users. Furthermore, there are a number of motivational features in Tinder that may even lead to addictive use; they include immediate positive feedback after a match, correlation between the time spent on the app and the amount of positive feedback received, and a seemingly unlimited number of potential mates making it hard to stop swiping [26].
- *Large decision space*: The large number of Tinder users worldwide leads to a very large set of possible candidates for matching. Even when restricting the search radius to just a few kilometres, thousands of profiles may be returned when using Tinder in a

big city. This issue is dealt with by the dichotomous selection mechanism: A Yes/No choice needs to be made for every profile shown before one can view and make a choice on the next one. Choices in Tinder are often done intuitively, based on the emotional response evoked by a profile photo rather than by any conscious analysis of the text describing the candidate. Such an intuitive, rapid way of thinking increases cognitive efficiency in decision making, as it radically reduces the set of options that would need to be considered when using only analytical thinking [27]. A match can always be reconsidered afterwards and easily undone via Tinder's "unmatch" function.

- *Distributed configuration tasks*: In Tinder, there are usually as many users as there are profiles (although some users, for whatever reason, may decide to use multiple virtual identities). Therefore, matching always involves two different users that need to mutually like each other. Their individual choices are completely independent of each other: They can occur at different times and at different physical locations (within the limits of their search radius). In addition, multiple matches can occur at the same time within the Tinder network, by different pairs of users. There is no single, central entity determining all the matches in the network.

3.2 Adapting the Tinder Dating Process to I4.0 Components

In this section we apply some of the concepts of Tinder to the I4.0 configuration process. This requires a few adaptations. Unlike humans, I4.0 components are not capable of selecting other components to interact with – at least, they are not assumed to have this kind of intelligence. The users of Tindustry are assumed to be the human owners of the respective I4.0 components rather than the I4.0 components themselves. For example, a robot expert would establish matches on behalf of a robot, and an automotive engineer would establish matches on behalf of a car body.

Other adaptations of the Tinder dating process relate to the individual steps of I4.0 configuration. They are elaborated in the remainder of this section.

Creating the Digital Twin (Mingling). User profiles in Tinder are kept very simple, mainly highlighting the users' physical appearance. Such an approach may be useful for I4.0 components too, given that many of them have a physical embodiment that can easily be recognized by domain experts. In addition, physical compatibility is an important aspect for production systems including I4.0 systems. Therefore, an iconic representation (which may be a photo or a 2D/3D model) may be used as part of the digital twin for purposes of "mingling" with other components. In the case of software components that do not have a unique physical embodiment, symbolic representations (e.g. text) or graphical metaphors (e.g., cylinders representing database components) may be used.

In the production context, there is an increased focus on function rather than on pure physical appearance. The equivalent of functional models in Tinder can be viewed as free-text descriptions one can use to (directly or indirectly) "advertise" what one can offer to potential mates. Examples include providing loyalty, financial stability, affinity for outdoor activities etc. The notion of function is generally understood as the teleology of a system or component (i.e., "what it is for") [28]. A standardised taxonomy of functions related to manufacturing processes (e.g. "drilling" and "milling") [29] may be used for function labelling in Tindustry 4.0 digital twins.

An example of a Tindustry profile for a welding robot, which comprises a photo of its structure and additional text describing its function, is shown in Fig. 2.

Fig. 2. Mockup showing a possible Tindustry profile for a robot

The information shown on the profile can be augmented with more detailed descriptions. In particular, input-output behaviours may be added to provide information about the way in which the given function may be realised, i.e. what kinds of material, energy or signal must be provided to the component and what kinds of material, energy or signal the component will produce in response. Such descriptions are widely used for functional modelling in the engineering domain [30, 31] and correspond to the notion of subjects in S-BPM interaction diagrams [32].

Selecting and Relating (Matching). The distributed selection mechanism can directly be transferred from Tinder to Tindustry. This includes the concept of a match requiring two reciprocal, positive decisions by potential interaction partners. It may also include some of Tinder's typical UI features such as the "swiping" motion, to make Tindustry an easy and enjoyable experience for domain experts.

One additional factor needs to be considered: the usefulness of algorithms restricting the set of profiles shown to a user and the order in which they are shown, aiming to increase the likelihood and therefore the speed of matches. Unlike other dating apps, Tinder's algorithms are fairly open and not based on compatibility scores.[4] While such an openness may have advantages in the case of Tinder, there may be good reasons to be more restrictive in the world of I4.0 configuration. For instance, a car body may be interested in mating only with those machine components whose function is welding

---

[4] https://www.theverge.com/2019/3/15/18267772/tinder-elo-score-desirability-algorithm-how-works.

or painting but not lathing or chemical etching. Without any automated preselection of potentially compatible components, domain experts are likely to be overwhelmed with large quantities of Tindustry profiles irrelevant for the configuration task at hand.

An algorithm for the preselection of potential matches can be devised based on the *functional basis* taxonomy of engineering functions developed by NIST [31], where functions are represented as transformations of material, energy or signal flows. Excerpts of the taxonomy are shown in Table 1 (transformations) and Table 2 (flows). A reasoning algorithm may use the functional basis to find components whose input and output flows are mutually compatible. For example, if component A requires rotational energy as input, component B may be found as compatible if its output includes that kind of energy. In contrast, component C whose output is translational energy may be considered incompatible.

In addition to this basic feasibility check, machine learning (ML) may be used to capture the usefulness of feasible component pairings. A suitable ML technique may be association analysis [33] that can extract correlations in a dataset. It may be used for identifying groups of components that are often matched together. For example, a component having the function to "optimize energy consumption" may frequently match with components having the functions to "measure energy consumption" and to "choose energy provider". Assuming a configuration task in which a match has already been established for two of these functions, a component having the third function would then be shown among the first profiles for further matching.

Arranging (Chatting). Matches are usually based on the assumption that a high-level compatibility exists between the components involved, considering the types of material, energy or signal flow to be exchanged. In a subsequent step, compatibility is to be established on a more detailed level, corresponding to Brown's [22] notion of "arranging": establishing specific (as opposed to abstract) relationships. This involves specialising the flow descriptions into exact interface specifications. For example, a flow of solid objects (one of the material subclasses, see Table 2) between two components may be specialised to include specific details of these objects, such as their physical dimensions, weight, colour and temperature.

Specifying interfaces is a collaborative activity involving the respective component owners. A major part of it is the negotiation of meaning, given that their individual viewpoints and terminologies may diverge. Approaches exist that can be used for the alignment of viewpoints in the industry 4.0 context [14].

Evaluating (Reality Check). After specifying the interfaces, a reality check is performed to test whether the interplay between the components works as expected. In the world of production engineering, this evaluation is increasingly carried out in a virtual reality (i.e., by means of simulation) rather than in the physical reality. This is because physical production resources are expensive and their installation on the shopfloor is disruptive, in the worst case leading to a complete stillstand of production.

The (virtual) reality check thus needs to be occur in a separate environment without affecting the physical production plant. At the same time, the effort required to move the digital twin between virtual and physical environments needs to be minimal, in order to ensure seamless engineering, simulation and reconfiguration.

Table 1. Transformations (excerpt) defined in the functional basis [31]

Class (Primary)	Secondary	Tertiary	Correspondents
Branch	Separate		Isolate, sever, disjoin
		Divide	Detach, isolate, release, sort, split, disconnect, subtract
		Extract	Refine, filter, purify, percolate, strain, clear
		Remove	Cut, drill, lathe, polish, sand
	Distribute		Diffuse, dispel, disperse, dissipate, diverge, scatter
Channel	Import		Form entrance, allow, input, capture
	Export		Dispose, eject, emit, empty, remove, destroy, eliminate
	Transfer		Carry, deliver
		Transport	Advance, lift, move
		Transmit	Conduct, convey
	Guide		Direct, shift, steer, straighten, switch
		Translate	Move, relocate
		Rotate	Spin, turn
		Allow DOF	Constrain, unfasten, unlock

A basis of such an approach is formed by the emerging standard architecture for I4.0 components [2]. I4.0 components are composed of an asset (i.e., any physical or virtual object of value for a company, including human operators, production machines, documents, workpieces, etc.) and an asset administration shell (AAS) that encapsulates the asset. This allows constructing modular I4.0 systems and is consistent with the notion of subjects in S-BPM [34].

The AAS provides a set of functionalities for standardised communication with other I4.0 components and for representing and managing the digital twin of the asset. The digital twin is organized in the following layers: The business layer includes interactions and behaviours of I4.0 components, in addition to contextual factors from the business environment. The functional layer includes a component's functions and services. The information layer includes various data models describing the component and its interfaces. The communication layer includes standard interfaces for message exchange between I4.0 components. The integration layer includes digital signals from the physical world.

The integration layer allows plugging in different assets inside the AAS. As shown in Fig. 3, physical assets (i.e. the actual production resources as they are used on the shopfloor) can be replaced with (virtual) test assets allowing test execution in a virtual environment separated from the productive environment. Substituting productive assets with test assets requires only minimal changes in the integration layer.

Table 2. Flows (excerpt) defined in the functional basis [31]

Class (Primary)	Secondary	Tertiary	Correspondents
Material	Human		Hand, foot, head
	Gas		Homogeneous
	Liquid		Incompressible, compressible, homogenous
	Solid	Object	Rigid-body, elastic-body, widget
		Particulate	
		Composite	
	Plasma		
	Mixture		
Signal	Status	Auditory	Tone, word
		Olfactory	
		Tactile	Temperature, pressure, roughness
		Taste	
		Visual	Position, displacement
	Control	Analog	Oscillatory
		Discrete	Binary
Energy	Human		
	Mechanical	Rotational	
		Translational	
	Pneumatic		

After integrating the test asset, the reality check can be realised by executing the component interactions step by step. This is similar to the notion of process validation in S-BPM [11]. As the number of components and interactions can be very large in an I4.0 system, there needs to be automated support for test execution and metrics for test management [8]. Research is currently under way by the authors to address these issues [35].

4   Application Example for Tindustry

In this section we illustrate the Tindustry approach using a simple example. A production company is assumed to have a (very) small I4.0 system already configured. It consists of only two I4.0 components, as shown in Fig. 4: a smart meter for measuring the electrical power consumption of a machine, and an SAP system for recording the consumption data.

It is now assumed that the company wants to adapt its production process to changes in electricity cost. This is because it has been notified by the electricity provider of a new, dynamic pricing model penalising extended periods of load peaks. The company decides

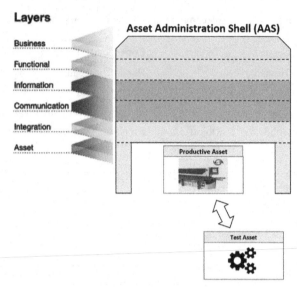

Fig. 3. Using the layered architecture of I4.0 components (according to RAMI 4.0) to replace the productive asset with a test asset

to extend the I4.0 system in a way to autonomously reduce the speed of production machines depending on real-time consumption data and current production goals. At this stage, the production manager has only a rough idea about which components may be useful for reconfiguring the existing system. For each of a number of possible components and all existing components a Tindustry profile is created and a dedicated domain expert is selected as the respective "component owner". After downloading and registering in the Tindustry app, the component owners are now ready to begin the reconfiguration process by swiping possible partner components.

Fig. 4. Initial state of an I4.0 system configuration

An algorithm calculates matching probabilities between different component combinations, based on ML techniques and compatibility analysis using input-output flows as described in Sect. 3. The probabilities are then used for determining the order in which potential partners are shown to component owners. In the example shown in Fig. 5, three likely matches are identified and ranked based on different probability scores.

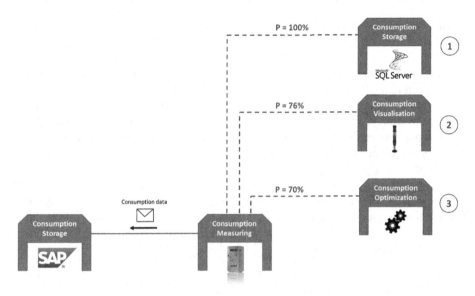

Fig. 5. Three potential matches are automatically suggested and ranked based using probability scores (P)

We assume for our example that the owner of "consumption measuring" selects the third component shown in the Tindustry app ("consumption optimization") as desired interaction partner. Similarly, the owner of "consumption optimization" swipes right when being provided with the profile of "consumption measuring". This produces a match between the two components. The resulting system configuration is depicted in Fig. 6.

Fig. 6. State of the I4.0 system configuration after matching the components "Consumption Measuring" and "Consumption Optimization"

The component owners can use the app in their own time, whenever their busy day-to-day schedules allow it. Matching between two components does not require their owners to be online at the same time. In addition, several options for matching may be explored, as component owners can swipe right on multiple possible component profiles that may represent alternative or complementary interaction partners. In the example, the owner of "consumption optimization" searches for complementary interaction partners. Here, the component "machine actuator" looks like a promising potential match, because it may use the optimization results produced by "consumption optimization" to bring about an actual effect – namely, a modified machine speed – on the production process. We therefore assume that the owner of "consumption optimization" swipes right on the Tindustry app.

A dashboard-style user interface for the role of I4.0 system owner continuously shows the progress of the evolving system configuration. This is done using a Subject Interaction Diagram (SID) that has been extended to distinguish matches that have been reciprocally established and those that have been only unilaterally proposed. A screenshot of the current SID implementation is shown in Fig. 7. It can be seen that the match between "consumption optimization" and "machine actuator" has not yet been confirmed in the example.

As our research in the Tindustry approach is still on-going, the example use case terminates here. The subsequent steps in the configuration process – relating the components in terms of specific interface definitions and evaluating the matches by executing them in a virtual environment – will be described and illustrated in future papers once more research results are available.

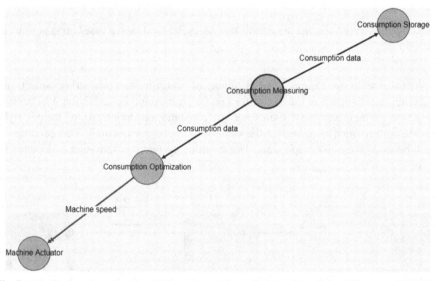

Fig. 7. Monitoring the emerging I4.0 system using a Subject Interaction Diagram (SID) that includes established (i.e. reciprocally selected) matches (represented as black arrows) and unilaterally proposed matches (represented as red arrows) between components (Color figure online)

What the example already demonstrates are the beginnings of how Tindustry can be beneficial for I4.0 configuration tasks with respect to the issues identified in Sect. 2:

- *Technical barriers*: can be assumed to be reduced, at least in the early stages of matching components, based on the simplicity and ease of use of the app. Here we refer back to the mockup example shown in Fig. 2, as the development of a productive app for Tindustry has not yet begun in this research project.

- *Large decision space*: The interplay of automated matching algorithms and intuitive decision-making by domain experts can quickly generate matches in a large pool of components. Domain experts are free to explore several alternatives in parallel (breadth-first strategy) or concentrate on a single alternative (depth-first strategy), depending on their individual expertise and their view of the current configuration task. Strategies can be modified dynamically, because matches can be quickly undone and previously refused matches (through left-swipes) may be presented to users again.
- *Distributed configuration tasks*: Although domain experts may be distributed in time and space, they can jointly produce a consistent system configuration using Tindustry. Their collaboration is completely asynchronous and does not interfere with their daily work routines. This is in contrast to the common "workshop approach" of system development, where all stakeholders need to find a common time and place for a project meeting.

5 Conclusion

In this paper an approach to the configuration of I4.0 systems is presented that is inspired by concepts of online dating using the Tinder app. As was shown conceptually and using an example, Tindustry can address some of the common challenges of I4.0 configuration, including technical barriers, large decision spaces, and task distribution. Bluntly speaking, this approach can make complex I4.0 system configuration look and feel like an everyday activity: forming and evolving social relationships. It is a capability that most of us have, independently of differences in cultural or professional backgrounds. While there are various societal rules and conventions impacting our behaviour, relationships are built at the most elementary level under control of two interacting individuals. In the world of industry 4.0, this may be a curse and a blessing. It is a curse because the local configurations established may not be effective at a larger system level. For example, the match between a measuring and an optimization component may be useless if the goal of the overall system is to predict (not optimize) maintenance times. However, the primacy of local control in industry 4.0 configuration can also be a blessing, because there is no need to do any "big design up front" involving lengthy requirements analyses at the system and subsystem levels. In many cases, new I4.0 systems are the outcomes of incremental changes to an existing system (as was presented in the example in Sect. 4) rather than greenfield development. Approaches based on local changes are arguably better suited here.

The general conflict between top-down and bottom-up approaches to system configuration has been studied in multi-agent system research at least since the 1980s. For building engineering applications including in I4.0 there needs to be a useful combination of the two approaches, by agents taking global goals into account in their local reasoning [36]. The representation of the evolving system using SIDs in the Tindustry approach can be seen as a first step towards considering global system goals. More work needs to be done to develop a governance framework around its use by stakeholders. For example, it may be used for allowing some form of top-down modifications of locally formed matches in case they turn out ineffective for given system goals. More thought also needs to be spent on the representation of non-functional goals, both on local and global levels.

While a number of fundamental research questions arise from this work, the next steps undertaken by the authors focus on the implementation of the concepts presented here. This will provide a validation of the basic ideas and a testbed for experiments that can help addressing some of the deeper research issues.

Acknowledgment. The research reported in this paper was funded by the Austrian Research Promotion Agency (FFG) via project no. 874906 (LINK).

References

1. Heidel, R., Hoffmeister, M., Hankel, M., Döbrich, U.: Industrie 4.0 - Basiswissen RAMI 4.0 : Referenzarchitekturmodell mit Industrie 4.0-Komponente. DIN Deutsches Institut für Normung e.V., Berlin, Germany (2017)
2. IEC: IEC PAS 63088:2017 Smart manufacturing - Reference architecture model industry 4.0 (RAMI4.0). International Electrotechnical Commission, Geneva, Switzerland (2017)
3. Moser, C., Kannengiesser, U.: Incremental implementation of automated guided vehicle-based logistics using S-BPM: experience report of a digitalization project at ENGEL Austria. In: S-BPM ONE 2019: Proceedings of the 11th International Conference on Subject-Oriented Business Process Management, Seville, Spain. Association for Computing Machinery (2019). https://doi.org/10.1145/3329007.3329015
4. VDMA: Guideline Industrie 4.0: Guiding principles for the implementation of Industrie 4.0 in small and medium sized businesses. Verband Deutscher Maschinen- und Anlagenbau (VDMA), Frankfurt, Germany (2016)
5. PwC: Global Digital Operations Study 2018. https://www.pwc.com/gx/en/industries/industry-4-0.html. Accessed 11 Feb 2020
6. Kannengiesser, U., Neubauer, M., Heininger, R.: Subject-oriented BPM as the glue for integrating enterprise processes in smart factories. In: Ciuciu, I., et al. (eds.) OTM 2015. LNCS, vol. 9416, pp. 77–86. Springer, Cham (2015). https://doi.org/10.1007/978-3-319-26138-6_11
7. VDI: VDI 2206 - Design Methodology for Mechatronic Systems. Verein Deutscher Ingenieure, Düsseldorf, Germany (2004). https://doi.org/10.1002/mawe.19740050417
8. VDI: Testing of Networked Systems for Industrie 4.0. Verein Deutscher Ingenieure, Düsseldorf, Germany (2018)
9. Harrison, R., Vera, D., Ahmad, B.: Engineering methods and tools for cyber-physical automation systems. Proc. IEEE **104**, 973–985 (2016). https://doi.org/10.1109/JPROC.2015.2510665
10. Aicher, T., Schutz, D., Vogel-Heuser, B.: Consistent engineering information model for mechatronic components in production automation engineering. In: IECON 2014 - 40th Annual Conference of the IEEE Industrial Electronics Society, pp. 2532–2537. IEEE (2014). https://doi.org/10.1109/IECON.2014.7048862
11. Fleischmann, A., Schmidt, W., Stary, C., Obermeier, S., Börger, E.: Subject-Oriented Business Process Management, 1st edn. Springer, Heidelberg (2012). https://doi.org/10.1007/978-3-642-32392-8
12. Paetzold, K.: Product and systems engineering/CA* tool chains. In: Biffl, S., Lüder, A., Gerhard, D. (eds.) Multi-Disciplinary Engineering for Cyber-Physical Production Systems, pp. 27–62. Springer, Cham (2017). https://doi.org/10.1007/978-3-319-56345-9_2
13. Biffl, S., Gerhard, D., Lüder, A.: Introduction to the multi-disciplinary engineering for cyber-physical production systems. In: Biffl, S., Lüder, A., Gerhard, D. (eds.) Multi-Disciplinary Engineering for Cyber-Physical Production Systems. LNCS, pp. 1–24. Springer, Cham (2017). https://doi.org/10.1007/978-3-319-56345-9_1

14. Kannengiesser, U., Müller, H.: Multi-level, viewpoint-oriented engineering of cyber-physical production systems: an approach based on industry 4.0, system architecture and semantic web standards. In: Proceedings - 44th Euromicro Conference on Software Engineering and Advanced Applications, SEAA 2018, Prague, Czech Republic, pp. 331–334. IEEE (2018). https://doi.org/10.1109/SEAA.2018.00061
15. Vogel-Heuser, B., Hess, D.: Guest editorial industry 4.0–prerequisites and visions. IEEE Trans. Autom. Sci. Eng. **13**, 411–413 (2016)
16. Sharpe, R., van Lopik, K., Neal, A., Goodall, P., Conway, P.P., West, A.A.: An industrial evaluation of an Industry 4.0 reference architecture demonstrating the need for the inclusion of security and human components. Comput. Ind. **108**, 37–44 (2019)
17. Kenett, R.S., Swarz, R.S., Zonnenshain, A. (eds.): Systems Engineering in the Fourth Industrial Revolution: Big Data, Novel Technologies, and Modern Systems Engineering. Wiley, Hoboken (2020)
18. Porrmann, T., Essmann, R., Colombo, A.W.: Development of an event-oriented, cloud-based SCADA system using a microservice architecture under the RAMI4.0 specification: lessons learned. In: IECON 2017 - 43rd Annual Conference of the IEEE Industrial Electronics Society, pp. 3441–3448 (2017). https://doi.org/10.1109/IECON.2017.8216583
19. Khaitan, S.K., McCalley, J.D.: Design techniques and applications of cyberphysical systems: a survey. IEEE Syst. J. **9**, 350–365 (2014)
20. Thramboulidis, K., Bochalis, P., Bouloumpasis, J.: A framework for MDE of IoT-based manufacturing cyber-physical systems. In: Proceedings of the Seventh International Conference on the Internet of Things - IoT 2017, pp. 1–8. ACM Press, New York (2017). https://doi.org/10.1145/3131542.3131554
21. Sabin, D., Weigel, R.: Product configuration frameworks - a survey. IEEE Intell. Syst. Appl. **13**, 42–49 (1998)
22. Brown, D.C.: Defining configuring. Artif. Intell. Eng. Des. Anal. Manuf. **12**, 301–305 (1998). https://doi.org/10.1017/s0890060498124034
23. Fuchs, J., Schmidt, J., Franke, J., Rehman, K., Sauer, M., Karnouskos, S.: I4.0-compliant integration of assets utilizing the Asset Administration Shell. In: 2019 24th IEEE International Conference on Emerging Technologies and Factory Automation (ETFA), pp. 1243–1247 (2019). https://doi.org/10.1109/ETFA.2019.8869255
24. Bauer, D.A., Mäkiö, J.: Hybrid cloud – architecture for administration shells with RAMI4.0 using Actor4j. In: 2019 IEEE 17th International Conference on Industrial Informatics (INDIN), pp. 79–86 (2019). https://doi.org/10.1109/INDIN41052.2019.8972075
25. Finkel, E.J., Eastwick, P.W., Karney, B.R., Reis, H.T., Sprecher, S.: Online dating: a critical analysis from the perspective of psychological science. Psychol. Sci. Public Interest **13**, 3–66 (2012). https://doi.org/10.1177/1529100612436522
26. Orosz, G., Tóth-Király, I., Bothe, B., Melher, D.: Too many swipes for today: the development of the problematic tinder use scale (PTUS). J. Behav. Addict. **5**, 518–523 (2016). https://doi.org/10.1556/2006.5.2016.016
27. Kahneman, D.: Thinking, Fast and Slow. Penguin Books, London (2011)
28. Gero, J.S., Kannengiesser, U.: An ontology of situated design teams. Artif. Intell. Eng. Des. Anal. Manuf. **21**, 295–308 (2007). https://doi.org/10.1017/S0890060407000297
29. Förster, R., Förster, A.: Einteilung der Fertigungsverfahren nach DIN 8580. In: Einführung in die Fertigungstechnik, pp. 23–136. Springer Vieweg, Heidelberg (2018). https://doi.org/10.1007/978-3-662-54702-1_2
30. Stone, R.B., Wood, K.L.: Development of a functional basis for design. J. Mech. Des. Trans. ASME **122**, 359–370 (2000). https://doi.org/10.1115/1.1289637
31. Hirtz, J., Stone, R.B., McAdams, D.A., Szykman, S., Wood, K.L.: A functional basis for engineering design: reconciling and evolving previous efforts. Res. Eng. Des. **13**, 65–82 (2002). https://doi.org/10.1007/s00163-001-0008-3

32. Fleischmann, A., Kannengiesser, U., Schmidt, W., Stary, C.: Subject-oriented modeling and execution of multi-agent business processes. In: Proceedings - 2013 IEEE/WIC/ACM International Conference on Intelligent Agent Technology, IAT 2013, pp. 138–145. IEEE Computer Society (2013). https://doi.org/10.1109/WI-IAT.2013.102

33. Agrawal, R., Imieliński, T., Swami, A.: Mining association rules between sets of items in large databases. ACM SIGMOD Rec. **22**, 207–216 (1993). https://doi.org/10.1145/170036.170072

34. Kannengiesser, U., Müller, H.: Industry 4.0 standardisation: where does S-BPM fit? In: S-BPM One 2018: 10th International Conference on Subject-Oriented Business Process Management, Linz, Austria. Association for Computing Machinery (2018). https://doi.org/10.1145/3178248.3178255

35. Kannengiesser, U., Krenn, F., Kornexl, M., Stary, C.: Testing of networked systems in industry 4.0: an agile, situated approach. In: AUTOMATION – 21. Leitkongress der Mess- und Automatisierungstechnik. VDI Verlag GmbH (2020)

36. Gero, J.S., Kannengiesser, U.: Towards agent-based product modelling. In: Borg, J.C., Farrugia, P.J., Camilleri, K.P. (eds.) Knowledge Intensive Design Technology. ITIFIP, vol. 136, pp. 3–17. Springer, Boston (2004). https://doi.org/10.1007/978-0-387-35708-9_1

Autonomy and Process Design

Richard Heininger[(⊠)]

Institute of Business Informatics, Johannes Kepler University Linz, Linz, Austria
richard.heininger@jku.at

Abstract. Openness is essential for autonomous actors to interact with others. The 2030 vision of Industry 4.0 includes autonomy as a key aspect and IoT as an essential technical component. Process design must take these developments into account.

Keywords: Openness · Industry 4.0 · Internet of Things · IoT · Process modelling

1 Introduction

This reflection paper summarizes the author's thoughts on openness, autonomy and process design. It is intended to contribute to (or start) the discussion on openness in the field of (subject-oriented) process design. The aim is to outline a research agenda on autonomy and process design.

Let us think for a moment of a murmuration - the flocking behaviour of starlings. Hundreds, if not thousands, of starlings gather in the evening and form huge formations in the air. We conclude from the observations of researchers that these formation flights usually never lead to crashes or collisions. The astonishing thing is that these formations do not need a leader and do not involve any central coordination. The starlings only have to follow a few simple rules. This is how one of the greatest collaborations in nature is created. It is an openness that involves sharing all kinds of information. And there is a real sense of interdependence that the individual birds somehow understand that their interests are in the interest of the collective [13]. In this way, following simple rules results in emergent behaviour [16].

2 Openness

A murmuration needs openness to cope with this specific situation. With respect to humans, openness describes the characteristic to deal with someone or something in an unbiased and willing way. It also means to communicate and act honestly without reservation. Openness to experience is one of the five main dimensions of a personality according to the five-factor model and has been researched extensively in psychology [15]. This also applies to the relation between openness and organizations, which has also been the subject of research for decades [3,11].

© Springer Nature Switzerland AG 2020
M. Freitag et al. (Eds.): S-BPM ONE 2020, CCIS 1278, pp. 195–199, 2020.
https://doi.org/10.1007/978-3-030-64351-5_13

Tapscott and Williams are convinced that openness revolutionizes all areas of our society [14].

However, openness can also lead to negative results. The Corona pandemic, for example, has shown that openness can have very worrying effects on health [12]. In the literature, openness is therefore often treated as a paradoxical phenomenon [4].

3 2030 Vision Plattform Industrie 4.0

Accordingly, openness plays a decisive role in the future of the manufacturing industry. Scholars and practitioners alike are currently working on the research, development and introduction of Industry 4.0 [5]. In its vision for the year 2030, Plattform Industrie 4.0 and its partners show how Industry 4.0 can look in the future. The 2030 vision introduces the concepts of autonomy, interoperability and sustainability as key factors for the implementation of Industry 4.0 [10] (Fig. 1).

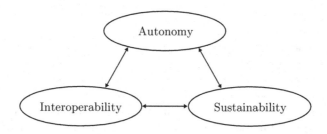

Fig. 1. Key factors for 2030 vision industrie 4.0 [10]

Autonomy stands for the self-determination of all actors participating in the market. They make independent decisions and compete fairly. Autonomy requires a digital infrastructure, security and safety, and technology-neutral research, development and innovation [10].

Interoperability therefore has an important role in Industry 4.0, as products and services are offered through a network of actors. This results in complex and decentralized business processes that can only be realized through a high degree of interoperability. Interoperability forces the use of standards, the introduction of a regulatory framework, and the use of artificial intelligence (Smart Data) in the decentralized units [10].

Sustainability concerns the social dimension of the 2030 vision. Industry 4.0 should, on the one hand, pursue goals of economic, ecological and social sustainability and, on the other hand, automatically strengthen these goals through its design. These include a decent workplace, social participation and the mitigation of climate change [10].

The three key factors are directly related to openness. In terms of autonomy, openness is a bridging function. It enables the communication and collaboration of autonomous units or agents. Although interoperability is achieved through standards and frameworks, open interfaces also promote cooperation. Sustainability and openness are closely linked; we can recognize this, for example, in the demand for social participation [10].

4   Process Design

With regard to process design, we focus on the key factor of autonomy. Interoperability is achieved through technical implementation and sustainability informs all phases (activity bundles) of the open control cycle [2, p. 30f]. Process design includes the activities analysis and modelling. When analyzing processes, we collect the tasks performed, their sequence, the data used, and the stakeholders involved (roles). Subsequently, the collected process knowledge is modelled. In this phase, the observed reality must be reduced to the notation of the model. In this abstraction, modelers focus specifically on the autonomy of the individual actors in the process as this is the focus of consideration in subject-oriented business process management (S-BPM) [2].

We recognise individual, autonomous actors through their behaviour and their interactions within the process. These are participants in the process, such as employees or workers, i.e. members of the workforce [2]. Process design in relation to Industry 4.0 must address one aspect in particular: the ability of the workforce to embrace new technologies, such as deep learning and IoT applications. According to Gartner, this will be the key to competitive advantage [9].

IoT applications, like all process participants from the perspective of S-BPM, are autonomous actors that must be considered in future process design [1]. The modelling of IoT applications requires both knowledge of IoT functionalities and knowledge of possible entry points into the business process. The latter is part of the process knowledge of those directly involved in the process. Therefore we suggest that these actors should actively participate and contribute to the process design of IoT applications. Research has shown that non-expert modelers are capable of doing process elicitation and modelling [7].

5   RFID Building Blocks

Non-experts usually do not model business processes or IoT applications. They find it cumbersome, have no time for it and see no immediate added value. Building blocks help to overcome barriers to entry [7]. They have a unique identifier and can even be used interactively via various technologies, such as table-top interfaces. However, the IT-supported, automatic processing of the models created with building blocks involves a high logistical effort. This is mainly due to the table-top interfaces [8].

Table-top interfaces, also known as modelling tables, allow the involvement of non-experts in an inviting environment. IT support is almost completely hidden and modelers are not distracted by technical shortcomings. It promotes communication, as people do not stare at a display, but can look at each other [8]. However, the need for a modelling table is less valuable if the modelling object focuses less on communication between people.. The organization of such an environment is a huge effort that is no longer worthwhile for other modeling tasks, such as modeling IoT applications.

Consequently, we derived the idea for our prototype from these conditions. Unlike a modeling table, it is an easily portable modelling environment with intelligent building blocks that can be set up and used at the desk. The building blocks are modularly expandable and the manufacturer of the building blocks strives to provide easy to develop and cost-effective IoT devices [6]. By means of RFID, the building bricks can be clearly assigned. We assume that there is a computer at the workplace that can visualize the model. Additionally, non-experts can learn about IoT applications.

For example, non-experts can learn IoT concepts by playing around with the building blocks. First of all, they understand that all the building blocks are interconnected as in IoT applications. Second, they grasp the extensibility of IoT devices. Third, they are able to describe (or even develop) the behaviour of the devices. And finally, people who were not experts at the beginning will understand the big picture when the behavior of their IoT application emerges.

6   Conclusion

The murmuration, the flocking behaviour of starlings, is an analogy to the imaginable 2030 vision of Industry 4.0. Like the individual players in the market, birds are autonomous. The cooperation works without a single leader or central control, but with clearly defined rules. And the system as a whole ensures and promotes sustainability.

According to Gartner, the workforce is crucial to ensuring that new technologies can contribute to the competitive advantage and thus make the vision a reality. From this it can be deduced that Industry 4.0 workplaces must be adequately designed to meet the requirements of autonomy and digital tools.

We are working on a solution to achieve these objectives. The prototype will support the process design of autonomous actors for non-expert modelers and provide a way to learn IoT technology. In addition, our tool will be designed to overcome the shortcomings of existing solutions for tangible modelling.

References

1. Brouns, N., Tata, S., Ludwig, H., Asensio, E.S., Grefen, P.: Modeling IoT-aware Business Processes - A State of the Art Report. Technical report, IBM (2018). https://arxiv.org/abs/1811.00652

2. Fleischmann, A., Schmidt, W., Stary, C., Obermeier, S., Börger, E.: Subject-Oriented Business Process Management. Springer, Heidelberg (2012). https://doi.org/10.1007/978-3-642-32392-8

3. Foster, P.A.: The Open Organization. Routledge, Abingdon (2016). https://doi.org/10.4324/9781315555003

4. Laursen, K., Salter, A.J.: The paradox of openness: appropriability, external search and collaboration. Res. Policy **43**(5), 867–878 (2014). https://doi.org/10.1016/j.respol.2013.10.004

5. Lu, Y.: Industry 4.0: a survey on technologies, applications and open research issues. J. Ind. Inf. Integr. **6**, 1–10 (2017). https://doi.org/10.1016/j.jii.2017.04.005

6. M5Stack: About Us – m5stack-store. https://m5stack.com/pages/about-us

7. Oppl, S.: Articulation of work process models for organizational alignment and informed information system design. Inf. Manag. **53**(5), 591–608 (2016). https://doi.org/10.1016/j.im.2016.01.004

8. Oppl, S., Stary, C.: Tabletop concept mapping. In: Proceedings of the 3rd International Conference on Tangible and Embedded Interaction, TEI 2009. pp. 275–282. ACM Press, New York (2009). https://doi.org/10.1145/1517664.1517721

9. Panetta, K.: Gartner Top Strategic Predictions for 2020 and Beyond (2019). https://www.gartner.com/smarterwithgartner/gartner-top-strategic-predictions-for-2020-and-beyond/

10. Plattform Industrie 4.0: 2030 Vision for Industrie 4.0 (2019). https://www.plattform-i40.de/PI40/Redaktion/EN/Downloads/Publikation/Vision-2030-for-Industrie-4.0.html

11. Steele, F.: The Open Organization: The Impact of Secrecy and Disclosure on People and Organizations. Addison-Wesley, Reading Mass (1975)

12. Stevens, H.: Why outbreaks like coronavirus spread exponentially, and how to "flatten the curve" - Washington Post (2020). https://www.washingtonpost.com/graphics/2020/world/corona-simulator/

13. Tapscott, D.: Four principles for the open world—TED Talk (2012). https://www.ted.com/talks/don_tapscott_four_principles_for_the_open_world

14. Tapscott, D., Williams, A.: Radical openness: four unexpected principles for success. In: TED Conference, LLC (2013)

15. Wikipedia: Big Five personality traits (2020). https://en.wikipedia.org/w/index.php?title=Big_Five_personality_traits&oldid=940108233

16. Wikipedia: Flocking (behavior) (2020). https://en.wikipedia.org/w/index.php?title=Flocking_(behavior)&oldid=940611100

Various Views on Business Process Management

Limitations of Choreography Specifications with BPMN

Albert Fleischmann[(⊠)]

InterAktiv Unternehmensberatung, Dr. Albert Fleischmann and Partner,
Pfaffenhofen, Germany
`albert.fleischmann@interaktiv.expert`

Abstract. Business processes cross borders of organizations and may cover the whole globe. The parties involved in a cross company business process coordinate their work by exchanging messages. Business processes in which interactions are a central aspect are called choreographies. The de facto language for describing business processes is BPMN. In this paper the choreography features of BPMN are investigated based on the author's practical experiences in industry projects. The practical experiences in industrial projects show that BPMN does not allow to model complex process choreographies because ofits limitations in structuring processes and the restrictions by exchanging messages.

Keywords: Business process management · Choreography · BPMN

1 Introduction

BPMN [15] is a wide spread language to describe business processes. It includes methods to describe so called process choreographies. The purpose of choreographies is to define interactions between different companies, suppliers, customers and other parties involved in a business network. With these messages, the involved parties day-to-day business is coordinated and the required data are exchanged. A choreography describes the interactions between multiple participants or services, whereas in orchestrations there is one single flow of control.

"The need for modeling choreographies, over and above conventional business process modeling, has become increasingly important as businesses shift their operations into wider value-chains featuring many collaborating partners and dynamic outsourcing and in-sourcing of services" [2].

In principle, BPMN includes two methods to describe choreographies: collaboration diagrams and choreography diagrams.

Based on practical experiences, in this paper we investigate whether BPMN is the right language to describe complex process choreographies with processes which have to handle defined exceptions like changing orders in an order handling process. Defined exceptions are events which are known but during the execution of a process they might or might not happen, and if they happen it is unknown when they happen. Depending in which execution state of a process exceptions

© Springer Nature Switzerland AG 2020
M. Freitag et al. (Eds.): S-BPM ONE 2020, CCIS 1278, pp. 203–216, 2020.
https://doi.org/10.1007/978-3-030-64351-5_14

happen the reactions can be different. In an order process the event "change order" can happen but don't have to ans the reaction can be different. If the goods are already on the way to the customer the order can not be changed.

In Sect. 2 we analyse the capabilities of the BPMN diagram types to define some common communication patterns and how complex processes can be described in a structured way. First, the term choreography is explained in more detail. Afterwards categories of languages for modeling choreographies are introduced. Then a short overview to BPMN is given especially to its diagram types for specifying choreographies. In the next section, choreography diagrams in BPMN are analyzed and some of their limitations are shown. Especially those identified in real projects. Finally, we describe how the restrictions of BPMN choreographies are covered in other choreography languages. In the last section an overview about other BPMN evaluations is given.

2   Choreography

The behaviour of business processes can be modelled from two distinct perspectives, orchestration and choreography [8]. An orchestration represents a single centralized executable business process in which the allowed sequences of actions or interactions are defined. In service orchestrations, a central control system manages the execution of a process orchestration. This control system envokes the execution of all parties involved in a business process according to the allowed sequences specified in the model. Orchestrations do not support the modeling of decentralized business processes. Service choreographies are global descriptions of all parties and services involved in a process. Essential in choreographies, is the exchange of messages between the participants. There is no central entity controlling the execution of a process. Figure 1 shows a simple example of a choreography. A customer sends an order to a supplier. The supplier sends back a confirmation. Afterwards it will send the ordered product.

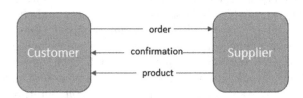

Fig. 1. Example of a choreography

In Fig. 1 only the involved parties and the messages exchanged between them are shown. The sequence in which the participants send and receive messages must be also defined. There are two principle ways to define the interactions [6]:

- Interaction model
- Interconnected Interface Model

In the case of interaction models, the focus is on the sequences in which messages are exchanged between the involved parties in a choreography. The communication between the participants is described from the viewpoint of an observer sitting in between. In the event of interconnected interface models the sequences of sending and receiving is defined separately per participant. Figure 2 shows these two methods defining choreographies.

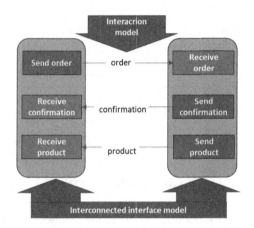

Fig. 2. Modeling choreographies

In [6] modeling languages for choreographies, these two categories are further divided into implementation independent and implementation dependent languages. Implementation independent models are for business people who are interested in the communication logic. They do not want to understand the implementation details which are important for developers. Figure 3 shows the various categories of the languages for modeling choreographies. BPMN and Let's Dance are implementation independent languages for defining process choreographies whereas WS-BPEL and WS-CDL are implementation specific languages.

In [7] a requirements framework for choreographies is presented which is along with existing choreography languages and which is assessed in that paper. Further evaluations of choreography languages can be found in [11,14].

In my opinion the paper [7] is up to date because a google scholar search of the author with key words "Process Choreography" showed that the topic choreography is not in the focus of the business process management community. This search has revealed that after 2010 nearly no papers are published about process or service choreographies.

BPMN is a de facto standard in defining business processes. In the following sections, the capabilities of BPMN for defining choreography models are investigated in greater detail. This assessment is not done on the basis of the criteria found in [7] or [14]. It is based on problems which arise in industry projects.

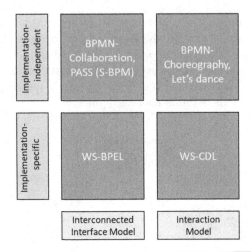

Fig. 3. Categories of languages for modeling choreographies

3 Modeling Choregraphies with BPMN

BPMN is the most used modeling language for business processes in industry.
There are many text books with introductions of the use of BPMN. In this paper,
only a short overview is given. First, the various types of diagrams in BPMN are
outlined. After that the choreography related diagrams are evaluated for their
capacity to express interaction issues which often arise in industry projects.

3.1 Overview BPMN

In BPMN four types of diagrams are used in order to express the various aspects
of business processes:

- Process Diagram
- Conversation Diagram
- Choreography Diagram
- Collaboration Diagram

Process Diagram. For structuring process models in BPMN a modeler can
use pools and lanes. A pool represents process participants. A Pool acts as
a container for a full business process. A process system can consist of several
pools. Pools can only interact by exchanging messages. Lanes are used to organize
and categorize Activities within a Pool. A pool can be divided in several lanes.
Each lane represents a party involved in the process. Between lanes no message
exchange is allowed.

A process diagram describes a process within a single business entity that is contained within a pool. This means that in the BPMN world one pool represents one process executed by one flow of control. This corresponds to an orchestration of services. Figure 4 shows an example of a very simple process diagram.

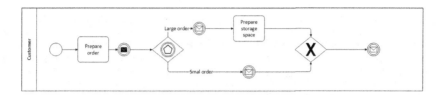

Fig. 4. Process diagram

The pool customer shows the execution logic of the order process like in a flow diagram. After the process started, the order document (paper or digital) is created and the order is sent. After the customer has received the order confirmation from the supplier he prepares storage space, which is not required for small orders.

Process diagrams are used for modeling process orchestrations. In general, parties represented by various lanes in one pool are tightly coupled and mostly belong to one company or organization. There is only one flow of control which wanders between the lanes. Processes with lanes can be seen as special cases of a choreography [8]. The involved parties are tightly coupled by one control flow. In this paper, pools with lanes are considered as choreographies. In this paper it is assumed that choreographies do not have a central control entity and it is essential for participants to exchange messages.

Conversation Diagram. Conversation diagrams give an overview of choreographies. It shows the involved parties and their message exchanges. Figure 5 presents a simple example of a conversation diagram. The shown conversation consists of two parties; Customer and Supplier. They exchange messages which belongs to the order communication. Order communication can be seen as a set of single messages which are exchanged for coordinating the order and delivery of products. In BPMN, the involved parties shown in a conversation diagram correspond to pools.

Conversation diagrams show only the involved parties and their communication relations. They do not describe the allowed sequences in which messages are exchanged.

Choreography Diagram. A new model type in BPMN 2.0 is the Choreography Diagram. Its purpose is to show the interaction between participants. It concentrates on the message flow instead of the individual detailed tasks of a process. Choreography diagrams in BPMN define interaction models. Sending

Fig. 5. Conversation diagram

and receiving of messages is considered as an activity like construct [2]. Figure 6 shows a simple example of a choreography diagram. Each rectangle represents an interaction. They show the receiver of a message in the shaded band, the name of the sender in the non shaded band and the name of the message in the middle. In Fig. 6, it is shown that the customer sends the message order to the supplier. After this message the message confirmation is sent from the supplier to the customer. Finally, the message product is sent from the supplier to the customer.

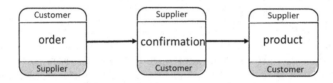

Fig. 6. Choreography diagram

In order to define complex choreographies all types of gateways available in BPMN (e.g. exclusive or, inclusive or, and, event based gateway) can be used. Hierarchies allow to structure complex choreographies.

Collaboration Diagram. Collaboration processes show the participants, their interactions and their internal behavior. In BPMN, a collaboration is any BPMN diagram that contains two or more participants as shown by pools which exchange message. Figure 7 presents an example of a collaboration diagram. It shows the pools customer and supplier. After the start the customer creates an order and sends the order to the supplier. The supplier checks the order and sends a confirmation to the customer. After the supplier has prepared the shipment, it sends the product to the customer.

4   Practical Problems Using BPMN Choreography

The following problems were identified during an industrial process project. In a team we described a process for handling a car accident or break down. The process system covers the whole chain from the incident call, organizing a towing service, workshop processes and it ends with the payment process. The process

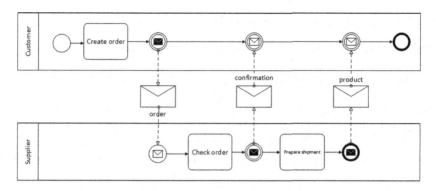

Fig. 7. Collaboration diagram

system was very large and without possibilities to structure it in a hierarchy and without simple and transparent mechanisms for specifying exception handling it was very difficult to keep the overview.

4.1 Assesment Criteria

The assessment of choreography modeling with BPMN is based on practical experiences. This paper does not claim to cover all aspects of modeling choreographies (Whatever "all" means). In the considered projects, the following aspects produced the most burdens:

- Hierarchies in choreography models
- Turing completeness of choreography diagrams (interactions)
- Flexibility in exchanging messages
- Exceptions (Arbitrary events)

In the following sections, the various diagram types in BPMN 2.0 for describing choreographies are assessed according these aspects.

4.2 Conversation Diagrams in BPMN

In conversation diagrams, only the parties involved in a choreography and their interactions are described. Complex process systems with many processes can not be structured in a hierarchical way. In one of our projects, a process system which consists of several sub process systems had been designed. A process system for handling car accidents consists of a process system for handling the direct impacts of the accident consisting of the entities, the call center, the towing company, the rental company etc. Another subsystems is the repair process and the payment process in which insurance companies may be involved. Because this complex process system could not be described with one layer in a transparent way a concept for describing hierarchies in complex process systems was developed. This concept originally created for BPMN has been generalized and integrated into S-BPM [9].

4.3 Choregraphy Diagrams in BPMN

In industry projects, many parties are involved in a process. The focus of choreography diagrams are on the interactions of two parties. This is mentioned in the standard document. "If there are only two participants in the choreography, then it is very simple – both participants will be aware of who is responsible for sending the next message. However, if there are more than two participants, then the modeler needs to be careful to sequence the choreography activities in such a way that the participants know when they are responsible for initiating the interactions" (see pp. 317 [15]). In situations in which messages are expected alternatively from different resources then you have to use event based gateways which causes very intransparent diagrams that we decided not to use them any more.

But the major problem of choreography diagrams is that they are not Turing complete (see Chomsky Hierarchy pp. 327 in [5]). This means that not all problems which can be solved by computers can be described with choreography diagrams. The reason for that is that "neither Data Objects nor Repositories are used in Choreographies" (see pp. 319 [15]). If variables are not allowed, only finite state machines can be described. If we have an order process similar as shown in Fig. 6 but we allow that a customer can send a unknown number of orders. The supplier confirms any order and delivers the ordered products. But it is possible that a customer has already sent n orders but has received n-x confirmations and n-y product deliveries. The number n can vary for each process instance based on the same process model. Such a process cannot be described with a choreography diagram because the number of messages can not be counted and there is no direct way to solve that problem by a work around (except some annotations in natural language). We had such a process. Workshops ordered the required spare parts in such a way.

4.4 Collaboration Diagrams in BPMN

In BPMN collaboration diagrams, it is not possible to structure complex process systems in a hierarchical way. As already mentioned in Sect. 4.2 for complex real life process systems, it is necessary to have the possibility to structure the complexity. In our projects we developed a concept to describe complex process systems in an hierarchical way (see [9]).

In the process system we developed, a lot of exceptions can occur, e.g. a spare part order must be changed, or an agreed appointment has to be postponed. In order to describe such situations in a transparent way it is very helpful to receive an event in several states. In BPMN, there is the restriction of a one-to-one relationship between send and receive events. This means that a message which is sent in a process can only be received in one path of the receiving process. However there are situations where a message is sent in one event but has to be received in two different paths. Figure 8 shows a simple example of such a situation.

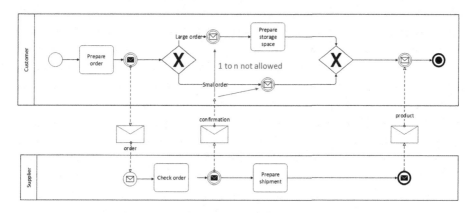

Fig. 8. Problems with one to one relationship of send and receive events

In principle, it is possible to overcome this problem by a work around. This is shown in Fig. 9. In this work around, there is a separate path concurrent to the main path in which all messages are received and stored in a message store. If a message has to be received in the main path it is checked whether the expected message is in the message store, if it is already there, it will be picked up, removed from the message store, and the process proceeds as defined. If the expected message is not in the message store, the process stops and waits for a signal which is thrown in the message receive path if a new message has arrived and stored in the message store. Now in the main path the message store is checked again whether the new message is the expected or not. The example shows that a work around to model such simple situation can become pretty complex and is not easy to understand.

Because of that one-to-one restriction, it is very difficult to discribe reactions on arbitrary messages. For an arbitrary message, it is not determined whether the message is sent or not and if it is sent it is open when it is sent. If such a message is received, the reaction depends on the state of the receiving process. An example of an arbitrary message is changing an order. Figure 10 shows an example. The process "customer" sends the message "order" and after that it waits for a "confirmation" message. But instead of waiting for the "confirmation" message, the customer decides to change its order (order must changed). He creates a "change order" message and send it to the "supplier".

The "supplier" process can either execute the action "check order" or "prepare shipment". Therefore the message "change order" is received via the receive path and deposited in the message store. After storing the "change order" message, the signal "supplier message arrived" is thrown. This signal is a border event of the activities "check order" and "prepare shipment". At the activity "check order" its an interrupting event, which means that the activity is interrupted and a message "change confirmation" is sent. In this state, the changing of orders is possible. The activity "prepare shipment" the signal "supplier mes-

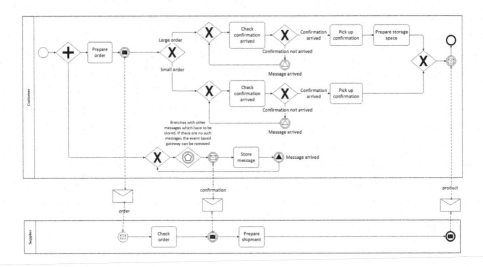

Fig. 9. Work around for receiving one event in more than one states

sage arrived" is non interrupting. This means that the activity is continued and a message "change rejected" is sent to the "customer".

The behaviour in Fig. 10 is very complex in spite of it is not completely described. The path for small orders is not contained and there may be situations where the message store has to be cleaned up (remove old messages). This simple example already illustrates how difficult it is to overcome the problem of arbitrary messages because of this one-to-one restriction. The handling of arbitrary messages is a very common situation, orders, dates, locations etc. may change.

The possible semantics of border events (interrupting or non interrupting) are also very weak. There are situations in which a sequence of activities may be interrupted but later after finishing the interrupt handling routine the sequence has to be continued where it has been interrupted or with any other activity inside the interrupted activity.

In order to describe the relationship between the receiving messages path and the main path signals have been used. The signals have the advantage that the relationship can be directly shown by a throwing and receiving event. But the semantica of signals defines that a signal can be received by any other process instance in a process system. In our case, this means that several process instances waiting for a message received signal can receive the signal independent in which instance the signal is thrown. This can cause that a process instance check the message storage inspite it has not received a message. The global visibility of signals may cause unnecessary look ups for messages.

In order to avoid that unnecessary loop a conditional event can be used. Instead of receiving a signal a conditional event is used and instead of throwing a signal an action which set the condition is used.

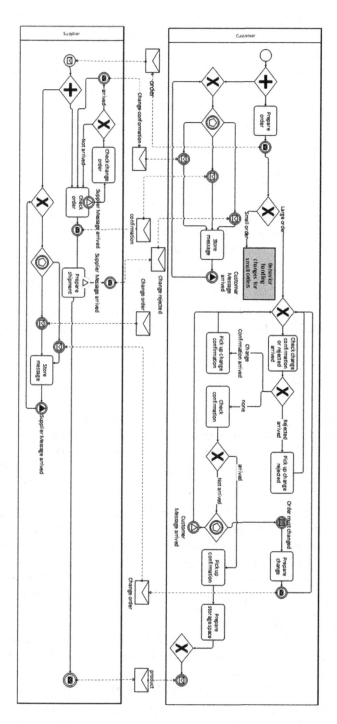

Fig. 10. Workaround for multiple receive events

5   Related Work

As mentioned, this paper is not a holistic evaluation of BPMN. A general evaluation of BPMN can be found in [1,3].

Several sets of criteria for the assessment of choreographies can be found in [7,11,14]. These criterias are used to evaluate several choreography languages. Until 2016, there was no common agreement about the criterias for evaluating choreography languages [11].

In [4] it is shown that the semantics of Exclusive and Event-Based Gateways in BPMN Choreographies are not precisely defined. It is shown that there use can lead to significant misinterpretations in process choreographies.

In [16,17] Liming Zhu et. al. illustrate inadequacies in BPMN through their experiences with a collection of real world reference business processes from the Australian lending industry. They observe that the most significant inadequacies include lack of resource management, exception handling, process variation, and data flow integration.

In [12] pp. 193–196, the limitations of BPMN in structuring complex processes are discussed and the need for a revised communication concept is required. In [13] a enhanced communication concept is described. This concept is influenced by S-BPM (see pp.119 in [13]). A detailed description of the communication concept of S-BPM can be found in [10].

6   Conclusion

The limitations of BPMN concerning choreography has been exposed in this paper. These limitations have been identified in industrial projects.

There are no features which allow to structure complex choreography systems in a hierarchical way. Only choreography diagrams allow hierarchy but they are not Turing Complete which means that some communication scenarios can not be described at all.

In collaboration diagrams, very common communication problems can be only described in very cumbersome ways. This leads to process descriptions which are very intransparent.The one-to-one relationship of send and receive events does not support the handling of arbitrary messages e.g. the change of orders. This scenarios can only be resolved with a pretty complex work around. Therefore some more powerful communication concepts are proposed in [10,13]. BPMN is a implementation independent specification language for business processes and has been designed for the usage by business people. But for real world processes with a certain complexity and the ability to react on business execeptions properly the work arounds require a deep understanding of the BPMN language. BPMN specifications become complex and are not easy to understand. Sure any business process can be described in BPMN but not always in an understandable and transparent way.

References

1. Aagesen, G., Krogstie, J.: BPMN 2.0 for modeling business processes. In: vom Brocke, J., Rosemann, M. (eds.) Handbook on Business Process Management 1. IHIS, pp. 219–250. Springer, Heidelberg (2015). https://doi.org/10.1007/978-3-642-45100-3_10
2. Barros, A., Hettel, T., Flender, C.: Process choreography modeling. In: Brocke, J., Rosemann, M. (eds.) Handbook on Business Process Management 1. IHIS, pp. 257–277. Springer, Heidelberg (2010). https://doi.org/10.1007/978-3-642-00416-2_12
3. Börger, E.: Approaches to modeling business processes: a critical analysis of BPMN, workflow patterns and YAWL. Softw. Syst. Modeling **11**, 305–318 (2012). https://doi.org/10.1007/s10270-011-0214-z
4. Corradini, F., Morichetta, A., Re, B., Tiezzi, F.: Walking through the semantics of exclusive and event-based gateways in BPMN choreographies. In: Alvim, M.S., Chatzikokolakis, K., Olarte, C., Valencia, F. (eds.) The Art of Modelling Computational Systems: A Journey from Logic and Concurrency to Security and Privacy. LNCS, vol. 11760, pp. 163–181. Springer, Cham (2019). https://doi.org/10.1007/978-3-030-31175-9_10
5. Davis, M., Sigal, R., Weyuker, E.J.: Computability, Complexity and Languages, Fundamentals of Theoretical Computer Science. Elsevier Science, San Francisco (1994)
6. Decker, G., Kopp, O., Barros, A.: An introduction to service choreographies. IT Inf. Technol. **50**(2), 122–127 (2008)
7. Decker, G., Kopp, O., Leymann, F., Weske, M.: Interacting services - from specification to execution. Data Knowl. Eng. **68**, 946–972 (2009)
8. Dumas, M., Kohlborn, T.: Service-enabled process management. In: Brocke, J., Rosemann, M. (eds.) Handbook on Business Process Management 1. IHIS, pp. 441–460. Springer, Heidelberg (2010). https://doi.org/10.1007/978-3-642-00416-2_20
9. Elstermann, M., Fleischmann, A.: Modeling complex processes systems with subject oriebted means. In: Betz, S., Elstermann, M., Lederer, M. (eds.) S-BPM ONE 2019, 11th International Conference on Subject Oriented Business Process Management, No. 85 in ICPC published by ACM Digital Library. ACM (2019)
10. Fleischmann, A., Schmidt, W., Stary, C., Obermeier, S., Börger, E.: Subject-Oriented Business Process Management. Springer, Heidelberg (2012). https://doi.org/10.1007/978-3-642-32392-8
11. Kopp, O.: Partnerübergreifende Geschäftsprozesse und ihre Realisierung in BPEL. Dissertation Universität Stuttgart (2016)
12. Kossak, F., et al.: A Rigouros Semantics for BPMN 2.0 Process Diagrams, pp. 29–152. Springer, Cham (2014). https://doi.org/10.1007/978-3-319-09931-6_4
13. Kossak, F., et al.: Hagenberg Business Process Modeling Method. Springer, Cham (2016). https://doi.org/10.1007/978-3-319-30496-0
14. Lässig, N.: Choreographiesprachen mit Datenmodellierungsfähigkeiten - eine Übersicht. Bachelor Thesis Universität Stuttgart (2017)

15. Open Management Group, (OMG): Business Process Model and Notation (BPMN). http://www.omg.org/spec/BPMN/2.0
16. Zhu, L., Osterweil, L.J., Staples, M., Kannengiesser, U., Simidchieva, B.I.: Desiderata for languages to be used in the defnition of reference business processes. Int. J. Softw. Inform. **1**(1), 37–65 (2007)
17. Zhu, L., Osterweil, L.J., Staples, M., Kannengiesser, U.: Challenges observed in the definition of reference business processes. In: ter Hofstede, A., Benatallah, B., Paik, H.-Y. (eds.) BPM 2007. LNCS, vol. 4928, pp. 95–107. Springer, Heidelberg (2008). https://doi.org/10.1007/978-3-540-78238-4_12

Technology-, Human-, and Data-Driven Developments in Business Process Management: A Literature Analysis

Matthias Lederer[1]([⊠]), Matthes Elstermann[2], Stefanie Betz[3], and Werner Schmidt[4]

[1] ISM International School of Management, Karlstr. 35, 80333 Munich, Germany
matthias.lederer@ism.de
[2] Karlsruher Institut Für Technologie, Kaiserstraße 12, 76131 Karlsruhe, Germany
matthes.elstermann@kit.edu
[3] Hochschule Furtwangen, Robert-Gerwig-Platz 1, 78120 Furtwangen, Germany
stefanie.betz@hs-furtwangen.de
[4] Technische Hochschule Ingolstadt, Esplanade 10, 85049 Ingolstadt, Germany
werner.schmidt@thi.de

Abstract. Approaches of business process management (BPM) are always changing, because underlying business strategies and technological implementation are constantly evolving. Likewise, methodical approaches, how business processes are planned, optimized, managed and controlled, come and go. This article collects and systematizes the trends discussed at major BPM conferences of the year 2019. The identified hot spots include e.g. process mining, predictive BPM, BPM trust, modeling, BPM platforms, team-driven BPM.

Keywords: Business process management · Trend analysis · Research discourses · BPM body of knowledge

1 Introduction

Even if business process management (BPM) as a discipline is not always mentioned, a classical process-oriented approach is often used in initiatives, research, or projects [1–4]. Currently, companies are trying to use digital transformation to change from product-/function-oriented designs to process-oriented approaches [5]. When this happens using intelligent data analysis or new technologies, the term "digital transformation" or simply "digitalization" is often used [2, 6, 7]. However, the underlying concepts result from and are enabled by the discipline of BPM [8], as has been shown in several studies for BPM [1, 4, 9]. Thus, many concepts used are not fundamentally new, but have already been used in previous BPM research. This transfer of ideas and approaches happens either *directly* (e.g. process mining has been known for decades as the analysis of process instance data, but is now content of numerous publication) or *indirectly* (holistic approaches such as smart home, smart cities, and smart grid are based on the control and data flows of workflow models or instances). However, many transfers conform to the core principle

© Springer Nature Switzerland AG 2020
M. Freitag et al. (Eds.): S-BPM ONE 2020, CCIS 1278, pp. 217–231, 2020.
https://doi.org/10.1007/978-3-030-64351-5_15

of BPM, namely the design of IT-supported or manual implementation and control of business processes [10].

As stated, there is a multitude of topics and challenges in the context of digitalization that are discussed either in the BPM discipline or are originally coming from the BPM discipline (e.g. Industry 4.0, Intelligent Business Models) [7, 11]. Possible reasons behind these developments have also been described. However, as these analyses were created two years in the past and with ever evolving business strategies, technological implementations, and research interest [4, 9], the authors of this paper saw the necessity for an update. This will be done analogous to [4, 9] with the following research questions:

(1) What catchwords is the scientific community using when discussing new concepts and methods?
(2) What are the current process management trends based on the catchword and which directions are they taking?

The concepts and terms in digitalization directly or indirectly relate to BPM and are subject to continuous change. This article is intended to help researchers and practitioners to gain an overview of current discussions. The analysis is also intended to renew and possibly expand one's own perspective on process management. The classification should help researchers to discover adjacent BPM discussions in related disciplines, avoid misunderstandings and uncertainties, and to discover relevant original research results in the different BPM communities.

Section 2 describes the applied methodology and Sect. 3 shows the classification of the individual topics and challenges (called catchwords). A discussion of the underlying developments as well as of the developments compared to the study before is presented in Sect. 4. A brief summary of the study can be found in Sect. 5.

2 Methodology

As mentioned above, this contribution serves as an update and extension to the results of [4, 9]. Therefore, the methods used will be applied again. Even if there are small adjustments, please refer to the core texts [4, 9] for a more detailed documentation of the procedure. As a major difference, the categories for the catchwords were not developed from scratch. Instead, after the topics were collected, they were classified into the dimensions known from the former study (human-driven, data-driven and case-driven). It turned out that it was also necessary to change one dimension.

The analysis with the goal of collecting relevant catchwords and assigning them to dimensions was carried out in a five-step qualitative content analysis. Specifically, the methodology followed the recommendations by [11–13] with the restriction that the classifications used are not conclusive or exclusive, but rather represent tendencies, i.e. dimensions. These dimensions thus stand for viewpoints, the respective papers take in order to investigate the catchword (e.g. more a human- or technology-driven view on topics).

For the *first step*, eight main BPM conferences (see Table 1) have been investigated[1], while WI (International Conference Wirtschaftsinformatik, engl. International Conference on Information Systems) and MKWI (Multikonferenz Wirtschaftsinformatik, engl. Multi Conference on Information Systems) being recorded once due to their merger. All analyzed conference proceedings have in common that (i) they have or have had a clear BPM focus, (ii) they are technically or business-oriented, (iii) they have a minimum of scientific quality (e.g. ranking), (iv) at least ten conference proceedings in the past are available, and (v) a sufficient degree of publicity is given. Note that, more and more upcoming conferences, which are originally organized by companies (e.g. software providers), were excluded because of possible bias in their topics.

Table 1. Identified BPM papers in the conference proceedings

Catchword	Conference								
	BPM	**WI**	**INF**	**ECIS**	**SEAA**	**CBI**	**S-BPM**	**BIS**	**Sum**
Process Mining	11	2							13
Conformance checking	2					2	1		5
Context awareness	1	1		1		1		2	6
NLP	1	1	1	1					4
Predictive BPM	1	3		2				3	9
Management	3			2	1		1		7
Modelling	6	6	2	2	1	1	1	2	21
BPM trust	2			4					6
User-centric BPM	1	1		4				1	7
Internet of Things (IoT)	1			1		2	2		6
Platforms		3				1			4

Legend: BPM = International Conference on Business Process Management; WI = International Conference Wirtschaftsinformatik, engl. International Conference on Information Systems; INF = Informatik, engl. Informatics; SEAA = Euromicro Conference on Software Engineering and Advanced Applications; CBI = IEEE International Conference on Business Informatics; S-BPM = International Conference S-BPM ONE; BIS = International Conference on Business Information Systems; NLP = Natural language processing

In a *second step*, from the total of 752 papers (all contributions from the conferences) only those with a clear BPM focus were selected. For this purpose, generic BPM-relevant elements (e.g. control flow, process orientation, recurring patterns) were screened in title, abstract and keywords.

---

[1] This implies only the main scientific conference and the according publications. Workshops, industrial forums, or poster presentations have been excluded.

Thus, 88 contributions went into *step three*. In this step the catchwords were grouped into topics by researcher triangulation. This means each researcher identified catchwords and grouped them to topics separately and then the results have been discussed and merged.

In *steps four and five*, categories were formed for identified topics. The researcher triangulation used in the former study was repeated to adjust and form the first categories. However, different to the former study, a Delphi study was conducted additionally. In two Delphi rounds the assignment of individual catchwords to the categories was evaluated on a quantitative 3-point scale and deviations were discussed afterwards. The four participating experts were BPM researchers with a doctorate, a total of more than 45 years of experience and more than 150 publications on BPM topics. This change in the methodology was necessary because the dimensions are no longer disjunct compared to the ones used in publications [4, 9]. Single topics (e.g. BPM 2.0) could be clearly assigned to one category in the previous study (e.g. social-driven), whereas many catchwords of this updated study (e.g. IoT, platforms) can be assigned to several categories (e.g. technology and people). The classification therefore becomes dependent on the viewpoint of the contributions analyzed in a multidimensional spectrum (see also Fig. 1).

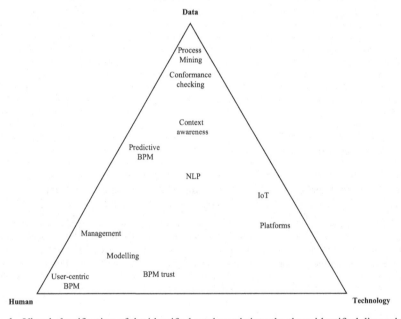

Fig. 1. Visual classification of the identified catchwords into the three identified dimensions

As a result, 11 single catchwords were grouped into three basic dimensions: data-driven, social-driven, and technology-driven BPM. Section 3 presents the identified trends and internal research discussions in greater detail. The originally existing category "case-driven" no longer appears in current discussions.

3   Results

Based on the distribution of the classified catchwords (see methodology), the following solution space can be spanned. It shows to which general view the identified catchwords tend to be assigned to within the respective proceeding papers.

In the following, the current research discourses on the individual catchwords are presented. Since the catchwords mentioned here are oriented directly after the analyzed publications (see previous section), naturally the descriptions differ in granularity.

3.1   Process Mining

Process Mining was already a relevant topic in the previous study. In the publications on this catchword, static methods, technique, as well as supporting tools are discussed. Generally, it stands for approaches that aim to extract information from real process executions (mostly recorded in event logs of information systems like Enterprise Resource Planning). In this analysis, again it was a very prominent topic with 13 publications.

This is probably due to increasing overall importance of the data and the focus on the intelligent evaluation (machine learning). Process Mining is seen as a solution to many BPM challenges (e.g. cost optimization, identifying bottlenecks, uncovering anomalies, or creating transparency/compliance). Even a contribution on how mining can be used to communicate conflicting goals can be found in the analysis. It is interesting to note that the business implications often reflect classic BPM optimization rules (e.g. remove activities, reorder resources, accelerate process paths).

In general (especially through the conference 'BPM'), more and more case studies on use cases of mining are published. Prominent examples are classical optimizations in Smart Factory, real-time evaluation/assessment of processes as well as Robot Process Automation (RPA). But also new ideas like interactions or the measurement of events at the transition between humans and machines are topics in papers. A first meta-study on application scenarios is also available.

Separated from use cases, research is being conducted on methodology in the narrower sense and on improving the mining basis. In the field of methodology, approaches exist on how declarative instead of descriptive information can be obtained from data. Furthermore, alternative mathematical/statistical methods are reported on the central question, how the accuracy of mining can be improved. There are also many publications on this topic in the research of Machine Learning. The central topic in BPM is still the question of how a reasonable consideration of certainly good (e.g. correct) data can be combined with less good (e.g. vague, old, generic) data for better decisions. In the area of improving the data basis, approaches are generally published that not only use flat event logs, but also enrich them or supplement them with additional data. For example, some papers discuss the urgent need for additional data for conformance checking. The ideas here range from labelling to describing the context. Some papers also apply mining techniques to other entities from process models. This includes classical elements (e.g. functions, actions) and is often analogous or complementary (e.g. labels for affected attributes to enrich semantics). However, extended elements are also used as a data basis for mining (e.g., business rules or best practices within processes).

Currently, less discussed is the question of suitable tools. The only papers on actual software focuses on the meaningful visualization of complex data and interrelationships. If this analysis were to be repeated in the coming years, special process mining conferences would also have to be considered.

3.2 Conformance Checking

The discipline of conformance checking can partially be considered a sub-domain of process mining [14]. In its most simple definition, it basically is concerned with methods, algorithms, and tools that can check whether event logs or traces comply with model definitions in formal process models [14–16].

Debatable is the question whether conformance checking can or should be considered the same as compliance checking. The fundamental premise in both cases is the same: there is a pre-definition of what is-supposed-to-be (process models or laws/regulations) and recording of what-is during execution (in both cases process or event logs of workflow tools but also specifications that describe process that should adhere to given regulations) [17, 18]. With compliance checking the chance that the is-supposed-to-be definitions are available in a formal computational form is less likely than with pure conformance checking. Partially NLP may be required.

3.3 Context Awareness

A simple and direct interpretation of context awareness would be research or studies that are geared towards more extensively and holistically considering more/all aspects in the surrounding execution system when executing BPM activities.

Into this category fall developments, analysis, and meta models that allow to define certain contexts for e.g. electronic marketplaces such as [19] or research regarding business process improvement activities with consideration of differences in organizational size, culture, and resources [20]. This broader interpretation is also covered in a study by Song et al. that is geared *Towards a Comprehensive Understanding of the Context Concepts in Context-aware Business Processes* [21]. The same researcher team also has extensively worked on a specialized technical oriented aspect of this domain, where modeling languages are required to describe *Context-Aware Business Process Models* [22] which in turn allows the integration of Internet of Things (IoT) technologies for Context-aware BPM Using IoT-integrated context ontologies and IoT-enhanced decision models [23].

3.4 NLP

Natural Language Processing (NLP) is a research and/or technology domain concerned with the computational analysis of natural human languages. As such, it is also a sub domain of artificial intelligence research. The goal is to allow computer systems to handle or be part of human information exchange. This encompasses text as well as spoken languages and includes aspects ranging from classical spell checking, thesauruses, to optical character recognitions (OCR), text-to-speech, voice recognition, but also more complex interaction systems that try to emulate human behavior on language level. In the context of BPM most research such as [17] is concerned with applying NLP technologies to their respective domain and in order to derive or generate formalized process models from natural language descriptions (usually in the English language). Other examples try to use chat-bots for service-desk customer interactions [24] or try to identify ambiguous, redundant, and missing roles in textual descriptions of workflow systems [25].

In all investigated cases, only textual descriptions were concerned and as far as discernable, other aspects of NLP such as voice recognition have not been applied to BPM concerns.

3.5 Predictive BPM

Same as Process Mining, Predictive BPM was already a catchword in the previous analysis and stands for data analytics approaches that aim to predict any kind of future behavior. The current research shows the classical use cases in digitalization (Predictive Maintenance, see the previous paper) is being continued. However, in the past, prediction systems with simple process data derived too imprecise predictions. The ongoing developments are to be seen in three areas: (i) In addition to structured data of processes, context information is increasingly used, which is nevertheless complicated to capture (see also Context Awareness). Therefore, mostly only specialized use-cases (e.g. document analysis) are being researched. (ii) Algorithms are also further developed (e.g. support vector machine/machine learning). Here two current trends can be seen. On the one hand, attempts are made to use patterns and to extend taxonomies in order to transfer predictions into known knowledge/open new fields of knowledge. On the other hand, other researchers show interest in individual and specific analysis methods, which use individual forecasts without patterns. (iii) Monitoring of processes was originally the goal of predictive BPM - but it is being expanded in ongoing research. Although there are still approaches that focus on classic KPI-based predictions with standard sets, many researchers are trying to explore individualized measures. These mostly originate from performance management and are currently only partially linked to concrete application scenarios (research from the energy industry and production planning was found).

3.6 Management

The topic management has already surfaced in [4, 9]. This is not surprising as is a basic theme and an inherent part of BPM. We identified seven paper belonging to this catchword. Simply speaking they cover research focusing on the improvement of Business Process Management approaches.

One research stream is to align Business Process Management with other management areas in an organisation in order to achieve a successful implementation and adoption of business processes. More specifically, one approach is for example suggesting aligning BPM with practices related to Human Resource Management (BPM - Understanding the Alignment of Employee Appraisals and Rewards with Business Processes) [26].

Another trend identified is to adopt software engineering approaches such as agile approaches for BPM. Here, the focus is on the transfer of agile models from software engineering to BPM (e.g. Synthesis of Design Parameters for the Transfer of Agility from Software Engineering to Process Management). On a more specific level the application of agile methods and personas to S-BPM is analysed in [27].

Other approaches are focusing on best practices and reference processes for different domains (e.g. research management processes and patient pathways). Lastly, one paper has quite a different focus. However, it is worth mentioning as it provides a BPM skills taxonomy drawn from an analysis of job ads to enable a better understanding of BPM Skill configurations and shifting business demands [28]. The work shows how the digitalisation has influenced the business demands and as such is important for the BPM curricula.

To summarize, in the management topic, we identified a trend to combine classical BPM approaches with human-centric approaches to enhance process implementation and adoption.

3.7 Modelling

Modelling of processes is a fundamental and traditional aspect of any concern in Business Process Management. As such, 'catchword' is not even a fitting term. Rather, BPM research concerned with modeling per se is very diversified and ties into many other domains, usually as a foundation to build further aspect on.

Examples range from proposals for specialized modeling languages and language extensions such as Annotated Textual Description of a Process (ADTP) for the field of Context Awareness [17, 29].

Papers may be concerned with declarative process descriptions and the according reasoning formalisms [30] or with the parameterized verification of Data-Aware BPMN [31].

Other possible topics that fall under the catchword modeling are e.g., more general consideration and overview studies review problems and challenges when using multiple conceptual models [32]. Some others try to give and overview and find themes and paths for future research regarding the learning of conceptual modeling [33]. Moreover, they derive a method-wise approach for selecting the most suitable business process modelling notation [34].

Just to name a few and provide an idea of the broadness of what could be implied with general topic of modeling.

3.8 BPM Trust

This topic is covering research focusing on techniques enhancing trust and transparency issues in BPM to enable secure and efficient processes. Half of the identified research papers investigate blockchain and its potential to realize (interorganizational) business processes and improve trust (e.g., [35, 36]).

Other research focuses on a more general approach and not a specific technique. For example, the paper Trust-Aware Process Design (Trust-Aware Process Design) introduces a conceptualization of trust for BPM and [37] provides examples on how to design useful transparency.

3.9 User-Centric

Research under that topic is focusing on how to support users in evolving their capabilities to improve employee alignment and process performance. Overall, we identified 13 papers belonging to this category showing the high importance of this category in current BPM research. The largest part of the research (6 papers in 2019) is concerned with user acceptance of organizational routines and new technologies. User acceptance and resistance can express itself in multiple forms including workarounds, and lack of cooperation as well as physical sabotage. User acceptance has a high impact on process performance. Interestingly, most of the current research is concentrating on workarounds and their dual nature. It investigates if a workaround is to be accepted or not accepted (e.g. [38]).

Another focus in this category is teaching, more specifically, in how to teach BPM using game-based approaches. This is due to its potential to enhance learning. Finally, there is another trend emerging in this category, this is the individualisation of processes. This research area is adding a micro perspective to the BPM body of knowledge for example by developing design patterns for Business Process individualisation (e.g. [39]). This is a trend that might become even bigger as BPM methods in general are focusing on process standardization and economies of scale, while the emerging digitalization enables process individualization and this in turn might enhance process performance [39].

3.10 Internet of Things (IoT)

The Internet of Things (IoT) describes a network of interacting devices (Things) connected via the Internet. The 'things' are for example sensors, actuators, or hardware/software combinations in embedded systems, etc. They generate and exchange data and are integral parts of technical as well as business processes. IoT technology supports the horizontal and vertical integration of such processes, in particular the transformation of the traditional automation pyramid (from bottom: Shop Floor, Manufacturing Execution Systems, Enterprise Resource Planning Systems, Supply Chain & Customer Relationship Management) into a networked environment across arbitrary enterprise architecture layers. IoT concepts and solutions involve Cyber-Physical Systems and also humans. They are not limited to industrial use-cases, but also occur in many other domains like health care or smart home. The increasing importance is reflected by the number of six papers we could assign to IoT in relation with BPM in the 2019 issues of the screened conferences. Like in previous publications, an emphasis is still on modelling. Topics reach from IoT-based business process layer, over IoT systems' architecture layer to IoT framework layer [40–42]. The high degree of integration in IoT settings mainly based on data and information flow causes vulnerability with respect to availability. To tackle this [43] suggest communication design and blockchain-based data sharing facilities in order avoid a single point of failure, while [44] present a modelling approach that depicts dependencies in IoT networks and allows to analyze threat propagation. An interesting path is followed by [45], who show how IoT technology in smart homes can be used for habit mining.

3.11 Platforms

Platforms are a cornerstone of digitalization. They match demand and supply of products, services, information etc. and support transactions between buyer and seller. Thus, platforms facilitate digital business models and enable ICT-based execution of business processes. For that reason, we consider platforms as a BPM-related topic and identified them as a relevant catchword in the publications under review, even if processes were not mentioned explicitly. [46] conceptualize a marketplace for production capacities, particularly for additive manufacturing, but also transferable to other use cases. Successfully kicking off an Industrial Internet of Things platform ecosystem is subject of the work of [19]. They conducted a case study that revealed conflicting horizontal and vertical aspects of a platform strategy. Helping SMEs to articulate needs and configure appropriate cyber-physical systems is the objective of [47]. The authors present a methodology for a respective matching platform. More general, not focusing on B2B platforms in industrial scenarios, [48] researched the combinability of strategic approaches of network economics in order to tackle the critical mass problem of two-sided marketplaces.

4   Discussion

In this discussion, a comprehensive summary and brief interpretation of the current BPM topics is provided. In addition, significant developments and changes to the study conducted 2017 will be highlighted.

In the previous study, the developments were classified into three clearly distinguishable categories (human-, data-, and case-driven). First, it should be noted that in the current proceedings no studies could be found which include the classic idea of case management for processes. At the same time, the constitutive characteristic of this research field, namely that the design and execution phases merge into one another, is found in some papers. Nevertheless, these new approaches (e.g. parts of conformance checking, process mining, predictive BPM) focus more on the data dimension. In the ideas of adaptive or emergent case management of the old study, the basic idea was to support knowledge workers with rough templates. These were then adapted manually for actual instances. With current data-driven developments, the focus is more on making digital data (and sometimes complex connections, e.g. with context data and varying data quality) available at short notice. This makes live monitoring or even automated adjustment of instances by machines possible. Nevertheless, in comparison to classical case management, where many applications and case studies have been reported, the current BPM papers mostly only show theoretical research results.

Topics that can be seen primarily to data-driven innovation have hardly changed in their naming. Process Mining was then and is now an important topic. Why exactly this form of Business Intelligence (partly also Business Analytics) has established itself in the BPM area or why it is not considered e.g. a sub-domain of machine learning, or business analytics ideas is an open question. Maybe it is because the starting point for these techniques is event tracking - an information that has always been important for automation in BPM for years. However, as with the other topics, simple ideas of data source usage or data analysis are no longer to be found in the publications. The main driver of many publications is the absorption of complexity, for example by compli-cated predictions or big data, and the consideration of many data and/or sources (e.g. in Predictive BPM). It is therefore not surprising that data or intelligence topics dominate the various conferences themes. It is also noticeable, when looking at the authors of the publications, that researchers who have previously investigated formal or generally ana-lytical topics now increasingly explicitly see data as the source of their research ideas. The Automated Knowledge Discovery to be found in the old study must now be viewed in a more fine-grained way, because many publications deal with partial aspects of this overarching topic such as the context, changed model entities (e.g. events plus actions) or even the people and machines involved in a process.

This leads to questions of technology as it is described as a new dimension in this paper. The use of technology has always been a driver for innovation in the information systems discipline, which naturally includes BPM. Technology-driven process innova-tion can happen through simple IT support of manual work, automation or even the digitalization of the market offer. No single topic identified in the study is – unlike the dimensions data and humans – purely seen in this dimension. Concepts related to the catchwords base on new technology in processes in order to use data potential (e.g. IoT) or to support people in their projects (e.g. modelling). Even if all proceedings contain pure technology topics (e.g. blockchain), only those described in the triangle (see Fig. 1) have a clear BPM reference. This shows that technology continues to be an enabler for processes and less the direct starting point for process innovation. Even though the question of whether technologies or business strategies are the drivers of innovation, this study comes to the conclusion that BPM communities tend to use technologies (e.g., connectivity in IoT, interfaces in platforms) to organize core BPM aspects (e.g., data and control flow).

A particularly interesting change has taken place in the dimension of human-driven topics. In the 2017 study, the topics mentioned in this area (e.g. Social BPM, BPM 2.0, Design Thinking) roughly all had the common goal of involving people in the design of processes, because their knowledge can be important for increasing effectiveness and efficiency. The topics analyzed 2017 not only had clearly different names than those in this new study, but also focused more on technical and operational issues (e.g. use of Web 2.0 tools, how workshops with process participants are to be organized, what quality assurance is required for ideas from teams). These user-focused concrete questions are still included (user-centric BPM), but the other topics go beyond this short-term view. They place people in a more individual and value-based context (e.g. trust, process individualization). The research topics are correspondingly a bit vaguer, but also often more challenging in study design. If one adds questions of culture as well as of trust, it becomes clear that the topics assigned to the human perspective tend to strive for greater values.

A scientific community such as S-BPM needs to measure its impact not only by core ideas (e.g. the further development of the modelling, the application of the concept in business practice). It has also do adapt or answer current scientific discourses from the parent BPM discipline. This paper can contribute to this, because for some of the concepts S-BPM is quite capable of providing suitable applications, theories or even descriptions.

5 Summary

This article followed in the research design of [4, 9] to give an overview of current research in the field of BPM. All eleven topics – referred to as catchwords – identified from academic conferences, were identified and their state of the art was summarized. All topics can be categorized as human-, technology- and/or data-driven.

Even though process management research is perhaps one of the oldest in the discipline of information systems, this study shows that many new developments and advancements are happening. Research at the scientific conferences tries to provide answers to classical questions of BPM with innovative ideas. The importance and drivers of people in processes was and is still a central question, as well as which technologies can support processes. A changed mindset (e.g. sustainability and sense making for people instead of operative integration of participants) and new technical possibilities (e.g. interoperability and computing power) find their ways into BPM. What they all have in common is that they attempt to promote incremental or radical process innovations using different ways and viewpoints. At the same time, due to a certain breadth of the digitization discussion, there are also papers that try to provide an overview (e.g. through taxonomies) on new trends. In general, data-based questions and solutions for processes are on the rise – a trend that BPM probably has in common with many other digital topics (e.g. Digital Health, Smart Energy).

References

1. Lederer, M.: What's going to happen to business process management? Current status and future of a discipline. In: Proceedings of the S-BPM ONE 2019. CEUR-WS, Sevilla (2019)
2. Felipe, M.: Process excellence the key for digitalization. Bus. Process Manag. J. **25**(7), 1716–1733 (2019)
3. Alt, R., Puschmann, T.: Digitalisierung der Finanzindustrie: Grundlagen der Fintech-Evolution. Springer, Heidelberg (2016). https://doi.org/10.1007/978-3-662-50542-7
4. Lederer, M., Knapp, J., Schott, P.: The digital future has many names - how business process management drives the digital transformation. In: Proceedings of the 6th International Conference on Industrial Technology and Management. IEEE, Cambridge (2017)
5. Bürck, A., Kaib, S., Seemann, J.: Business Process Management – der Weg zu agileren Prozessen. Kienbaum Consultants International (2015)
6. Koch, A.: Prozessmanagement-Trends im Langzeitvergleich (2016). https://blog.ibo.de/2016/03/21/prozessmanagement-trends-im-langzeitvergleich/. Accessed 03 May 2016
7. Mertens, P., Barbian, D.: Digitalisierung und Industrie 4.0 – Moden, modische Überhöhung oder Trend? Working Paper University Erlangen-Nuremberg (2016)
8. Rosemann, M.: Proposals for future BPM research directions. In: Ouyang, C., Jung, J.-Y. (eds.) AP-BPM 2014. LNBIP, vol. 181, pp. 1–15. Springer, Cham (2014). https://doi.org/10.1007/978-3-319-08222-6_1
9. Lederer, M., Betz, S., Kurz, M., Schmidt, W.: Some say digitalization - others say IT-enabled process management thought through to the end. In: Zehbold, C., Mühlhäuser, M. (eds.) Proceedings of the S-BPM ONE 2017. ACM, New York
10. Duman, M., La Rosa, M., Mendling, J., Reijers, H.A.: Fundamentals of Business Process Management. Springer, Heidelberg (2018). https://doi.org/10.1007/978-3-662-56509-4
11. Weber, R.: Basic Content Analysis. Sage, Newbury Park (1990)

12. Mayring, P.: Qualitative content analysis. In: Forum Qualitative Sozialforschung, vol. 1, no. 2 (2000)
13. Elo, S., Kynglas, N.: The qualitative content analysis process. J. Adv. Nurs. **62**(1), 107–115 (2008)
14. Dunzer, S., Stierle, M., Matzner, M., Baier, S.: Conformance checking: a state-of-the-art literature review. In: Proceedings of the S-BPM ONE 2019. ACM, Sevilla (2019)
15. Artamonov, K., Lomazova, I.: What has remaindes unchanged in your business process model. In: 21st Conference on Business Informatics CBI. IEEE, Moscow (2019)
16. Bauer, M., van der Aa, H., Weidlich, M.: Estimating process conformance by trace sampling and result approximation. In: Hildebrandt, T., van Dongen, B., Röglinger, M., Mendling, J. (eds.) BPM 2019. LNCS, vol. 11675, pp. 179–197. Springer, Cham (2019). https://doi.org/10.1007/978-3-030-26619-6_13
17. Sànchez-Ferreres, J., Burattin, A., Carmona, J., Montali, M., Padró, L.: Formal reasoning on natural language descriptions of processes. In: Hildebrandt, T., van Dongen, B., Röglinger, M., Mendling, J. (eds.) BPM 2019. LNCS, vol. 11675, pp. 86–101. Springer, Cham (2019). https://doi.org/10.1007/978-3-030-26619-6_8
18. Colombo Tosatto, S., Governatori, G., van Beest, N.: Checking regulatory compliance: will we live to see it? In: Hildebrandt, T., van Dongen, B., Röglinger, M., Mendling, J. (eds.) BPM 2019. LNCS, vol. 11675, pp. 119–138. Springer, Cham (2019). https://doi.org/10.1007/978-3-030-26619-6_10
19. Freichel, C., Hofmann, A., Fischer, M., Winkelmann, A.: Requirements and a meta model for exchanging additive manufacturing capacities. In: Ludwig, T., Pipek, V. (eds.) Proceedings of the WI 2019. University Siegen, Siegen (2019)
20. Beerepoot, I., van de Weerd, I., Reijers, H.A.: Business process improvement activities: differences in organizational size, culture, and resources. In: Hildebrandt, T., van Dongen, B., Röglinger, M., Mendling, J. (eds.) BPM 2019. LNCS, vol. 11675, pp. 402–418. Springer, Cham (2019). https://doi.org/10.1007/978-3-030-26619-6_26
21. Song, R., Vanthienen, J., Cui, W., Wang, Y., Huang, L.: Towards a comprehensive understanding of the context concepts in context-aware business processes In: Proceedings of the S-BPM ONE 2019. ACM, Sevilla (2019)
22. Song, R., Vanthienen, J., Cui, W., Wang, Y., Huang, L.: A DMN-based method for context-aware business process modeling towards process variability. In: Abramowicz, W., Corchuelo, R. (eds.) BIS 2019. LNBIP, vol. 353, pp. 176–188. Springer, Cham (2019). https://doi.org/10.1007/978-3-030-20485-3_14
23. Song, R., Vanthienen, J., Cui, W., Wang, Y., Huang, L.: Context-aware BPM using IoT-integrated context ontologies and IoT-enhanced decision models. In: 21st Conference on Business Informatics CBI. IEEE, Moscow (2019)
24. Espig, A., Klimpel, N., Rödenbeck, F., Auth, G.: Bewertung des Kundennutzens von Chatbots für den Einsatz im Servicedesk. In: Ludwig, T., Pipek, V. (eds.) Proceedings of the WI 2019. University Siegen, Siegen (2019)
25. Aysolmaz, B., Iren, D., Reijers, H.A.: Detecting role inconsistencies in process models. In: 27th European Conference on Information Systems ECIS. AIS, Stockholm (2019)
26. Heuchert, M., Barann, B.: BPM2TPM: the knowledge transfer from business process to touchpoint management. In: 27th European Conference on Information Systems ECIS. AIS, Stockholm (2019)
27. Forbrig, P., Dittmar, A.: Applying agile methods and personas to S-BPM. In: Proceedings of the S-BPM ONE 2019. ACM, Seville (2019)
28. Lohmann, P., zur Muehlen, M.: Regulatory instability, business process management technology, and BPM skill configurations. In: Hildebrandt, T., van Dongen, B., Röglinger, M., Mendling, J. (eds.) BPM 2019. LNCS, vol. 11675, pp. 419–435. Springer, Cham (2019). https://doi.org/10.1007/978-3-030-26619-6_27

29. Houhou, S., Baarir, S., Poizat, P., Quéinnec, P.: A first-order logic semantics for communication-parametric BPMN collaborations. In: Hildebrandt, T., van Dongen, B., Röglinger, M., Mendling, J. (eds.) BPM 2019. LNCS, vol. 11675, pp. 52–68. Springer, Cham (2019). https://doi.org/10.1007/978-3-030-26619-6_6

30. Artale, A., Kovtunova, A., Montali, M., van der Aalst, W.M.P.: Modeling and reasoning over declarative data-aware processes with object-centric behavioral constraints. In: Hildebrandt, T., van Dongen, B., Röglinger, M., Mendling, J. (eds.) BPM 2019. LNCS, vol. 11675, pp. 139–156. Springer, Cham (2019). https://doi.org/10.1007/978-3-030-26619-6_11

31. Calvanese, D., Ghilardi, S., Gianola, A., Montali, M., Rivkin, A.: Formal modeling and SMT-based parameterized verification of data-aware BPMN. In: Hildebrandt, T., van Dongen, B., Röglinger, M., Mendling, J. (eds.) BPM 2019. LNCS, vol. 11675, pp. 157–175. Springer, Cham (2019). https://doi.org/10.1007/978-3-030-26619-6_12

32. Ong, D., Jabbari, M.: A review of problems and challenges of using multiple conceptual models. In: 27th European Conference on Information Systems ECIS. AIS, Stockholm (2019)

33. Rosenthal, K., Ternes, B., Strecker, S.: Learning conceptual modeling: structuring overview, research themes and paths for future research. In: 27th European Conference on Information Systems ECIS. AIS, Stockholm (2019)

34. Reggio, G., Leotta, M.: A method-wise approach for selecting the most suitable business process modelling notation. In: 45th Euromicro Conference on Software Engineering and Advanced Applications SEAA. IEEE, Kallithea-Chalkidiki (2019)

35. Wickboldt, C., Kliewer, N.: Blockchain for workshop event certificates-a proof of concept in the aviation industry. In: 27th European Conference on Information Systems ECIS. AIS, Stockholm (2019)

36. Jahanbin, P., Wingreen, S.C., Sharma, R.S.: Blockchain and IoT integration for trust improvement in agricultural supply chain. In: 27th European Conference on Information Systems ECIS. AIS, Stockholm (2019)

37. Vössing, M., Potthoff, F., Kühl, N., Satzger, G.: Designing useful transparency to improve process performance—evidence from an automated production line. In: 27th European Conference on Information Systems ECIS. AIS, Stockholm (2019)

38. Wolf, V., Beverungen, D.: Conceptualizing the impact of workarounds – an organizational routines' perspective. In: 27th European Conference on Information Systems ECIS. AIS, Stockholm (2019)

39. Wurm, B., Goel, K., Bandara, W., Rosemann, M.: Design patterns for business process individualization. In: Hildebrandt, T., van Dongen, B., Röglinger, M., Mendling, J. (eds.) BPM 2019. LNCS, vol. 11675, pp. 370–385. Springer, Cham (2019). https://doi.org/10.1007/978-3-030-26619-6_24

40. Venkatakumar, H., Schmidt, W.: Subject-oriented specification of IoT scenarios. In: Proceedings of the S-BPM ONE 2019. ACM, Seville (2019)

41. Kychkin, A., Deryabin, A., Neganova, E.: IoT-based energy management assistant architecture design. In: 21st Conference on Business Informatics CBI. IEEE, Moscow (2019)

42. Fayumi, A., Sutanto, J., Maamar, Z.: The socio-net of things modeling framework. In: 21st Conference on Business Informatics CBI. IEEE, Moscow (2019)

43. Fleischmann, A., Stary, C.: Dependable data sharing in dynamic IoT-systems. In: Proceedings of the S-BPM ONE 2019. ACM, Seville (2019)

44. Berger, S., Bogenreuther, M., Häckel, B., Niesel, O.: Modelling availability risks of IT threats in smart factory networks: a modular petri net approach. In: 27th European Conference on Information Systems ECIS. AIS, Stockholm (2019)

45. Leotta, F., Marrella, A., Mecella, M.: IoT for BPMers. challenges, case studies and successful applications. In: Hildebrandt, T., van Dongen, B., Röglinger, M., Mendling, J. (eds.) BPM 2019. LNCS, vol. 11675, pp. 16–22. Springer, Cham (2019). https://doi.org/10.1007/978-3-030-26619-6_3

46. Wanner, J., Bauer, C., Janiesch, C.: Two-sided digital markets - disruptive chance meets chicken or egg causality dilemma. In: 21st Conference on Business Informatics CBI. IEEE, Moscow (2019)
47. Xu, T., Bernardy, A., Bertling, M., Burggräf, P., Stich, V., Dannapfel, M.: Development of a matching platform for the requirement-oriented selection of cyber physical systems for SMEs. In: Ludwig, T., Pipek, V. (eds.) Proceedings of the WI 2019. University Siegen, Siegen (2019)
48. Schermouly, L., Schreieck, M., Wiesche, M., Krcmar, H.: Developing an industrial IoT platform – trade-off between horizontal and vertical approaches. In: Ludwig, T., Pipek, V. (eds.) Proceedings of the WI 2019. University Siegen, Siegen (2019)

Subject-Oriented Value-Stream Mapping with SiSi

Matthes Elstermann(✉), Jakob Bönsch, and Jivka Ovtcharova

Karlsruhe Institute of Technology, Karlsruhe, Germany
matthes.elstermann@kit.edu
http://www.imi.kit.edu

Abstract. Value Stream Analysis (VSA) is an important tool to assess areas of improvement in manufacturing according to lean principles. Prior research conjectured the hypothesis, that it is possible to use tools from the S-BPM context for this task. This work follows up on this hypothesis and investigates the possibilities to execute value stream mapping using subject-oriented PASS modeling and evaluation via the simulation tool SiSi to determine causes of inefficiency. For this purpose extensions to PASS and SiSi have been developed to better fit the requirements of VSA. The resulting models indicated that the value stream perspective is a good starting point, but often lead time considerations are not comprehensive enough to detect problems in a company's information flow and business processes. Therefore we further propose an agile methodology to scale initial VSA consideration to a full-blown (S-)BPM approach.

Keywords: S-BPM · PASS · Value Stream Mapping (VSM) · SiSi · Value Stream Design (VSD)

1 Introduction

Value Stream Design (VSD) and the accompanying analysis and description method of Value Stream Mapping (VSM) are widely used and applied in the industry as a relatively simple and fast means for the investigation of a production process.

In [11] Kannengiesser proposes and describes a hypothetical mapping between VSD/VSM and the domain of Subject-Oriented Business Process Management or Modeling (S-BPM). His argument however, is purely theoretical and also doesn't really differentiate between S-BPM as a methodology and modeling with the subject-oriented (SO) process modeling language that is the Parallel Activity Specification Scheme (PASS).

© Springer Nature Switzerland AG 2020
M. Freitag et al. (Eds.): S-BPM ONE 2020, CCIS 1278, pp. 232–250, 2020.
https://doi.org/10.1007/978-3-030-64351-5_16

This work further explores the hypotheses that applying SO/PASS for the tasks of value stream mapping is possible and possibly advantageous[1]. This is not only done theoretically, but also evaluated practically by applying and consequently extending modeling and evaluation tools.

Additionally to the results of that investigation, we present a simple and compact method that, depending on actual needs, encourages to dynamically change scope and extent of process improvement activities. This includes the whole range from pure and relative simple VSM, over extensive business and information flow process considerations, up to complete business process modeling and (S-)BPM efforts, and everything in between.

2 Theoretical Foundation: Value Stream Analysis

Improvements to a company's value streams as a whole, instead of production, logistics, and business processes on their own is a well renown tool in the production industry. The value stream analysis is an integral part of this Value Stream Method [14]. Its principle procedure consist of four steps [6]: 1. Start: Deduction of product families. 2. Preparation: Analysis of customer demand. 3. Execution: Value Stream Mapping (VSM). And 4. Evaluation: Potential for improvement. Often the result of such an endeavor is a so-called value stream map, a graphical representation and overview of the findings of the analysis and the identified areas of improvement. Commonly this activity feeds into or can be considered a part of Value Stream Design (VSD) which is a methodology that uses lean principles to improve the overall value stream [6].

Value Stream Mapping (VSM) itself usually is done by hand with a pencil and paper (or aided with a spreadsheet program, which is essentially the same). During analysis, the method-practitioner follows "the value stream" through the shop floor from ramp to ramp and takes notes before drawing a value stream map. A classical value stream map consists of standardized symbols as seen in Fig. 1.

Even though the method of VSM supports a broader view and should reflect the whole value stream from raw material to final consumer (or even recycling efforts), most often, only the own production facility is regarded [14]. This commonly leads to linear VSMs from "ramp to ramp", that fit nicely onto a single sheet of paper. But even only identifying the supposedly main value stream may be much more complex than the overall single page description would reveal.

Also an interesting and at the least debatable aspect is, that this concept differs between business processes and the value stream, where the value stream is a somewhat abstract and incomplete idea of a production process. The exact

---

[1] Later considerations incorporate the works of Moser [8,13] and argue that VSM as a sole approach not sufficient to analyze actual problems occurring in modern, complex production systems. However, for simplicity reasons that argument is made later and the initial focus of this work is on the simpler task of considering the usage of PASS/S-BPM as a means for conducting VSM as was proposed by Kannengiesser.

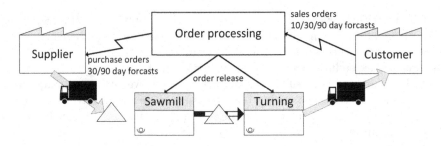

Fig. 1. Example of a classic value stream map design

differentiation is somewhat unclear and intermixed as the importance of information flow and thereby business processes is naturally acknowledged in the literature, however still considered as something different with the business process often being a black box without direct impact on the value stream [6].

3   Theoretical Foundations: S-BPM, Subject-Orientation, PASS, and SiSi

In his work [11], Kannengiesser mapped VSD/VSM, by title, with *S-BPM* which stands for Subject-Oriented Business Process Management.

S-BPM: As any BPM approach, S-BPM is a general management approach with two dimensions to it [15]: Firstly, it is an economic management philosophy with consideration of factors like costs, time, or amounts of resources regarding the design and execution of processes. Secondly, BPM encompasses technologies, tools, and methods to document and automate business processes. This can also be referred to as digitization [12].

The specialty of S-BPM [7] is, that for these purposes and activities, it puts the focus on the active entities, the involved people. A main aspect within this approach is the usage of subject-orientation (SO) as the main modeling paradigm for processes in the according BPM activities.

PASS: Currently, the only explicit subject-oriented modeling language in existence is the Parallel Activity Specification Schema (PASS). To comply with the idea of SO, PASS consist of two different diagram types. Firstly, in a Subject Interaction Diagram (SID) (Compare Fig. 2) the active entities of a process - the *Subjects* - and the information objects they exchange - the *Messages* - are described. Afterwards and in dependency to the SID, the activities of each subject are modeled in individual Subject Behavior Diagrams (SBD) (Compare Figs. 3 and 4), where, next to individual activities, especially interaction with other subjects is explicitly modeled via *Do*, *Send*, and *Receive* states.

In some cases there are so called *Interface Subjects* on the SID level. These subjects do not posses individual SBDs and function as black boxes who's behavior is unknown or irrelevant for a given process model or described in another model.

SiSi: There are currently several tools that allow to create subject-oriented process models [2]. One of these, is a self developed plug-in tool for MS Visio that contains a static simulator component called *Simple Simulation (SiSi)* [4]. This tool allows to compute run-times of linear processes from start to finish for individual process runs, based on dedicated timing/duration/transmission information that need to be modelled into the SBD-states and messages of PASS diagrams.

Next to the jSim tool mentioned in [7], SiSi is the only process simulation allowing numerical process analysis for SO/PASS models, and, as far as known, the only one currently still being used and compatible with the official PASS OWL standard [1,3]. In its original configuration, the SiSi tool enables to add the run-time duration to individual tasks of an SBD and transmission times of message in the SIDs of PASS models. With this information it can calculate the according overall run-time of complex (but linear) processes.

One of the explored hypothesis of this work is, that SiSi can be used to conduct and support Value Stream Mapping. In principle this has proven to be possible. However, to facilitate VSM, SiSi was extended to better express important aspects of VSM. This mainly allows now to categorize Do-States, message types, and subjects according to the VSM-terminology. Next, the individual results of the existing overall run-time calculation for each VSM specific sub-type can be computed and presented separately.

3.1 S-BPM vs. PASS

As a side note, in his work, Kannengiesser does not mention PASS, however he describes it and refers to SIDs and SBDs as being S-BPM diagrams. Therefore, it is somewhat unclear if his work implies a mapping and usage of PASS diagrams/process models for VSM or if he envisioned a synthesis of methodological concepts of VSD and S-BPM. The title claims the later. However, the content indicates only the former.

This analysis is geared toward the clarification of this gap.

4 Value Stream Mapping with PASS and SiSi

In essence, a Value Stream Map is nothing but an informal, single-page process model, while PASS is a modeling language for processes. And *"In order to be able to map the various productive activities of a factory as comprehensively as possible, a suitable modelling is necessary"* [6].

As Kannengiesser argued, S-BPM, or, as can be assumed, PASS, is a good tool to conduct the modeling aspect and support the creation of the actual value stream map (VSM). The principles of value stream mapping as proposed by Rother and Shook [14] and explained further in [6] do not change by using PASS for the description and analysis, instead of pen and paper. However, using formalized and especially subject-oriented process models opens the possibility for improved analysis capabilities and is beneficial especially for calculating cycle times, which are an important aspect in VSM.

There are several aspects that need to be considered when creating subject-oriented VSMs. There are, however, a couple of different possibilities to approach VSM using PASS.

4.1 Methodology

To test the initial hypothesis, multiple exemplary use-case VSMs were recreated using PASS. In principle, as Kannengiesser had assumed, this was found to be conductible, however in its pure form with several missing details and inconveniences, due to lacking information depth of existing informal value stream maps.

Based on the experience during creation, the modeling guidelines for how to approach VSM with PASS were created iteratively. In parallel, the modeling capabilities of the MS Visio PASS modeling tool and SiSi were extended to better fit the specific needs of practitioners of classical VSA/VSM. The following sections introduce the resulting guidelines and modeling practices, together with the discussion of their adoption.

4.2 SID and Basic Structural Elements

According to Erlach [6] there are six basic elements to any value stream map: production processes, business processes, material flow, information flow, the customer and the supplier. If PASS is to be used, these need to be expressed in or mapped to PASS' elements. The first step to modelling a process system with PASS is the creation of a Subject Interaction Diagram (SID). Therefore, it is important to analyze the basic structural elements of a value stream map and decide which ones and how to model them using the concepts of SIDs [11]. In most (obvious) cases we use the same or at least a similar mapping of modelling concepts as Kannengiesser [11]. In some instances, a different approach is used to accommodate for more flexibility or to improve the performance of SiSi.

As a side note: The resulting SID of the production process as a whole could or should graphically resemble the typical visual layout of a common value stream map. This is not necessary for PASS, but, supposedly, will help to avoid or at least reduce aversions of classic VSM practitioners, otherwise caused by unfamiliar formalism. However, with realistic but complex network-like process, it very well will not be possible to achieve an according layout.

Production Processes include all activities to transform material in a value adding way into the final product. This means technical processes (e.g. manufacturing, assembling) and logistic processes (e.g. sorting, shipping) alike. On the shop floor these *processes* will be seen as resources like machines or work stations and their operators. Modelling of production processes in PASS is done directly using standard subjects that have SBDs.

If for one or more production step a subcontractor is used and no information about the behavior is available, it is advisable to use an interface subject for these steps instead. However, due to the limits of SiSi, such a construction will hinder correct computations. If an interface subject is "interrupting" the value stream and no further modelling considerations are taken, following subjects, that only receive message from the interface subject, are considered as being active from the beginning of the overall process. Their internal times are still being computed correctly nevertheless [4].

Business processes provide and process information in regards to order processing. They enable the whole production process. As most order processing, business process activities are expected to be aided or executed entirely by or within according IT-systems.

For representation of business processes in PASS again subjects or interface subjects can be used. The choice depends on the grade of detail the VSM-analyst wants to achieve. In most cases it doesn't make sense to go into too much detail on the business process at the stage of VSA/VSM. Firstly, the logic of business processes may differ quite profoundly from a straight forward and linear value stream description. Therefore, very detailed and especially cyclic models could limit the performance or usefulness of SiSi. Secondly, as business processes tend to be quite complex themselves, a truthful, in-depth process analysis most likely requires resources (time/effort) that should rather be invested in a larger BPM approach than a smaller scale, focused VSA.

Note however, that the results of a VSA may indicate, or, in a more complex industry 4.0 context, are almost expected to show that problems do indeed lie in the communication and business process domain. In that case, a further, in-depth process analysis of the coordination processes is necessary since the actual causes of inefficiency are *"hidden"* there.

Customer and Supplier are the external elements in any value stream map. They embody the start and the end point of any ramp-to-ramp VSA. Similar to subcontractors and business processes, in PASS they are best represented as interface subjects, since either no information about their behavior is available or, at the very least, there is no interest or purpose in modelling their behaviour. Neither the customer nor the supplier subjects have to be a single company. The customer is simply the destination for the finished product of the analyzed product family and the supplier is the source of (raw) material for the production. If graphical representation of multiple suppliers or customers is wished, their subjects can be declared as Multi-(Interface-)Subjects. This would have no impact on the calculations as SiSi is ignoring the Multi-Subject mechanism.

Material Flow has three components to it: movement, storage, and handling. As these functions are quite different in nature, they call for different representation in PASS.

Movement describes the reallocation of physical goods. This includes intra-plant conveyance as well as external transport between production processes or storage areas. The best representation of movement in PASS is as a message, sent between processes.

Storage describes the temporary placement of physical goods in an allocated area. As storage facilities are, in contrast to goods in transit, usually independent areas of activities, they are best represented in PASS as subjects. There is no distinction between storing (stock) and staging (WIP) necessary in VSA. Hence storing/storage can always also regard WIP in the following descriptions.

Handling is the movement of physical goods within a production process or a storage area. Significant amount of handling can call for it's own (logistical) *production process*. Other than that, handling should be represented simply as Do-States within the SBDs of according production- or storage-subjects and most minor handling may not even be represented within a value stream map at all to keep it lite and focused.

Information Flow transmits information regarding the material flow or order processing. As this links subjects in PASS, information flow is naturally modelled as message. Kannengiesser [11] suggested to verbally distinguish between material flow messages as 'material messages' and information flow messages as 'control messages'. Technically there is no differentiation between message types in PASS. However, for the logic of VSAs a distinction is required. With standard PASS, a classification is a purely graphical or textual annotation for what a message is supposed to represent. However, for the extension of the Visio-Shapes and SiSi we have integrated an according message classification mechanism that allows to differ the various message types.

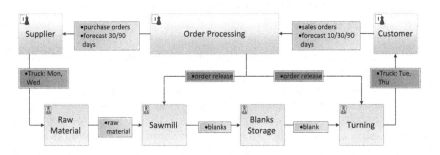

Fig. 2. Example VSM in PASS

4.3   Process vs. Subject

That most of the supposedly *"processes"* of a VSM can be descried directly as subjects, without even compromising the original meaning, is testimony to another hypothesis: Namely that here, as well as in many other rather abstracted process models there is a creeping, barely perceivable and subtle shift from consideration of a *"process"* with a classical, linear input-task-output logic to that of a *"processor"* or *"area of activity"* as described in [5].

More bluntly put: while the VSA applicants may refer to the individual stations as *processes*, they are actually already considering and handling them as subjects, however without acknowledging that there is a steep conceptual difference between the classical, unidirectional input-task-output concept of *"process"* and that of an area of activity that may have multi-directional input and output channels that allows them to form complex netted process structures (if required).

According to [5], the classical concept severely limits consideration and description means for analysts if applied strictly. In consequence it is rarely followed through. Hence high level (and especially non-formal) process descriptions tend to follow a classical paradigm only in name (e.g. by referring to stations or subjects as *processes* but actually using SO logic[2] in all arguments.

To some degree it can be claimed that SO thinking, with its simple but strict separation of activity and actor, is what is being done anyway already. However, in order to actually benefit from using PASS/S-BPM for VSM, any analyst or modeler should be aware of this and embrace SO fully.

Consequently, we are using the terms *storage **subject*** and *production **subject*** instead of ***process***. We also encourage to consider that as the correct term.

4.4   SBDs for VSM

Every non-Interface subject in the value stream map has a Subject Behavior Diagram (SBD). In the SBD the actual activities and their corresponding run-times, which are used for SiSi, are modeled. For a process consideration on VSA level, it is not necessary to try to model every single operation. Most *production subjects* and *storage subjects* follow the same principles and therefore will have the same standardized behavior. Of course, if more complex and detailed behaviors are necessary it is always possible to deviate from the proposed schema.

It is important to note, that each modeled behavior needs to describe the activities of a workstation that are executed **for a single unit** or element from start to finish. While PASS can also easily be used to correctly describe the continuous behavior of any station, SiSi is not intended to simulate overall production systems. It rather is conceptualized for the start-to-finish logic of VSA/VSM. As a consequence, a value stream analyst using PASS needs to be aware to measure and map all times in the model according to the correct batch sizes.

A standard VSM **production subject SBD** is displayed in Fig. 3. As long as input (e.g. material) is required, any production subject will have a Receive-State as Start-State. The second input requirement is often an order release from an organisational structure[3]. As order processing can be quite different depending on the organizational structure in various scenarios, this first part of the production SBD is more likely to be changed than the second part.

The central part of the production SBD consists of three Do-States. They are used to distinct and note down (See Fig. 5) the different VSA concepts or types of processing times that make up the cycle time.

---

[2] The core assumption or logic of subject-orientation is that there is clearly defined difference between action, actor, and process (as collection of actors with actions).
[3] As long as order processing is an interface subject this message is considered available instantaneous and no additional time is added.

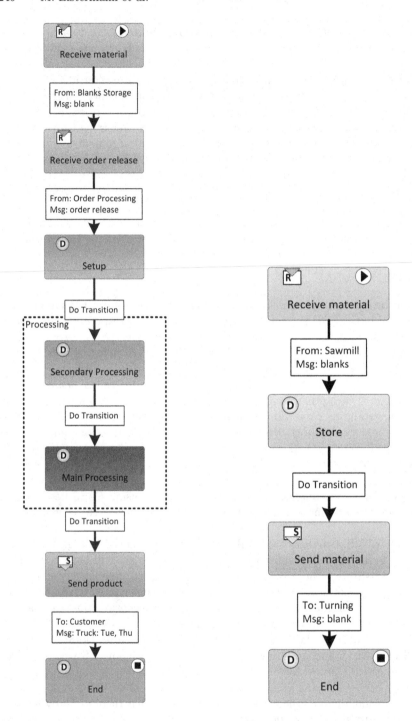

Fig. 3. Example of a proposed standard SBD for production process subjects

Fig. 4. Example of a proposed standard SBD for storage subjects in a Push production

The first Do-State regards the setup-time. This operation describes any necessary changeover on the machinery or of the work station. Setup-time is accounted just once per batch.

The actual processing time is split up further into two Do-States. First the 'Secondary Processing Time' and then the 'Main Processing Time'. The former time represents the no-value-adding time (e.g. clamping), the latter the value-adding time (e.g. machining) for every piece in a considered batch.

The 'Setup Time' in this regard counts as 'Secondary Processing Time' as well and will be computed together with that. The distinction is needed to differ between time that will be divided between all elements of a typical batch and the individual secondary processing time. If no such differentiation is necessary, one state is enough.

The last part of the SBD is a Send-State and concludes the production process by passing on the material to the next storage area or production station. After this the End-State is reached and the (single) iteration is complete. In accordance to the companies order processing procedures another Send-State for a control-message reporting the completion of the task can be included.

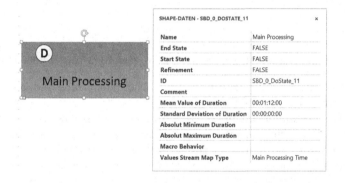

Fig. 5. Example Time Input and VSM Type Choice

An example **storage subject SBD** is shown in Fig. 4. The actual SBDs of storage subjects might vary quite a lot depending on the kind of storage area one wants to model. The given example is a simple FIFO storage area in a push production. The storage process starts by receiving material. This material is going to be put in storage. If this and/or taking goods out of storage is significant for the overall production run-time these activities can be modeled as Do-States of the type 'Secondary Processing Time'. Otherwise one Do-State (excluding the end state) of type 'Waiting Time' is sufficient. After taking material out of storage it is sent to the next production process or storage area.

4.5   Transportation Times

The transportation times of messages, be it information or (more likely) material flow is entered in the SID where the SiSi mechanism allows to note the transmission times of messages. Depending on the VSM category chosen for a given message the results will be summarized accordingly (See Fig. 6).

Fig. 6. Example Time Input and Message Type Choice

For fully specified subjects with SBDs, all other times will be noted down in the individual behavior diagrams.

For Interface Subjects (Customer, Suppliers or Subcontractor), time is only relevant if they are in the middle of the value stream and time will pass between them receiving a message and sending a reply (excluding transmission times). For this, SiSi allows to define the according response times in the SBD (not shown).

4.6   Additional Subject Information in the SID and Data Boxes

In addition to the times for transport, production and storage, there are further key information used in VSM.

The two most important parameters for storage subjects are *inventory* and *days' supply*. The former is the actual number of items in the storage area and the latter refers to how many days the *inventory* will last on average. As both are not dependent on the behavior run-time, they simply are added as shape data to the subject in the SID by the modeler based on measured times or feasible assumptions.

Production subjects take more than two parameters to be described properly. The central attributes *main process time* and *secondary process time* as well as the *waiting time* are computed via SiSi from the information in the SBD. Based on those values, the probably most looked at parameter in value stream maps can be computed: the *cycle time*.

Information such as the *process quantity* are entered manually. This parameter reflects the number of cycles it takes to complete the production of one batch. In most cases this number will be the same as the batch size. Some production stations, however, have the possibility to work on more than one piece at a time. This will change the *process quantity* in relation to the workflow and work station at hand.

In addition to that, an analyst is provided with the ability to add the information about *quality rate* and *availability* as percentage values to a subject shape. These values reflect diminished efficiency based on e.g. rework, scrap, maintenance, and repair.

All fields that are computed by SiSi are not displayed and not allowed to be changed by hand. To view them, data boxes are necessary to show all relevant information about a subject. There are plenty of parameters that could make sense to be displayed in different instances. Erlach [6] collected an extensive list of possible parameters and how to calculate or measure them. A subset of those with the most commonly mentioned and used indicators was chosen to be depicted in the PASS/SiSi approach.

The depiction of internal shape data is not part of standard PASS. In the graphical depiction of a value stream map it is however expected. Therefore, as part of this research, according data boxes were implemented to better facilitate VSM with PASS. Figure 7 shows examples for these data boxes. A short version for storage subjects, and a more extensive one for production subjects. Both give information for the *Active Time* and *Waiting Time* as computed by SiSi based on the duration of any Do-State for active time and waiting time in Receive-States[4].

For storage subjects the added information includes the display of the *Inventory*-Value and the internal *Waiting Time* that is only dependent on the inputted time in the SBD for specialized *Storage* Do states and not on the reception of any messages (See Fig. 4).

For the production subjects the data box contains more extensive information, including all the previously mentioned values as well as *Main Processing Time*, *Secondary Processing Time*, and *Cycle Time* that are computed by SiSi.

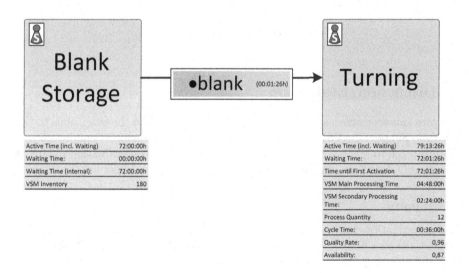

Fig. 7. Data Box information

---

[4] With the default behaviors proposed, there will be no normal waiting time since no messages are internally waited for.

The given information is on a per-subject basis. As the VSM methodology requires an overview and summary of the overall considered process, the functionality to automatically create a *VSM Summary Shape* has been added. Figure 8 shows the summary shape for our arbitrary example. All the times in the summary shape are color coded throughout the whole Visio extension. All the VSM parameters from the data boxes are added up according to their specified type of time. This allows for a quick overview of the total time domain and the time splits between value adding and no value adding activities.

VSM – Total Times:	
VSM Main Processing Time Mean:	05:02:24h
VSM Secondary Processing Time Mean:	04:04:48h
VSM Cycle Times Mean:	09:07:12h
VSM Internal Waiting Time Mean:	240:00:00h
Message Transmission Time (Overall):	144:04:36h
- Conveyance Time (internal)	00:04:19h
- Conveyance Time (external)	144:00:00h
- Information Flow Time (internal)	00:00:17h

Fig. 8. Summary shape

5   Discussion/Evaluation

The previous sections described how to facilitate PASS (and the extensions to the MS Visio Shapes) for VSM. This section therefore discusses limits and benefits of this approach to VSM. The main focus in this chapter lies on evaluating the merit of using SO/PASS in contrast to pen and paper, or spreadsheet applications.

5.1   Limits

The investigation was not able to disproof the initial hypothesis and the the tool extensions created during investigation make VSA/VSM with PASS a very powerful approach. However, in addition to a few already mentioned restrictions, there are some limits to it.

First of all the behaviour of all the subjects has to be modeled linearly and on a per-batch-run basis to enable SiSi[5]. This does not compromise the integrity of

---

[5] In contrast to modelling continuous activities of individual production areas, which could be done with PASS but will not be computed correctly in SiSi. Since SiSi is a simple process analysis tool and not a comprehensive production simulation tool.

the model, but makes modeling in some instances less intuitive (e.g. for Kanban logic). Because of this need of SiSi for linearity, the modeler must preemptively decide on, and base and measure all values on the processing times for a pre-determined batch size, rather than necessarily for single pieces. Consequently, the user has to manually enter the processing times for the whole batch and the product quantity which could be an inconvenience and/or lead to inconsistencies.

Secondly, as with any modelling solution, determining the right flight level and/or grade of abstraction is a general challenge. This weights even heavier for bigger value stream models because of increasing simulation times. As a result it might be impossible to pinpoint the exact cause of value stream inefficiencies or overly long lead times within a VSA application. The power of PASS may even tempt practitioners to spend more resources (time) on the creation of models that are more detailed or complex than necessary for a simple value stream map.

Lastly and in the same direction, PASS is a formal process modelling language and not a tool specifically designed for VSM only. In some instances it might be beneficial to opt for a dedicated value stream management application. Especially if a very simplified user guidance is necessary and it is definitely clear that nothing beyond a simple VSM will ever be required. In those cases, learning to model with PASS could be more time-consuming without benefit, especially if the possibilities of extended SBDs or networked value streams in the SID are not likely used.

5.2   Benefits

Nevertheless, using PASS for VSM is feasible and has a number of potential benefits to it.

A mayor advantage is gained in contrast to classic, informal, non-tool-supported VSM where calculations have to be done by hand. This can be time consuming (e.g. when different possibilities to improve the value stream are being analyzed) and a source for errors. Using our developed tool, instead of putting effort into making a spreadsheet, automatizes this activity to a great degree. With SiSi, this even includes the possibility to not only calculate means, but also statistic confidence intervals and possible time spreads to gain a more realistic insights beyond the idealized happy path. In addition, more parameters (e.g. transportation times) are being analyzed by default than would be in the case of a simple spreadsheet VSM. And, as shown before, even the distinction between value adding, non value adding, and different kinds of wasted time can be investigated.

Tool wise, using a process modeling program comes with its own benefits. Most modeling tools for PASS posses syntax checking functionality that is able to support VSM by reminding of missing or forgotten elements or incorrect usage of description elements. Also, during creation of VSM, constantly developing and changing layouts and routings of the map are to be expected if the investigated production process is not a textbook example that fits the schema of the standard map. This customizing of layouts and structure or adding/removing model elements is much more easily and intuitively done with a free-form graphical process modeling/lay-outing tool rather than with non-visual spreadsheets or purpose build tools with fixed graphical layout that may have not envisioned specific real-live situations.

The advantages gained form tool usage are benefits that, in principle, could be gained from using any process modeling tool. However, a core benefit lies in the employed paradigm of subject-orientation and the language PASS itself.

It was already analyzed that the *"process"* concept in the VSM context is more akin to the concept of *"subjects"* than to that of a singular task in an input-task-output context. This implicates that an SO-based approach may be what is actually required or "thought" by VSA practitioners and fits with the observation that the paradigm of subject-orientation is designed to reflect the way humans think and speak in general (and thereby is actually rather intuitive and understandable) [5,7].

Still, PASS is more flexible than standard VSM notation. The SBD-mechanism concept offers a whole extra layer of information about complex interactions, that is available to viewers upon request while being hidden otherwise. At the same time, PASS is a Turing-complete, formal, and executable process modeling language that can be fitted to varying situations that are likely to be encountered in different use cases. The aspect of formality is the key that enables tool-support for verification, error finding and allows for other formal investigation methods of value streams or inclusion into 3D simulation environments as envisioned by Häfner [10].

The ultimate argument for using PASS for VSM, however, does lie in the possibility to flexibly, dynamically, and easily extend any given value stream model. This includes mapping of complex, not-necessarily-linear value stream networks as depicted in Fig. 9. It allows to include more information in VSM without the need for more and more shape types and notation standards (while still being as formal and accurate as needed). PASS therefore can be considered a kind of multi-purpose tool.

Furthermore, in the context of modern production systems[6] the hypothesis arises, that non-linear, complex, decentralized, networked systems, will be the norm, rather than specialized cases. Consequently, it should be expected, that any tool used for modern value stream analysis and design will need to cope with such situations correctly and an approach using SO/PASS is able to fulfill this role [9]. To elaborate on this point we have further explored this aspect in the following section.

6   From Value Streams to Indiscriminate Process Modeling - A Methodology Concept

As shown in the last section VSA/VSM, especially if executed with PASS, is a powerful tool to assess value streams. However, we found that in our modern

---

[6] In the context of buzzwords like Industry 4.0, cyber-physical systems, driverless transport systems, machine learning, object-tracking, batch size 1, Internet-of-things, block-chains for production coordination, etc.

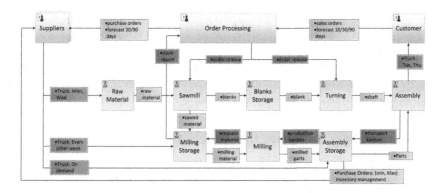

Fig. 9. Example of complex networked VSM in PASS

world manufacturing and business processes are getting more and more intertwined. This calls for an approach that does not discriminate between various different kinds of processes but considers all conditions equally.

6.1 Initial Situation

The expectation of encountering complex value streams in real-life are partially based on the findings of C. Moser [8,13], who stated that in their real-life use-case at a larger Austrian machine production company, they initially started out with a VSA approach but found that to be lacking very quickly. What they required was a full but integrated investigation of all production processes with a special focus on the according coordination processes and information flow. The actual problems they encountered were found in the interplay between all involved activities, and they found that via a full subject-oriented process modeling and analysis approach they conducted after reaching limits with simple (non SO/PASS) VSA/VSM.

In contrast, classic VSM commonly puts all business processes in one black box called 'production planning and control' [14].

However, under the assumption that the demands for order processing are rising as the variant diversity, individuality and complexity of products is escalating, it is almost mandatory to emphasize more on the business process side of production for identification of the most urgent areas of improvement (opposed to only focusing on the materialistic value stream). Proof to that is that according to [6], more modern approaches of VSM try to depict much more detail about business processes and information flow.

(Without PASS) This leads to even more new, non-standardized symbols and modeling practices that essentially are just informal process modeling techniques (or simply put: pictures). Additionally the VSM approach is inherently limited by its need to deploy all information on one sheet of paper. The lack of possibilities to describe more complex information flow in detail calls for another approach to analyze value streams and more importantly the accommodated information flow.

In essence these are the problems that have been reported by Fleischmann et al. in [8,13]. However where Moser/Fleischmann used a classical VSM approach, found it to be lacking, and only then started with subject-oriented process modeling and analysis, we encourage to start with PASS from the beginning.

6.2   Nucleus for a Seamless, Integrated Agile Effort

Using subject-orientated process modeling is a possible better approach, however going to the extreme of starting out with a full blown S-BPM approach has the potential for being inefficient in its own regard. For one, quite possibly, not all stake holders will be acquainted with the methodology and might initially not see any benefit in it. This holds especially true when their mind is strictly routed in an engineering mindset, that is closely focused on the physical value stream and deems the information flow of less or even no importance.

While that mindset may be counterproductive, value stream analysis is still an established, accepted, and useful methodology, even if it is very likely to turn out to be insufficient in more complex situations [13].

Therefore, our methodology simply proposes to start with a standard VSA/VSM approach as the initial task for the analysis of the production process. This is a very low-threshold starting point, but it requires to do so by using PASS and it requires stakeholders to understand that it is only the beginning.

Participants must be aware that problems beyond the simple material value stream will most likely exist. Therefore it is required to be open minded to identify them. PASS as a modeling language supports this behavior. A subject-oriented process model initially focused on the value stream can be the nucleus of further investigation. Especially if no deeper systematic insight into the actual processes does exist at the start of the activities[7].

In regular, ideally time-boxed, intervals stakeholders have to decide how to proceed with the investigation and how much effort/resources can and should be invested into further activities. The most recent considered and created process models (at least the SID) will serve as anchor for discussion and further planning. Decisions on what to focus on for the next iteration or agile sprint should be made dynamically to facilitate continuous and evolving agile resource allocation.

With this and in consideration of a complex coordination process system, it can be expected, that at some point there will most likely be the situation where the stricter linear-logic of VSA/VSM and SiSi have become impractical and should be left behind. To avoid confusion practitioners should always have a clear understanding of the angel and scope of the current modeling considerations. In accordance they have to keep in mind the possibility of shifting the point of view and fully embrace this change in their models.

---

[7] If such insight would truly exist, either there would not really be a need for an analysis or at least the planning of activities could be directed better towards problematic areas of processing.

7   Summary and Outlook

In our work we have investigated the hypothesis that the subject-oriented, formal process modeling language PASS is suitable and advantageous to be used for VSD/VSA/VSM concepts. We have presented the principles of a practical approach to model VSMs with their inherent logic in PASS and have analyzed which possible drawbacks and benefits can be gained from using this approach. We could not find any indicators that would disproof the initial hypothesis nor additional assumptions and consideration that formed during the research.

However, we got to the understanding that strict and pure adherence to the principles of VSD/VSA/VSM must not be the initial goal when starting a value stream analysis. Rather, the quick and relatively simple VSM analysis can be the nucleus or starting point of an continuous process that leads to a better understanding and in effect to improvements of value streams.

Using subject-oriented process modeling with PASS is not only possible here, but is possibly the best choice since it can serve as a uniting element that allows shifting analysis and consideration efforts seamlessly from pure value stream considerations towards information flow centered business process analysis models.

Next to that, since PASS is being completely formal and executable, models created throughout such ventures are very well suited for further formal evaluation and may also be used as the foundation for simulation, automation, and similar efforts.

SiSi on the other hand is a very practical tool that is most suitable for VSM and similar considerations. It is however only suitable for linear considerations and future research can be conducted to develop tools that allow simulations of non-linear PASS models as foundation for extensive production simulation which in turn could open up new ways and possibilities for production planning.

References

1. A standard for subject-oriented specification of systems. https://github.com/I2PM/Standard-Documents-for-Subject-Orientation. Accessed 13 Jan 2020
2. Fleischmann, A., Borgert, S., Elstermann, M., Krenn, F., Singer, R.: An overview to S-BPM oriented tool suites. In: Proceedings of the 9th International Conference on Subject-oriented Business Process Management. S-BPM ONE. ACM (2017)
3. Elstermann, M., Krenn, F.: The semantic exchange standard for subject-oriented process models. In: S-BPM ONE 2018 - Linz, Austria, 4–6 April (2018)
4. Elstermann, M., Ovtcharova, J.: Sisi in the ALPS: a simple simulation and verification approach for pass. In: Proceedings of the 10th International Conference on Subject-Oriented Business Process Management. S-BPM One 2018. Association for Computing Machinery, New York (2018)
5. Elstermannn, M.: Executing Strategic Product Planning - A Subject-Oriented Analysis and New Referential Process Model for IT-Tool Support and Agile Execution of Strategic Product Planning. KIT Scientific Publishing (2019)
6. Erlach, K.: Value Stream Design: The Way Towards a Lean Factory. Lecture Notes in Logistics. Springer, Heidelberg (2013). https://doi.org/10.1007/978-3-642-12569-0

7. Fleischmann, A., Schmidt, W., Stary, C., Obermeier, S., Börger, E.: Subject-Oriented Business Process Management. Springer, Heidelberg (2012). https://doi.org/10.1007/978-3-642-32392-8

8. Fleischmann, C., Říha, K., Stangl, G.: Logistics processes modelled in S-BPM and implemented in sap to reduce production lead times. In: Sanz, J.L. (ed.) S-BPM ONE 2016, pp. 1–4 (2016)

9. Friedl, A.: Meeting Industrie 4.0 challenges with S-BPM. In: Stary, C., Krenn, F. (eds.) S-BPM ONE 2018, 10 years, ICPS. The Association for Computing Machinery, New York (2018)

10. Häfner, V.V.: Polyvr - a virtual reality authoring framework for engineering applications (2019). https://doi.org/10.5445/IR/1000098349

11. Kannengiesser, U.: Supporting value stream design using S-BPM. In: Nanopoulos, A., Schmidt, W. (eds.) S-BPM ONE 2014. LNBIP, vol. 170, pp. 151–160. Springer, Cham (2014). https://doi.org/10.1007/978-3-319-06065-1_11

12. Lederer, M., Betz, S., Kurz, M., Schmidt, W.: Some say digitalization - others say it-enabled process management thought through to the end. In: Proceedings of the 9th Conference on Subject-Oriented Business Process Management. S-BPM ONE 2017. Association for Computing Machinery, New York (2017). https://doi.org/10.1145/3040565.3040574

13. Moser, C., Říha, K.: Digitalization of information-intensive logistics processes to reduce production lead times at ENGEL Austria GmbH: extending value stream mapping with subject-oriented business process management. In: Urbach, N., Röglinger, M. (eds.) Digitalization Cases. MP, pp. 293–312. Springer, Cham (2019). https://doi.org/10.1007/978-3-319-95273-4_15

14. Rother, M., Shook, J.: Learning to See: Value-Stream Mapping to Create Value and Eliminate Muda. A Lean Tool Kit Method and Workbook. Lean Enterprise Inst, Cambridge, Mass., version 1.4 edn. (2009)

15. Schmidt, W., Fleischmann, A., Gilbert, O.T.: Subjektorientiertes geschäftsprozessmanagement. HMD Praxis der Wirtschaftsinformatik **46**, 52–62 (2009). https://doi.org/10.1007/BF03340343

Author Index

Printed in the United States
By Bookmasters